Flourishing in Faith

Flourishing in Faith

Theology Encountering Positive Psychology

Edited by
GILLIES AMBLER,
MATTHEW P. ANSTEY,
THEO D. MCCALL,
& MATHEW A. WHITE

Foreword by
KRISTJÁN KRISTJÁNSSON

CASCADE *Books* · Eugene, Oregon

FLOURISHING IN FAITH
Theology Encountering Positive Psychology

Cascade Books
An Imprint of Wipf and Stock Publishers
199 W. 8th Ave., Suite 3
Eugene, OR 97401
www.wipfandstock.com

PAPERBACK ISBN: 978-1-4982-9640-3
HARDCOVER ISBN: 978-1-4982-9642-7
EBOOK ISBN: 978-1-4982-9641-0

Cataloging-in-Publication data:

Names: Ambler, Gillies, editor. | Anstey, Matthew P., editor. | McCall, Theo D., editor. | White, Mathew A., editor

Title: Flourishing in faith : theology encountering positive psychology / edited by Gillies Ambler, Matthew P. Anstey, Theo D. McCall, and Mathew A. White.

Description: Eugene, OR : Cascade, 2017 | Includes bibliographical references.

Identifiers: ISBN 978-1-4982-9640-3 (paperback) | ISBN 978-1-4982-9642-7 (hardcover) | ISBN 978-1-4982-9641-0 (ebook)

Subjects: LCSH: Well-being—Religious aspects—Christianity.| Quality of life—Religious aspects—Christianity. | Christianity—Psychology. | Positive psychology.

Classification: LCC BV4598.3 F5 2017 (print) | LCC BV4598.3 (ebook)

Manufactured in the U.S.A.   06/20/17

Contents

Contributors

Foreword—Kristján Kristjánsson (PhD, University of St. Andrews) is Deputy Director in the Jubilee Centre for Character and Virtues and Professor of Character Education and Virtue Ethics at the University of Birmingham, UK. His interests lie in research on character and virtues at the intersection between moral philosophy, moral psychology, and moral education. He has published six books on those issues; the latest one, *Aristotelian Character Education*, was published by Routledge in 2015. His previous books include *Virtues and Vices in Positive Psychology* (Cambridge University Press, 2013). In 2011, Kristján was awarded the Ása Wright Award, the most prestigious award given annually to an Icelandic scholar. In addition to leading a number of the Jubilee Centre's flagship projects, he oversees all research activities in the Centre. As a member of various international organizations and editorial boards, Kristján collaborates with colleagues in Asia, Europe, and the USA on issues that relate to the cultivation of virtuous character.

Editor—The Rev'd Dr Gillies Ambler, a retired Uniting Church minister, is a former high school teacher with an honors degree in mathematics. He has been privileged to be a teacher throughout his life. He was a Uniting Church parish minister for over twenty-five years and has a Master's degree in theology. He is passionate about empowering marginalized people. For over twelve years he has counseled women wounded by domestic violence, as well as being an advocate and fundraiser for a major Adelaide metropolitan Domestic Violence Service. In 2014, he was honored with Campbelltown Citizen of the Year for his outreach to the local community.

His doctorate (2008), unique in its field, applied qualitative methodologies to the narration and analysis of personal grief. Dr Ambler has lectured on grief and spirituality and supervised postgraduates exploring personal and corporate grief issues in contemporary society. He has self-published a book, developed from his doctorate, entitled: *Grief Wounds. Love Heals. Insights of a Bereaved Husband and Bereaved Parent*. He is an adjunct faculty member of St Barnabas College, Adelaide, and Charles Sturt University, Australia.

Editor—The Rev'd Canon Dr Matthew P. Anstey moved to Adelaide in 2010 to take up the position of College Principal at St Barnabas College, Adelaide. Prior to this, he was an Australian Research Council Postdoctoral Fellow at Charles Sturt University (2006–2009) working in the area of Biblical Hebrew linguistics. His research interests include Biblical Hebrew linguistics, Old Testament, theology, narrative, lament, and homiletics. His academic webpage www.bhgrammar.com is used by Hebrew specialists around the world. He is Canon Theologian of the Anglican Diocese of Adelaide and speaks regularly at churches and conferences. Matthew is a board member of the Council of Governors at St Peter's College—Adelaide, the Australian Research Theological Foundation, the Anglican Church of Australia Doctrine Commission, and the National Association of Professors of Hebrew. He is also a Visiting Research Fellow, School of Humanities (Linguistics), University of Adelaide (2016–).

Editor—The Rev'd Dr Theo D. McCall is Chaplain at St Peter's College, Adelaide, and works across the whole school (ELC-Year 12). He graduated PhD in Theology from Flinders University and his thesis was published as *The Greenie's Guide to the End of the World* (ATF, 2011). He is a board member of St Barnabas College and Adjunct Lecturer at St Barnabas College and Charles Sturt University. Theo is keenly interested in the dialogue between systematic theology and positive psychology, particularly from a practical point of view in delivering chaplaincy services and Religious and Values Education (RAVE) lessons. In October 2013 he attended a meeting in Canterbury of spiritual leaders and psychologists, led by Martin Seligman. He co-edited the proceedings of this meeting in a book entitled *Being Called* (Praeger, 2015). Theo has presented and run workshops on wellbeing widely. He authored a chapter for *Evidence-based Approaches to Positive Education* (Springer, 2015). He is currently writing for a new publication, *Selected Essays on Future Directions in Wellbeing*, due for publication in

2017. He enjoys cycling (his collection of bicycles seems to increase yearly), singing and music, bushwalking, good food and red wine, and making connections between movies and theology.

Editor—Associate Professor Mathew A. White (PhD, The University of Adelaide) is the Director of Wellbeing and Positive Education at St Peter's College—Adelaide in Australia. He is a Principal Fellow in the Melbourne Graduate School of Education at The University of Melbourne and an affiliate of Cambridge University's Well-being Institute. Mathew has co-authored two of the six most read articles in the *Journal of Positive Psychology*. He is co-editor of *Evidence-based Approaches to Positive Education* (Springer). His work has been published in *the Oxford Handbook of Happiness, International Journal of Well-being, Psychology, International Journal of Appreciative Inquiry, International Education Journal,* and *Dialogue Australasia.* Mathew is a member of the South Australian Health and Medical Research Institute Wellbeing and Resilience Centre's Education Committee (SAHMRI-WRC); Academic Advisory Board of the Positive Psychology Centre, Melbourne Graduate School of Education, The University of Melbourne; Academic Committee at St Mark's College, Adelaide's largest residential university college; and The Reach Foundation's Research Impact Committee. The International Positive Education Network (IPEN) appointed Mathew as one of fifty representatives from twenty-eight different countries who help bring IPEN's mission to a global audience.

The Rev'd Dr James Burns IVD is Interim Dean, Woods College of Advancing Studies at Boston College. Dr Burns is a native of St. Paul, MN. He worked as an accountant for a pharmaceutical company before enrolling in seminary. Ordained as a Catholic priest in 1993, he served as a parish priest for six years (three as a pastor) before returning to graduate school in psychology. After a pre-doctoral psychology internship at Yale School of Medicine he completed a Postdoctoral Fellowship at McLean Hospital/ Harvard Medical School, as well as at the Danielsen Institute's Center for the Study of Religion and Psychology and the Boston Psychoanalytic Society. He became an Assistant Professor of Psychology at the University of St Thomas in St Paul, MN since 2003. Beginning in September 2007, he joined the Boston University School of Theology Faculty, while continuing work in the research center and clinic of the Danielsen Institute. Dr Burns' dissertation research examined the relationship between levels of anger and aggression in adolescent males and their levels of spirituality. He continues to be interested in mental health issues in adolescence and the relationship of these issues to religion and spirituality. Current interests and research include the way the sexual abuse crisis in the Catholic Church and church closings have impacted the morale of priests, pastoral leadership, and community dynamics. He is also interested in studies of peace and conflict, particularly as these impact globalization and mental health resources. In his private practice he treats individuals and couples with mood and anxiety disorders, along with a focus on ministry personnel, especially priests.

Professor Ellen T. Charry is the Margaret W. Harmon Professor of Theology at Princeton Theological Seminary. She earned an MA and PhD in Religion from Temple University following an MSW from Yeshiva University and a BA from Barnard College. Her interest is in human flourishing from a Christian perspective. Her monographs include *By the Renewing of your Minds* (1997) and *God and the Art of Happiness* (2010). She was a member of the Pursuit of Happiness Project at the Center for Law and Religion at Emory University, sponsored by the Templeton Foundation (2007–2010). Charry has served on the editorial boards of *Theology Today*, *Scottish Journal of Theology*, and *Pro Ecclesia*. She currently serves as an editor-at-large for *The Christian Century*.

Professor Shane Clifton is Dean of Theology at Alphacrucis college in Sydney, editor of the journal *Australasian Pentecostal Studies*, and author of *Pentecostal Churches in Transition* and *Globalisation and the Mission of the Church* (co-authored with Neil Ormerod). He is married to Elly and together they are the parents of three young men. In October 2010, Shane's career and family life were interrupted by a serious accident that left him a quadriplegic (C5 incomplete). During the lengthy process of rehabilitation, Shane drew on the combined resources of the virtue tradition (Aristotle, Aquinas, and Macintyre) and the related discipline of Positive Psychology to help him reclaim his own happiness. Since that time he has published his memoir, *Husbands Should Not Break*, and various articles exploring the intersection of disability and Christian theology, such as, "Disability, Theodicy, and Fragility" (*Theological Studies* 76.4, Dec. 2015).

Dr Jameela Conway-Turner graduated from George Mason University with her PhD in Applied Developmental Psychology. She is an executive policy fellow for the Society for Research on Child Development (SRCD). She is placed within the National Institute of Justice. Jameela also holds a

Masters degree in Applied Developmental Psychology from Boston College and a Bachelors degree in Psychology from Penn State University.

The Rev'd Dr J Harold Ellens holds a PhD in Psychology and a PhD in Second Temple Judaism and Christian Origins. His lifetime of professional work has been as a pastor, university professor, psychotherapist, and army chaplain (Colonel). His 311 volumes of scholarly publications, 171 journal articles, international lectureships, and university teaching have been focused entirely upon the interface between psychology and religion/spirituality. He is a noted preacher and much admired lecturer.

Carla Ford, a part time lecturer and Co-Director of Mindful Edge, works with individuals, schools, and organizations in the area of wellbeing, resilience, and performance. She emigrated from the UK in 2007 with an Honors degree in Theology (London School of Theology) and a PGCert in Education (Roehampton University), and completed a Masters in Applied Positive Psychology (MAPP) at the University of Melbourne, Australia. A qualified teacher with ten years' classroom experience, Carla previously led the education work at the South Australian Health and Medical Research Institute's Wellbeing and Resilience Centre, a statewide wellbeing initiative. Following on from her MAPP capstone project, Carla is currently researching the impact of gratitude interventions on relationships with God.

Andrew Ford is Co-Director of Mindful Edge, a training, coaching, and consulting business that works with schools and organizations to enhance wellbeing and performance. He is a qualified Personal Coach and is currently studying a Masters in Applied Positive Psychology and Coaching Psychology from the University of East London. He holds a DipHE in Christian Life and Ministry from the London School of Theology and has over twenty years' leadership experience as a pastor, trainer, coach, and mentor. Passionate about discovering how to live the abundant life, Andrew is excited by the contribution Positive Psychology can bring to the Christian faith.

The Right Rev'd Dr Tim Harris has combined thirty years of grassroots local church ministry with academic studies and over two decades' experience as an educator in theological education. Formerly the founding Dean of Bishopdale Theological College in Nelson, NZ, he is now based in Adelaide and focused on preparing people for ministry with a strong understanding of the mission of God, serving the Anglican Diocese of Adelaide as an Assistant Bishop. He is Vice Principal and Lecturer in New Testament Studies at St Barnabas College.

Dr Matthew T. McGonagle is a Board Certified Adult Psychiatrist with a private practice in Wellesley, Massachusetts. Matthew obtained his Medical Degree from Loyola University Chicago - Stritch School of Medicine in 2003 and completed his residency at Tufts Medical Center-Adult Psychiatry Residency Training Program (where he served as Chief Resident of Emergency and Outpatient Services from 2006–2007). He was former Medical Director of Outpatient Psychiatry and Addictions Services at Mount Auburn Hospital and Clinical Instructor of Psychiatry at Harvard Medical School from 2007–2012. He graduated from Boston College in 1998. Matthew has worked with religious organizations in a variety of ways ranging from mental health service delivery and management to workshops, educational activities, and consulting roles. Most of his practice is focused on working with clients struggling with depression, anxiety, stress related illness, and trauma. He has a clinical interest in the relationship between a person's spirituality, health, and wellness.

Melaine Malcolm is a Child Welfare Data Analyst at the Massachusetts Trial Court. As an analyst, Melaine supports the use of data to inform decision-making. Her research interests center on understanding risk and protective factors in the child welfare system, achieving permanency outcomes for children, and improving wellbeing outcomes for vulnerable youth. Among her responsibilities, she serves on the Massachusetts Court Improvement Program and the Trial Courts' Innovation Grant Team. She is also a Guest Lecturer for the Seminar of Government and Families course at Tufts University. Melaine holds an Executive Certificate in Information Sharing from Georgetown University's Center for Juvenile Justice Reform. She holds an MEd from the Lynch School of Education and a Bachelors degree from Morrissey College of Arts and Sciences at Boston College.

James Nelson currently enjoys the role of Director of Student Development at St Andrews Lutheran College. He is engaged by the opportunity to create stronger links between teachers across the years; enhancing links between chapel and Positive Education; promoting teachers as leaders and learners; encouraging student leadership and service; and building skills and awareness of a life lived with renewed focus on truth, hope, and joy. These are natural and energetic pursuits for his strengths as an activator, connector, relator, and ideator. He is even more passionate about his faith and opportunities for relationships and institutions to be transformed as we encounter and celebrate grace. He is currently involved in action research on explicit teaching and its impact on high achieving students; the broad and positive outcomes of Stillness practices in the classroom; literacy in the Middle Years; and the effects of growth coaching on teacher efficacy. These are some of the strategies he supports for a college focused on student and staff flourishing as part of the mission "Celebrating the Gospel, nurturing the individual, empowering lifelong learning." He currently enjoys marriage, life, and worship on the Gold Coast, where there are abundant opportunities for surfing before work and hiking with his children on the weekend.

The Rev'd Lisa Spargo is an Australian Anglican Priest who ministers as a School Chaplain. She enjoys the challenges that chaplaincy brings, especially the call to inspire faith in all members of the school community and help them to value the spiritual aspect of human life. Given that schools are such busy places for staff, students, and families, she sees a significant part of her role as nurturing wellbeing so that fullness of life may be found.

Christopher Staysniak is a PhD candidate in American religious history at Boston College. His areas of specialty include the development of religious volunteer and service programs, Catholic higher education, and twentieth-century American social and political movements. Additionally he works for Boston College's Institute for Advanced Jesuit Studies and serves as a managing editor for the *Journal of Jesuit Studies*.

Foreword

Giving Transcendence and Spirituality Their Due

Kristján Kristjánsson

It may seem odd to ask someone who is neither a theologian nor a psychologist, let alone a "positive" one, to write the foreword to a book about how these two disciplines can learn from one another: to "exchange gifts," as Ellen T. Charry explains so well in Chapter 1. The editors probably asked me because I have written at length about the need for more interplay and reciprocity between philosophical virtue ethics, especially of the Aristotelian kind, and Positive Psychology. I have pointed out how Positive Psychology misses a trick by not incorporating, more explicitly, Aristotelian elements into its theory of character strengths and virtues: for example, the idea of an overarching meta-virtue of *phronesis*, which integrates the virtues and adjudicates value conflicts, and by not rejecting less half-heartedly than it does the notorious fact-value distinction—although positive psychologists may want to keep the is-ought distinction to retain their "scientific" credibility. Conversely, I have argued that Aristotelian virtue ethicists have a lot to learn from the way in which Positive Psychology undergirds its finding with empirical evidence and how it cleverly operationalizes and brings down to earth some of Aristotle's more cryptic concepts: for example, his "pleasure in unimpeded activities" reconceptualized as "flow."

To cut a long story short, I have long thought that a similar argument could be made for the value-added-ness for both theology and Positive

Psychology of entering into a dialogue. After reading through the chapters in this excellent book, this is now not only something that I or others may "think" or hypothesize; the whole volume is both an extended *argument* for the potential constructiveness of crossover work between the two disciplines and a *plea* for more efforts of that kind. I know many people in Positive Psychology who would take well to this suggestion. It seems, however—to an outsider at least—that theology has traditionally been quite a cloistered discipline and often slow to react to developments in areas to which it could potentially contribute. For instance, as interest in moral education has swayed in latter days towards conception of character-and-virtue cultivation and towards an ideal of flourishing as an overall educational aim, theologians have failed to make a significant impact on the discourse. Yet these "new" ideals should be right up their street. I hope this volume encourages theologians to acquaint themselves with the new paradigm of Positive Psychology and to participate in the discourse on how people can best lead flourishing lives.

Just one example of an area to which theology could contribute—but where Aristotle is all at sea—has to do with one of the six overarching virtues in Positive Psychology, namely *transcendence*, and one of its five subordinate character strengths, namely *spirituality*. The positive psychological conceptualization of "virtues" and "character strengths" draws heavily on historical precedents, not least Aristotelian ones. However, although Aristotle is strong on virtues directed at other people, such as compassion, and at oneself, such as proper pride, he has little if anything to say about virtues directed at transpersonal ideals. Aristotle is not alone here; while moral philosophers have traditionally been deeply interested in "self-transcendence" in a *horizontal* sense, where people abandon the obsession with their own "fat ego" and reach out to others, they have often had little to say about self-transcendence in a *vertical* sense, where people direct their attention to higher, non-transpersonal ideals. Plato was obviously an exception here, and recently moral philosophers and positive psychologists have given considerable attention to *moral elevation* (targeting moral ideals rather than just admired moral exemplars). Yet if one really seeks enlightenment on the virtue of transcendence, the best bet is still to study the views of the great founders of theology, such as Aquinas. A search for enlightenment in those sources does not necessarily come with the baggage—too heavy for some—of buying into a *particular* religious framework, or even *any* such framework. There is for instance, in my view, more gained—even for secular thinkers—from trying to get a grip on the potentially virtuous emotion of *awe* by reading theological texts and studying religious art than by scouring the available philosophical sources.

A similar argument could be made for *spirituality*. Lots of psychological research seems to indicate that people have a deep psychological need for spiritual experiences. Yet philosophical, psychological, and educational writings on the nature of spirituality are often lacking in depth and sophistication—only skimming the surface of the deep-rooted needs that draw people towards ideals of spiritual transcendence. For example, what goes by the name of "spiritual education" in schools is often watered-down beyond belief, for the sake of mistaken liberal neutrality. Again, theologians should not be shy to enter the relevant discussion and offer their insights. That is not the same as proselytizing or telling people what their objects of self-transcendent awe or spirituality should be.

I have only given brief examples here of areas in Positive Psychology where crossing the fence between theology and empirical science would potentially be productive. The following chapters in this book are brimming with other examples. To give not only transcendence and spirituality their due, but also many other positive psychological constructs, theology offers resources that cannot be ignored with impunity. Analogously, if theologians are really interested—as they should be—in helping ordinary people in the modern world identify ways in which they can "flourish in faith," they can only disregard the evidence provided by Positive Psychology at their peril. Crossing fences may not always be more profitable than mending them, but this book speaks volumes for the former option in the case of theology and Positive Psychology. I congratulate the editors and authors on a job well done.

Introduction

GILLIES AMBLER, MATTHEW P. ANSTEY,
THEO D. MCCALL, AND MATHEW A. WHITE

THIS BOOK AROSE FROM a landmark Australian conference run at St Peter's College-Adelaide in September 2014, *Flourishing in Faith: Positive Psychology and Theology*. The conference was jointly hosted by St Barnabas College, an Anglican theological college, and St Peter's College, an Anglican school for boys (K-12).

The conference was a result of the creativity and tenacity of an organizing committee chaired by the Rev'd Canon Dr Matthew P. Anstey, with representation from Anglican, Roman Catholic and Lutheran denominations. Committee members included Mary Carmody from Catholic Education South Australia; Associate Professor Mathew A. White, the Rev'd Dr Theo D. McCall, Emily FitzSimons, and Jason Haseldine, from St Peter's College; Jim Raw, the Anglican Schools Liason Officer from the Diocese of Adelaide; and Stuart Traeger, the Spiritual Development Leader for the Lutheran Schools Association of South Australia, Northern Territory and Western Australia.

With over 200 delegates from nearly every state across Australia and international delegates from the United States of America, the conference was the first to explore the relationship between the Christian tradition and the emerging field of Positive Psychology, a branch of psychology that conducts scientific inquiry into factors that help individuals, communities, and organizations to thrive. Both institutions have a keen interest in this conversation.

St Peter's College, Adelaide, and St Barnabas College have a historical connection and share close links, extending back to the influence of the first Anglican Bishop of Adelaide, Augustus Short, who accomplished the immense task of establishing the Church of England in South Australia and Western Australia. In the early years of the colony of South Australia, Bishop Short sent his first candidates for ordination to St Peter's College for tuition in theological subjects. Now, over 130 years later, it is fitting that a book like this emerges from connections between the two institutions.

Today, St Barnabas College is a member of the Charles Sturt University School of Theology and is engaged in exploring the theological issues at stake in human flourishing. St Peter's College is renowned internationally for the quality and depth of its integration of Positive Psychology into all aspects of school life, for students and staff, in the curriculum and co-curriculum. This has come to be known as Positive Education, an umbrella term used to describe empirically validated programs of Positive Psychology in educational settings. In 2015, St Peter's College published the landmark book *Evidence-based Approaches to Positive Education in Schools: Implementing a Strategic Framework for Well-being in Schools*, co-edited by Mathew A. White and Simon Murray with Springer Press.

Our initial vision for the conference was for there to be an equal measure of theologians encountering Positive Psychology and psychologists encountering theology. As the planning proceeded there were, however, many more speakers in the former category and the book has developed likewise. Hence our decision to amend the conference title of the subsequent monograph to, *Flourishing in Faith: Theology Encountering Positive Psychology*. The contributions to this book accordingly reflect a slight lopsidedness to the conversation, which in our view is important for readers to recognize but in no way detracts from the worthiness of the project.

The keynote speaker was Professor Ellen T. Charry, Margaret W. Harmon Professor of Theology at Princeton Theological Seminary, who has had a long academic interest in the interface between Christian theology and human wellbeing. Her two addresses constitute the first two chapters of this book and develop the metaphor of two friends exchanging gifts as an evocative and thoughtful lens through which to consider the relationship of theology with Positive Psychology. Though at times the friendship has been tense, given their respective philosophical frameworks, Ellen deftly explores the relationship and what each might be able to hear from, and offer as a gift to, the other. Together with an introduction to Positive Psychology by Associate Professor Mathew A. White, Director of Wellbeing and Positive Education at St Peter's College and Principal Fellow in the Melbourne Graduate School of Education at The University of Melbourne; these chapters act to frame the conversation for the remainder of the book.

The editors have divided the remaining chapters into three sections: Biblical, theological, and practical perspectives. In Biblical Perspectives, two chapters seek to discern the place of human flourishing within the broad sweep of the Biblical story: Matthew P. Anstey explores the notion of wellbeing within the first account of creation in Genesis 1 and its eschatological trajectory (Chapter 4), while Tim Harris considers wellbeing as an expression of God's mission to bring *shalom* "wholeness" to all creation (Chapter 5). Mathew White takes a deeper focus in exploring how the story and life of Mary, the God-bearer (*theotokos*) can be read through the lens of Positive Psychology (Chapter 6).

In Theological Perspectives, Theo D. McCall, who lectures at St Barnabas and is Senior Chaplain at St Peter's College (and Senior Chaplain for Anglican Schools in the Diocese of Adelaide), investigates the conversation from a Trinitarian perspective and shows the many areas of convergence between the two disciplines, some of which are perhaps unexpected (Chapter 7). Carla and Andrew Ford take a different approach by focusing on one specific idea, namely, gratitude, and the different ways it is construed in theology and psychology (Chapter 8), while Harold Ellens concludes this section with an exploration of the (relatively common) experiences people have of the "numinous," posing the question whether such experiences are basically human or encounters with the divine (Chapter 9). Again, much common ground is evident when one takes time to listen attentively to theological and psychological literature in these areas.

The final section is Practical Perspectives and it covers a diversity of topics and approaches. The first two chapters tackle significant negative human experiences, grief and disability respectively—topics "at home" in theological discourse given its traditional emphasis on human brokenness—and ponder the ways in which theology and Positive Psychology approach these when brought into conversation with one another. Gillies Ambler explores his profound personal experiences of grief and the ways in which he applied his insights to the counselling of others (Chapter 10). Shane Clifton was a plenary speaker at the conference but was not able to contribute a chapter to this book. Shane's reflections on Positive Psychology, as a systematic theologian in the Pentecostal tradition and as a quadriplegic, are always thought-provoking and at times unsettling. We judged his voice too important to omit. He kindly agreed to an interview, which appears in edited form in Chapter 11.

The contributions of Lisa Spargo and James Nelson in Chapters 12-13 are both at the "coal-face" of secondary school educational contexts (Anglican and Lutheran respectively) where Positive Psychology is being implemented. They provide insights into how this conversation plays out in practice. The final chapter in the book is distinctive in several ways: it is authored by a multidisciplinary team with theological, psychological, statistical, psychiatric, and justice studies expertise; and it adopts an empirical approach to investigate the measurement of hope and faith in human flourishing (Chapter 14). This chapter demonstrates the potential for rich and probing conversations to be explored further through empirical research into the contribution of spirituality to wellbeing, and more broadly to research projects evaluating evidence of the contribution Christian theology and Positive Psychology make to the project of human flourishing.

The editors would like to acknowledge those who assisted in the publication of this monograph. The Right Reverend Dr Jeffrey Driver, Archbishop of Adelaide, Visitor and President of the Council of Governors of St Peter's College (2005–2016) and the Headmaster of St Peter's College, Mr Simon Murray (2010–), have been enthusiastic supporters of the collaboration between the two institutions that led to the conference and this book. The Council of St Barnabas College and the Council of Governors of St Peter's College likewise provided support and financial assistance for this project.

St Barnabas College is a member of the Charles Sturt University School of Theology and acknowledges its support, and St Peter's College acknowledges the support of the Centre for Positive Psychology, Melbourne Graduate School of Education at The University of Melbourne, with whom it collaborates in the study of Positive Education. Finally, the editors would like to thank Dr Doug Rowston (St Barnabas College, Adjunct Lecturer), the Rev'd Melinda Cousins (St Barnabas College, PhD candidate) and Leeston McNab, who assisted in the preparation of the manuscript for publication.

St Barnabas College—Adelaide
St Peter's College—Adelaide
Feast of St Aidan of Lindisfarne, August 31, 2016

Framing the Conversation

Chapter 1

Positive Psychology
and Christian Theology

An Exchange of Gifts
❀

ELLEN T. CHARRY

AT FIRST GLANCE IT may appear unlikely that Christian theology and Positive Psychology would be friends, or even consider being friends. In this chapter, though, I will argue that these two approaches to human flourishing should become friends, because each bears gifts that will benefit the other on its own terms. I will begin by offering an image of what friendship between the fields might look like, set against a backdrop of common objections. I will even argue that the objections on each side provide solid ground for such a friendship and then discuss ways that theology should open itself to a friendship with Positive Psychology. In Chapter 2, I will argue that Positive Psychology should open itself to friendship with theology. Although not exact parallels, the two chapters are intended to be considered alongside one another.

WHAT IS FRIENDSHIP?

Friendship was highly prized in antiquity. Sophocles, Aristotle, Xenophon, and Cicero all lauded it. Cicero's "Laelius on Friendship" notes the uplifting nature of friendship as well as its limits and its fragility. Cicero writes that we cannot be friends with those we fear; friendship is grounded in trust. He also argues that to seek friendship is natural to us; it is not sought from a sense of personal inadequacy. I shall return to these two points anon. Probably because it was written in Latin, Cicero's treatise particularly influenced the Cistercian monk, Aelred of Rievaulx's "On Spiritual Friendship" written in the twelfth century. Spiritual friendship is as demanding as it is rewarding. We do well to heed Aelred's words.

> First, there should be a mutual caring; friends should pray for each other, blush and rejoice for one another, each should weep over the other's lapse as though it were his own, and look on his friend's progress as his own. In whatever ways he can, he should encourage the timid, support the weak, console the sorrowful and restrain the hot-tempered. Moreover, he must respect the eyes and ears of his friend, and never presume to wound them with an unseemly act or an unfitting word. A becoming reserve is friendship's best companion: take reserve away from friendship and you deprive it of its greatest ornament. How often has a sign from my friend damped down or quenched the smoldering fire of anger, already on the point of flaring out! How many times have his graver features checked the undignified remark already on the tip of my tongue! How often when I have needlessly dissolved into laughter, or fallen into idle chatter has his arrival restored me to a proper gravity! Besides, if there is something that needs saying, it comes better from a friend and leaves a deeper mark. A recommendation must carry real weight when the giver is known to be loyal and yet not given to flattery. Therefore, between friends sound advice should be given confidently, candidly and freely. Mutual admonishment is an integral part of friendship; it should be kindly and not roughly given, and patiently, not resentfully, received. For believe me, there is no scourge of friendship like flattery and complaisance, the characteristic vices of the light-minded and smooth-tongued, those who say what's sure to please and never what is true. So let there be no hesitation between friends, none of the pretence that is so utterly incompatible with friendship. One owes a friend the truth; without it the word friendship has no meaning.[1]

1. Aelred, "Spiritual Friendship," 187.

The elements of this paragraph that I think speak to our topic are that friends are invited to admonish one another when needed, yet always kindly and with reserve. They are also called to check the other's rashness or frivolity; that is, they are called to provide a second set of eyes on oneself to prevent one from looking foolish. One might argue that Aelred disagreed with Cicero at this point because offering mutual admonition to protect one's friend from embarrassment does expose one's weakness. But I would argue that two heads are always better than one, that other people's experience, knowledge, temperament and insight should enhance one's own judgments. The capacity to embrace friendship, and especially the capacity to welcome and offer loving criticism, are signs of strength, not weakness. With this outlook in mind I turn to the relationship at hand.

OBJECTIONS TO FRIENDSHIP

Hesitation to befriend the other occurs within both disciplines. To put the point sharply, I think that the basic issue dividing theology from psychology, or more accurately, Augustinian theology from modern secular psychology, is autonomy. The Augustinian tradition denies that we are autonomous, insisting that we are tethered to God whether we admit it or not, and that we need God to have proper self-understanding, a properly modest identity. Modern secular psychology denies this theological foundation of the self, insisting that we are free to define ourselves as we see fit, perhaps within circumstantial limits.

From my perch in theology, minimally perusing psychology's landscape, I have the impression that this fundamental disagreement makes psychology, a scientific discipline based on repeatable evidence, more nervous about engaging theology, than theology is about engaging psychology. I believe that the reasons underpinning this nervousness are both principled and personal. Although I address psychology's concerns more fully in Chapter 2, I provide an initial outline here.

Objections from Psychology

Modern research-driven psychology was nurtured from the placenta of high modernity, where self-directedness[2] and moral independence were

2. The term "autonomy" is more often used than "self-directedness." "Autonomy"

seen as strengths that enable self-expression and thereby flourishing. Post-modernity may be nuancing that belief slightly but modern science is established on the belief that we are not tethered to God and do not require any notion of a transcendent realm in order to understand ourselves rightly. We do not need to face ultimate reality in order to make sense of our lives. That is quite counter to Voltaire's famous quip that "If God did not exist, it would be necessary to invent him."

The very idea of standing before God by virtue of being creature implies dependency, elegantly articulated by Friedrich Schleiermacher, the father of modern theology, as "utter dependence." Secular psychology, based as it is on modern scientific method, rejects theology's insistence on another ontological realm as essential to our wellbeing. The idea of an essential transcendent realm has been replaced with the notion of autonomy, the idea that we can and should determine our own destiny so far as practically possible.

To this end, angels, demons, and "satanic forces," sometimes externalized and concretized as existent beings, have been psychologized and internalized to create the notion of psychological pathology and the possibility of its being overcome.[3] Both disciplines may agree that such forces are harmful. From time to time they may be willing to cooperate to address them. But they are not having a single conversation.

Modern psychology's goal has generally been to address such psychological limitations by improving personal skills, through techniques such as cognitive behavioral therapy (CBT), medication (with psychiatric management), or insight-oriented psychotherapy. The idea that we are tethered to a "higher power," to which we are responsible and before which we are accountable and inherently inadequate, infringes on modernity's conviction that we are self-propelled. More than this, it is considered by some to deter attempts to maximize strengths if it teaches helplessness before God.[4] Religion, in particular some forms of Christianity, is rejected, because it casts us as victims of both ourselves and of the divine will. It is seen to undercut

comes from Immanuel Kant, *Grounding*, but he meant something narrower than psychology means by self-directedness.

3. It is possible that ancient use of such terms was intended to be understood psychologically and existentially but at least in the Middles Ages they were objectified.

4. The evidence on whether religion improves wellbeing or not is mixed although often positive. See Koenig et al., *Handbook*, 53–73, 123–44, 298–314; Pargament and Mahoney, "Sacred Matters." Some positive findings may be attributable to the sociality of religious belonging rather than to a specific system of belief.

precisely the strengths, emotions, and enjoyments that modern psychology and particularly Positive Psychology seek to maximize.

Mainstream and positive psychologies reject the idea of a need for salvation by an external transcendent source. They do not recognize a ubiquitous and uniform character defect from which all need to be healed and that only God can heal. Mainstream psychology recognizes character disorders, of course, but does not single one out as central and universal. Perhaps the closest psychological term for the Augustinian insistence on sin (*superbia*) as vanity is *narcissism*. Translating the theological into the psychological potentially begins building a bridge between the two discourses, although modern psychology would not see narcissism as a universal flaw, as held by Augustinian theology.[5]

There is an ongoing debate about which therapeutic strategies best address character disorders, but the tenor of the times in the US, influenced by modern psychology, does not generally recognize faith in God as one of them. Rather than see sin as a congenital illness, modern psychology and social psychology may attribute psychological dysfunction to untoward circumstances. The culture of poverty and difficult family circumstances (recall the schizophrenogenic mother of a few decades ago) protect the patient from self-incrimination. More recently, biochemical and genetic research are complexifying our understanding of the origins of the major mental illnesses.

Another prominent theme of Positive Psychology is the preferential value placed on positive emotions. Although these may be seen as stemming from an optimistic personality, they are also cultivated through various exercises and personal practices. Western Christian theology, by contrast, does not generally discuss specific emotions, but values fear of divine punishment and self-examination stemming from feelings of guilt and remorse at sin.

Having identified some potential principles behind the psychology profession's friendship hesitations, I now turn to some personal reasons that individual psychologists might have for resisting theology. One relates to the scientific outlook that dominates modern culture, leading psychology to scientize. Here are the children of Feuerbach, who consider the idea of a transcendent realm to be spurious because it cannot be quantified. To legitimate itself, modern psychology scientized, insisting on the necessity of quantifying its hunches in order to give them credibility. Modern

---

5. Augustine, "On Free Will"; "To Simplician"; *Confessions*; "Literal Meaning."

psychology patterned itself on the hard sciences, distancing itself from the humanities: literature, philosophy, and theology. Framing the point more personally, as religion became incredible, some psychologists came to see theology and religion as either irrelevant to their work, fraudulent and therefore unworthy of consideration, or perhaps even inimical to psychology's scientific claims. Religion is to be "got beyond" as eighteenth-century French revolutionaries generally hoped. It is also probable that the secular terms of the modern discipline attract scholars and clinicians who may be personally sympathetic to those terms.

A yet more individual reason for some psychologists' resistance to theology is personal experience. Some practitioners may have chosen the psychology discipline in their efforts to disrobe following debilitating religious experiences. In their zeal to press their opposing case, practitioners portray religious customs and practices as restrictive and even psychologically damaging. Personal experience of theological malpractice understandably influences how researchers and clinicians approach these matters.

Objections from Theology

Having suggested why modern psychology may resist befriending theology, I now turn to classical western theology's distrust of modern psychology. Following reflections on Scripture, his own adolescence, and his observations of children and adults, Augustine of Hippo proposed the controversial idea that all people incline toward self-centeredness, arrogance, or vanity. He called this original (or inherent) sin, *superbia*—we think that we are superb.[6] It is a congenital spiritual defect, a basic weakness in every human personality that powers bad behavior and sullies one's reputation and relationships with others. All people are characterologically flawed and we cannot rid ourselves of the defect by personal effort. Indeed, character disorders are notoriously difficult to treat. Modern psychology would hold that we can make at least some strides against our limitations with effort, therapy, learning new skills, or cultivating more constructive optimistic attitudes. The Christian west, on the other hand, that followed Augustine, claims that we are helpless before God and only God's grace can release us from these shackles. Although the modern pastoral care movement steps somewhat outside theological tradition in utilizing secular psychology, in

6. Augustine, *Confessions*, 2.

strict theological terms, the Augustinian view is that God is the only reliable therapist.

Reading the Bible, Augustine, Anselm, and Calvin all theorized that there was a primordial time before this fundamental character flaw overtook people, but it is long gone. We now, all of us, are narcissistic, curved in on ourselves and for Augustine that meant that we enact twisted love. We both love the wrong things and we love them inordinately. Even when we love good things, we tend to love them badly. All our loves should be God-directed. God-directed love is accomplished only by recognizing Jesus Christ as having given his life gratuitously for our sakes and, from his example, learning to live sagaciously, justly, and responsibly. It is only by embracing Christ that we come to know God and learn to love well. Loving God better, even if never perfectly, straightens our twisted loves, perhaps not curing the defect, but at least meliorating it, by orienting our love toward the beauty, wisdom, and goodness of God rather than toward less worthy goods. So concludes the Augustinian heritage.

At the end of the eleventh century, Anselm of Canterbury, as well as the lesser-known Odo of Tournai, offered a significant tweak of the Augustinian heritage. Augustine's idea that we are all narcissists but that our love could be partially straightened, was interpreted as a permanent state of sinfulness; which must be forgiven in order for us to move on. The western Christian theological tradition had been elaborating the theme of the wrath of God since before Augustine's time, but the western medievals focused on that suggesting that God's punishing wrath and gracious love were in tension with one another.

While it would not be right for God to look away from human sinfulness, neither would it be right for God's punishing anger to have free reign. Anselm proposed a solution.[7] Although from God's perspective we deserve capital punishment for our narcissism, the Son of God became incarnate in order to undergo our punishment for us, thus displaying God's love for us. The idea was to apprise people of what they truly deserve, yet recognize what they have received and so humble them. Thus they may both learn what justice demands and live gratefully, given that God executed his wrath on Christ in our place. Since, in Christian terms, Christ is the Son of God, ontologically the same as God the Father, the point is that forgiving narcissism is actualized by an action that takes place within the divine life, made visible to humanity for a pedagogical purpose. It aims to draw our

---

7. Anselm, *Why God Became Man.*

attention to the loving goodness of God so that we wrap our lives around that knowledge.

To protect divine sovereignty, the Augustinian heritage, particularly in its Protestant expressions, denies us the power of repair, even with God's help. Even the hope of it is a symptom of the disease. Arguments about the possibility and extent of repair divided Catholic and Protestant interpretations of their common Augustinian patrimony. The staunchest Protestant position is that the most we can hope for is to be included among those whose sins God forgives through the undeserved death of Christ, that God takes the "hit" that we deserve. Those who trust that interpretation of Christ's accomplishment experience relief from the fear of divine punishment, believing that God looks away from their guilt. Relief from dread of God's wrath does not, however, heal the basic narcissism. Luther drove this point home with his *simul justus et peccator*. This Latin tradition in its Protestant form became truncated into the idea that the central dilemma of a human life is the need to experience oneself as forgiven rather than blameworthy. This is based on the hope that belief in our forgiveness acts to transform our behavior for the better. The spiritual transformation is from fearful to joyful living.

Although we cannot know for sure who is accepted by the gift of Christ's atoning death, because God's judgment on each is unknown to us, the Augustine heritage urges people to turn away from themselves and toward God as the energy fueling their life, trusting that they are among those favored. Elaborating on this theme, Calvin encouraged self-denial and self-abnegation as means to that end, on the principle that the less we think of and about ourselves, the more we will think of God and about others. Similar sentiments are cited in Galatians: "I have been crucified with Christ; it is no longer I who live, but it is Christ who lives in me" (2:19–20), or perhaps Colossians "you have died, and your life is hidden with Christ in God" (3:3), reflecting the idea that Christians are to abjure themselves and rest in warranted humility before God.

Having previously noted the position of modern psychology on human nature it is easy to see why western Christian theology might not welcome its friendship. Augustinian theo-psychology construes all people as permanent victims of moral scoliosis, while modern psychology admits of no such thing as original sin (or perhaps of actual sin either). It does acknowledge, however, that we make mistakes and poor judgments that can lead to dysfunctional behavior and unstable relationships. But it generally does not label the cause of these impediments to a flourishing life as "sin." The goal of therapy or retraining behavior is to manage the obstacles to a flourishing life by developing the skills needed to maximize strengths, recognizing and learning to control character defects, and, within Positive Psychology, cultivating positive emotions and an optimistic attitude that encourages persistence, territory that western theology distrusts.[8]

All of this is to say that theology and psychology see similar phenomena but name them differently. When we push the linguistic boundaries on both sides, though, we might find more commonality than one might expect, despite philosophical objections. Disagreements about how to interpret behavioral and character flaws are not readily bridged, even when vocabulary can be shared, as with "narcissism" or "character flaw." Each perspective is grounded in principles that the other denies; acquiescing to the terms of the other would encroach on its principles. I suggest that basic disagreement stems from the modern notion of autonomy. Theology thinks that we are tethered to God by virtue of being created by him in his image. Psychology thinks that this God-given identity denies the self-determination that enables people to direct their lives and this may include taking no account of God.

That said, classical western theology and mainstream modern psychology do have common interests. Although neither uses precisely this language, I think they both hope to help people become excellent persons, at least so say the supporters of eudemonic flourishing.[9] The Church thinks of that in moral terms, while Positive Psychology thinks of that in terms that moderately correlate with wealth, health, mental health and other factors assessable by subjective wellbeing measurements. Still, they all want to help people flourish. There is no strong reason why they should not be able to respect the perspective of the other and use it to broaden their own.

Before moving on, I would add that some of these disagreements may be rhetorical, as suggested by translating *superbia* as narcissism. Modern psychology, for example, certainly understands that we have only limited control over our lives and that we live mutually interdependent lives on the horizontal level. Of course, it denies that all people are somewhat narcissistic, as western Christian theology claims. For its part, Augustinian theology recognizes that we make choices and decisions about how to live our lives every waking moment. We are not morally paralyzed or helpless on

8. Peterson and Seligman, *Character Strengths.*
9. Keyes, "Well-Being"; Keyes and Haidt, *Flourishing.*

the horizontal plane; the problem is only that we cannot justify ourselves before God. Such areas of agreement provide opportunity for interesting conversation but are insufficient to overcome the neuralgia that plagues the relationship.

In conclusion, I now turn to gifts that Positive Psychology can offer theology. In Chapter 2 I examine the gifts that theology offers Positive Psychology.

POSITIVE PSYCHOLOGY'S GIFTS TO THEOLOGY

1. Embracing Strength as a Christianly Warranted Moral Position

When I first began talking about happiness a decade ago, I offered two lectures at a Christian liberal arts college, using the word "happiness." As people were filing out of the hall, a gentleman passed by me and said, *sotto voce*, "There are more important things to think about." What did he mean? I think he was instructing me that Christians should not be concerned about being happy but about being good. Indeed, for some, perhaps wanting to be happy is itself an expression of the narcissism that affects us all. One can hear echoes of deontological ethics applauding in the background.

The modern idea that happiness and goodness sit in different life compartments, stems largely from a particular reading of Immanuel Kant's ethics that proposed praiseworthy behavior as dutiful behavior, unpleasant as it may be. While Kant admitted that acting dutifully might arouse some sort of personal satisfaction, he insisted that for the most part being good is unpleasant and praiseworthy precisely for that reason. That line of thought fits well with Christian agapeism that advocated self-sacrifice and self-denial to correct basic narcissism, though at times it slid the value of Christian love into advocating self-hatred as praiseworthy. Indeed, Kant himself was informed by this strand of Protestant Pietism. This reading of Kant has been basic to modern Protestant ethics. I believe that the idea is flawed although I do recognize its origin deep in western Christian spirituality and ethics.

The Christian objection to seeking enjoyment of life and self stems from the tradition of agapeistic ethics, which is focused on the idea that we should imitate Christ's sacrifice on the cross by taking up our own cross to follow him (Matt 10:38; 16:24; and parallels). Agapeistic ethics is the idea that moral strength is unconditional and requires painful self-sacrifice for the sake of "the other." One is to give and give and give, and when one has nothing left to give, one gives more. In a counter-intuitive move, the tradition holds that it is in suffering voluntarily that we flourish. This is the heart of Nietzsche's objection to Christianity, an objection that was deeply influential throughout the twentieth century and spawned reform movements within Christian theology.

I do not think that this view pleases or honors God. God did not create the world for its languishing. Self-sacrifice to the point of self-damage is not desirable, not only because God laments our languishing, but more importantly because languishing prevents us from enabling the world to flourish and may lead us to take others down with us. When we flourish truly, including but not limited to moral flourishing, we enable others and the world around us to flourish because flourishing is built from positive experiences that enable us to navigate the world successfully. Living successfully strengthens and motivates us to think about challenges broadly and assist others confidently to do the same. That is, the ability to "use" ourselves well is essential to being an instrument of creation's flourishing and that is to be obedient to God. Trust in one's strength to use oneself well in the service of creation's flourishing is a deep source of pleasure in being who one is continuously becoming.

Espousing adroit self-use may be off-putting to some Christians, but if heard within a Christian theological frame of reference in which life is lived in the joy, and to the glory, of God, I think there is protection from distorting the idea and using it in the service of crass selfishness. Theologically proper self-centeredness encourages discerning self-knowledge that powers a well-directed life. Recognizing that using oneself well not only benefits others but enhances our own wellbeing is a theological rendition of Barbara Fredrickson's "broaden and build" theory as I understand it. This leads me to a corollary of embracing strength: embracing self-repair within a Christian theological framework.

2. Embracing Self-Repair as Christianly Appropriate

Augustinian theology's insistence that we are dependent upon God to the point of helplessness to save ourselves from sin does not mean that we are helpless to repair ourselves, although it has sometimes been taken that way. Since second millennium western soteriology focused on belief in the forgiveness of sin as constituting salvation, I think what is being suggested in that case is rather that we should not imagine that we are warranted in dismissing our own iniquities as inconsequential, for that amounts to self-deception. Highlighting our character flaws and the untoward behavior that they generate impresses upon us that there are things about ourselves to which we must attend for our own wellbeing and that of those around us.

Unfortunately the denial of any possibility of lasting self-improvement, which is inherent in some Christian theology, invites despair. Is it not possible to learn to control anger better, control inappropriate jealousy, become more attentive to others' needs, become a better listener? We may not realize our hopes for ourselves, but here Christians should welcome help from psychology and medicine. Self-repair strategies such as building on personal strengths also enable those around us to flourish better, so that the positive effects of self-repair lateralize.

3. Embracing Psychological Individuation as Basic to Human Nature

A key difference between Augustinian theology and modern psychology lies in Augustinian theology's identification of a univocal personality that applies to all people, while modern psychology identifies a range of personality types that affect individuals differently. Even more importantly for this conversation, psychology believes that it is possible to be psychologically healthy without tarring everyone with the brush of narcissism or some other uniform defect.

While Augustine may have been correct that we all sin, it is also true that we do not all sin exactly as he seems to have proposed. Character and behavioral weaknesses vary from one person to the next. One is too timid while another is too bold. One is greedy, another generous to a fault. One is overprotective of those in their care, another is indifferent, as Aristotle taught us long ago.

Temperamental differences among people were recognized in ancient humoral theory that predates Christianity, but Augustine did not utilize these findings. He gave us a uniform picture of "human nature" that is inattentive to individual differences. Christian counselors have to set aside what can look like a caricature of the human personality in order to really see the person who comes for treatment, making it difficult to bring theology into the clinical setting. The recognition of individual differences would not entail giving up the notion of sin so central to all Christian theology. It could be nuanced and rendered more accessible to a psychologically attentive public.

4. Embracing Positive Emotions

Positive Psychology does not highlight moral flourishing but stresses positive feelings and attitudes that reflect enjoyment of life, with such enjoyment being seen as an appropriate personal goal. These ideas are likely to be viewed with suspicion by theology, having logged onto the idea that obedience to God, following the model of the cross, requires self-sacrifice, or, as Kant put it, "obeying bitter duty." And yet, at least in the Eastern-Orthodox (Greek) Christian theological tradition, represented by both Irenaeus[10] and Athanasius,[11] God wants us to flourish, is genuinely distressed when we languish, and intervenes in history to turn situations around.

If welcoming strength, creativity, confidence, resilience, and fun sound odd to western Christian ears, I would encourage a pause for reflection. Why would God create a world to embrace its languishing? That would only reflect ill upon him. Indeed, why would God create at all except to be accompanied by creatures both great and small who reflect his beauty and goodness by flourishing themselves? I would even go so far as to say that enjoying ourselves is central to God's own flourishing as suggested by Isaiah: "For as a young man marries a young woman, so shall your builder marry you, and as the bridegroom rejoices over the bride, so shall your God rejoice over you" (Isa 62:5). Zephaniah also affirms this idea; "The Lord, your God, is in your midst, a warrior who gives victory; he will rejoice over you with gladness, he will renew you in his love; he will exult over you with loud singing" (Zeph 3:17). God rejoices in our happy times, exults in being among us when we succeed, renewing us with his love. If God truly wants creation's flourishing he must exult when we love well, when we enjoy success at challenging tasks, and when we create adroitly. We, in turn, are encouraged by God's celebration of us as we succeed in living beneficently. At least these two verses suggest that between God and us there is a win-win expectation. Christian theology has yet to drink deeply from it. Positive Psychology can awaken Christian theology to this perspective.

10. Grant, *Irenaeus of Lyons.*
11. Athanasius, *Contra Gentes.*

5. Embracing Pleasure

Western Christianity has stumbled over material pleasure and not without reason. Physical enjoyment is the source of much suffering in life. Presently, the pleasures of the table threaten the health of North Americans as the food industry exploits the human preference for carbohydrates and the salt-sugar cycle not to speak of the dangers of sexual impropriety that leaves women trapped in poverty and fatherless children in its wake. Despite these excesses, the pleasures of table and bed, along with the pleasures of accomplishment, creativity, and the beneficent use of power, promote creation's wellbeing. Western Christian theology has hesitated to celebrate pleasure for fear of encouraging the debilitating potential of these desires. Theology has functioned rather as a watchdog on unruly emotions, inclinations, and behavior, and understandably so. Positive Psychology, in its seeking to strengthen morally discerning strength, may warrant guidance from theology about how to do that constructively. Theology's warning about the abusive possibilities of poorly guided pleasure-seeking is indeed warranted. When enjoyed judiciously however, material pleasures serve creation's flourishing.

MOVING FORWARD

Here I have proposed that modern psychology generally, and Positive Psychology within it, can help Christian theology appreciate a broader understanding of human nature than has often been the case. This is possible without compromising theology's deep commitments to life with God as basic for wellbeing, its belief in the sinfulness of human nature that requires divine aid, or its appreciation of the potentially positive effects of negative emotions like fear, jealousy, and greed. Mainstream modern psychology, in dealing with similar problems to theology, can encourage theology to expand its understanding of sin to encompass not only the emotions behind bad behavior but also to appreciate individual differences in temperament and personality because individuals sin differently. Since Christianity is interested in encouraging self-examination, the nuancing of its doctrine of sin will forward this important Christian value. Conversation with psychology will also encourage Christian theology to encourage strategies for self-improvement, not that they compromise commitment to the saving grace of God, but that they encourage pro-social behavior on the horizontal plane. Further, psychology's interest in defense and coping mechanisms and Positive Psychology's interest in building resilience,[12] creativity, and resourcefulness in negotiating life's vicissitudes, will encourage theology to value adaptability and flexibility[13] as properly Christian habits and virtues.

Theology need not agree with all of Positive Psychology's presuppositions and methods in order to appreciate its interest in cultivating positive emotions, and without jeopardizing its insistence on the positive role of negative emotions in a well-ordered life. Indeed, the character strengths and virtues that many Christian psychologists study, including gratitude, forgiveness, love, and hope, resonate deeply with, even derive from, Christian sensibilities. Theological language may well be "dusty" in a psychologically oriented culture and exchange with psychology will surely enhance and respect theology's understanding of some of its own deepest commitments. Let the conversation commence!

REFERENCES

Aelred of Rievaulx. "Selections from On Spiritual Friendship." In *Cistercian World: Monastic Writings of the Twelfth Century*, edited by Pauline Matarasso, 169–90. New York: Penguin, 1993.

Anselm. *Why God Became Man: Cur Deus Homo*. Translated by Jasper Hopkins and Herbert Richardson. Queenston: Mellen, 1985.

Athanasius. *Contra Gentes* and *De incarnatione*. Translated by Robert W. Thomson, Oxford Early Christian Texts. Oxford: Clarendon, 1971.

Augustine. *Confessions*. Translated by Henry Chadwick. Oxford: Oxford University Press, 1991.

———. "On Free Will." In *Augustine: The Earlier Writings*, edited by J. H. S. Burleigh, 102–217. Philadelphia: Westminster, 1958.

———. "The Literal Meaning of Genesis." In *On Genesis*, edited by Michael Fiedrowicz, 168–506. Hyde Park: New City, 2002.

———. "To Simplician on Various Questions Book 1." In *Augustine: The Earlier Writings*, edited by J. H. S. Burleigh, 370–406. Philadelphia: Westminster, 1958.

Conway, Anne M., et al. "The Broaden-and-build Theory of Positive Emotions: Form, Function, and Mechanisms." In *The Oxford Handbook of Happiness*, edited by Susan A. David et al., 17–34. New York: Oxford University Press, 2013.

Fredrickson, Barbara L. "The Broaden-and-Build Theory of Positive Emotions." In *A Life Worth Living: Contributions to Positive Psychology.*, edited by Mihaly Csikszentmihalyi et al., 85–103. New York: Oxford University Press, 2006.

12. Glantz and Johnson, *Resilience and Development*; Masten and Reed, "Resilience"; Titus, *Resilience and the Virtue of Fortitude*.

13. Leeming and Hayes, "Parents"; Marshall and Brockman, "Relationships"; Salande and Hawkins, "Flexibility."

————. "The Role of Positive Emotions in Positive Psychology: The Broaden-and-build Theory of Positive Emotions." *American Psychologist* 56 (2001) 218–26.

Glantz, Meyer D., and Jeannette L. Johnson. 1999. *Resilience and Development: Positive Life Adaptations, Longitudinal Research in the Social and Behavioral Sciences*. New York: Kluwer Academic/Plenum, 1999.

Grant, Robert McQueen. *Irenaeus of Lyons, The Early Church Fathers*. New York: Routledge, 1997.

Kant, Immanuel. *Grounding for the Metaphysics of Morals*. Translated by James W. Ellington. Indianapolis, IN: Hackett, 1981.

Keyes, Corey L. M. "Subjective Well-Being in Mental Health and Human Development Research Worldwide: An Introduction." *Social Indicators Research* 77 (2006) 1–10.

Keyes, Corey L. M., and Jonathan Haidt, eds. *Flourishing: Positive Psychology and the Life Well-lived*. Washington, DC: American Psychological Association, 2003.

Koenig, Harold G., et al., eds. *Handbook of Religion and Health*. 2nd ed. New York: Oxford University Press, 2012.

Leeming, Emily, and Steven C. Hayes. "Parents are People too: The Importance of Parental Psychological Flexibility." *Clinical Psychology: Science and Practice* 23 (2016) 158–60.

Marshall, Emma-Jane, and Robert N. Brockman. "The Relationships between Psychological Flexibility, Self-compassion, and Emotional Well-being." *Journal of Cognitive Psychotherapy* 30 (2016) 60–72.

Masten, Ann S., and Marie-Gabrielle J. Reed. "Resilience in Development." In *Handbook of Positive Psychology*, edited by C. R. Snyder et al., 74–88. New York: Oxford University Press, 2002.

Pargament, Kenneth I., and Annette Mahoney. "Sacred Matters: Sanctification as a Vital Topic for the Psychology of Religion." *International Journal for the Psychology of Religion* 15 (2005) 179–98.

Peterson, Christopher, and Martin E. P. Seligman. *Character Strengths and Virtues: A Handbook and Classification*. New York: American Psychological Association, 2004.

Salande, Joseph D., and Raymond C. Hawkins, II. "Psychological Flexibility, Attachment Style, and Personality Organization: Correlations Between Constructs of Differing Approaches." *Journal of Psychotherapy Integration*. Advance online publication. http://dx.doi.org/10.1037/int0000037 (April 18, 2016).

Titus, Craig Steven. *Resilience and the Virtue of Fortitude: Aquinas in Dialogue with the Psychosocial Sciences*. Washington, DC: Catholic University of America Press, 2006.

Tugade, Michele M., et al. "Infusing Positive Emotions into Life: The Broaden-and-build Theory and a Dual-process Model of Resilience." In *Handbook of Positive Emotions*, edited by Michele M. Tugade et al., 28–43. New York: Guilford, 2014.

Chapter 2

Flourishing and Languishing

Testimony from the Psalms

E<small>LLEN</small> T. C<small>HARRY</small>

I<small>N CHAPTER</small> 1, I argued that theology and Positive Psychology would benefit from talking to one another because, although they have different discourses and philosophical commitments, they share some common concerns about human wellbeing. Theology would benefit from Positive Psychology's emphasis on strengths and abilities to maximize them as well as its emphasis on building on positive experiences. Here, I propose that Positive Psychology would benefit from theology's emphasis on the ability of failure and weakness to stimulate self-examination and repair relationships. Each perspective without the other gives us a limited view of how to maximize our ability to live well.

Positive Psychology would benefit from theology's focus on the negative aspects of life, not only because avoiding them is unrealistic, but because, at least from a Christian perspective, we tend to exaggerate our strengths and minimize our weaknesses. Meanwhile the weaknesses of others may be more salient to us than they are to the people themselves.

Western Christian theology calls this the sin of *superbia,* that in Chapter 1 I translated as narcissism.[1] At its best, the point of encouraging people to humility is not to make them feel helpless, but to encourage them to accept criticism so that they gain a more realistic self-understanding and live more successfully as a result. So, the point I wish to make is that languishing can contribute to flourishing by stimulating self-reflection and strengthening the self for the healing of relationships.

To offer Positive Psychology the strength of self-examination I turn to Scripture shared by Jews and Christians. The 150 canonized poems of ancient Israel are central to and beloved by both communities. They are embedded in Jewish and Christian liturgy, devotion, and private prayer. They are sung, chanted, and recited in public worship, carried in hip-pockets, purses, and glove compartments by travelers, and puzzled over by interpreters who find many of them perplexing. Yet despite their strangeness to modern readers the Psalms remain implacably in the forefront of devotional attention.

While Christianity (unlike Judaism and Islam) inherited a strong dose of Stoicism from ancient philosophy, the poets of ancient Israel know nothing of it. They embrace life's highs and lows, its flourishing and languishing, with equal gusto. They have no inkling of a "suck it up" apathy, no desire to escape the emotional exhilaration and trauma of life's vicissitudes with Stoic passionless-ness or Epicurean tranquility. On the contrary, the psalmists cavort in every emotion with gusto. They know the exuberant joy of triumph in combat, in politics, in marriage, and in the daily thrill of awakening once again to the world's beauty. At the same time, they carry us into the psychological and physical experiences of humiliation, fear, frustration, fretting, shame, and dishonor, where sleep and eating disorders, depression, and anxiety rob us of what could have been joy-filled days.

Athanasius of Alexandria stated the power of the Psalter some seventeen hundred years ago: "he who recites the Psalms is uttering the rest as his own words, and each sings them as if they were written concerning him . . . he who chants these will be especially confident in speaking what is written as if his own and about him . . . these words become like a mirror to the person singing them, so that he might perceive himself and the emotions of his soul."[2] The poems carry us deep within to disclose our soul to our own gaze.

---

1. Some of this may be gender related. See Key and Shipman, *Confidence Code.*
2. Athanasius, "Letter to Marcellinus," 110–11.

Israel's poets are not for hiding one's lamp under a bushel, but for ebulliently celebrating success with pomp and circumstance, and downfall with candor and regret. In short, Israel's hymnists and liturgists welcome human life in its full vividness from vivacious triumph to profound vulnerability. In that, they are particularly well-suited for our own moment in which flourishing is broadly construed and not confined to cognitive or moral categories. In our day, the membrane between principle and virtue is porous, the indissolubility of emotion having intervened. Since the advent of modern psychology, we cannot envision a virtuous life based on principle alone, as Kant hoped. If a flourishing life is a morally healthy one, we cannot imagine it without emotional support, that is, without personal engagement.[3]

One further prefatory comment is apposite before turning to the texts. As we think about flourishing and languishing, at least two distinct scenarios present themselves for consideration. On one hand, flourishing and languishing are inevitably tied to material circumstances. We either have access to resources for health, safety, peace, adequate wealth, and a stable political environment with access to opportunity and personal striving; or we do not. Even if we do, however, the unforeseeable threat of accident, natural disaster, terrorism, political upheaval, or perhaps even the business cycle or the specter of death, inevitably cast a pall on our aspirations.

Another scenario is that flourishing and languishing are beyond the reach of material circumstance and lie within the psychological realm. Here we meet the first great western psychologist, Augustine of Hippo, who probed the inner life's loves, desires, fears, jealousies, and anger that jostle one another for control. Here, flourishing is not enjoying the benefits of positive material circumstances but the pleasure of self-mastery. Having the energy to persevere towards one's goal, the courage to benefit from criticism, the self-control to resist anger's urgings, and so on, are the strengths of flourishing, satisfaction, and joy. Satisfaction from a task well-completed, contentment with how one handled a delicate situation, or pleasure from having helped another through a difficult moment; this is the stuff of a flourishing life quite apart from one's material circumstance. With this bifocal lens on the parameters of a flourishing life, I turn to a few snippets from the Psalter.

---

3. Nussbaum, *Upheavals of Thought*; Roberts, *Emotions*; Solomon, *Passions*.

TESTIMONY FROM PSALMS

Numerous Psalms are laments, many of which appear early in the canonized collection. The speakers raise their voices, complaining to God of being
trapped in untoward circumstances. Enemies humiliate, shun and demean
them and many protagonists cannot fathom the grounds for such insulting
treatment. The complainant throws himself on God's mercy to rescue him,
either because he believes he does not deserve such treatment, on account
of his faithfulness, or because God's prior rescue operations lead him to
expect rescue now. At the same time, the complaints are studded with accounts of God's rescue operations, both within Israel and among broader
constituencies. Almost all conclude with celebratory shouts of joy at victory over suffering, to support the claim that "Weeping may linger for the
night, but joy comes in the morning" (Ps 30:5). This became the distinctive
Christian dynamic of crucifixion-resurrection: life follows death offering
hope of eternal life.

An assumption of the Psalter is that God responds to those in distress
precisely because it is his nature to be "merciful and gracious, slow to anger,
and abounding in lovingkindness and truth, sustaining lovingkindness to
the thousandth generation, forgiving iniquity, transgression and sin" (Exod
34:6–7, my translation). The psalmists adhere to this characterization of
God whether suffering is unwarranted, self-inflicted, or justifiable. While
some Psalms explode with joy and others implode in pain, most know both
experiences and stubbornly hold out for the joy of being rescued from both
material and psychological suffering. Here I examine four psalms, two
that illustrate circumstantial joy and misery, and two that illustrate non-
circumstantial joy and misery.

Circumstantial Misery and Joy

Psalms 106 and 107 identify material circumstances that are causing misery
and grope toward the joy that anticipated rescue will bring. These two long
poems may have been placed next to one another in the Psalter because
they both open with the phrase, "Give thanks to the Lord, for he is good;
for his lovingkindness endures forever," echoing the sentiments of Exod
34:6–7. Further, they both urge pious behavior and devotion, although that
is a ubiquitous psalmic theme. Perhaps they are from the same hand. I think
that these two psalms target different publics and consequently they have

different messages and employ different strategies to convey them. Psalm 106 focuses on Israel in its turbid love affair with God, while Psalm 107 looks beyond Israel to all "humankind." Together they insist upon God's universal sway.

Psalm 106

Psalm 106 scolds Israel for forgetting God, since they should know better and should honor God's grace from which they have so richly benefitted. The Psalm's message about joy appears forthrightly by verse 3: "Happy are those who observe justice, who do righteousness at all times." It is a central theme of the Psalter. The poem adjures Israelites to return to their ancestral faith, having strayed away to worship foreign gods. It scurries forth and back among God's gracious rescue operations on Israel's behalf when in tight straits and Israel's forgetting these redemptive experiences and falling into idolatry over and again. God is hurt and angry. The psalmist portrays God as rescuing and punishing Israel, by turns creating further suffering on the ground for Israel.

The hope of punishing bad behavior is, of course, to avert it in the future by creating fear in the wrongdoer. It is probably the oldest and one of the more ubiquitous strategies for deterring bad behavior known to humankind. Yet when undertaken therapeutically, from settled disapproval rather than reactive anger, thoughtful punishment should stimulate self-reflection rather than simply raw fear. That was the motive behind the invention of the "penitentiary." Here God's anger is fueled by the ingratitude he experiences, given his track record of dealing with Israel in the past. The poet offers us a transparent view of God.

The candor with which the poet portrays God's anger and mercy by turns most surely influenced later Christian theologians, who unfortunately used this text to provide scriptural support for their anti-Judaism and anti-Semitism, redirecting God's punishing anger at Israel. In the original case, however, the poet gives us a candid shot of God's inner conflict about how to handle Israel, when neither rescue nor punishment seem to keep Israel "at home" with him. We see God exasperated, struggling, that his compassion might overwhelm the hurt being inflicted by "his people" (v. 40), for he is roused even to hate Israel (v. 41). After all, those whom we love have great power to hurt us.

The bottom line of the drama here is that, although Israel has forgotten God's covenant (vv. 13, 21) God remembers it (v. 45) and that enables compassion to prevail over his righteous indignation. This window onto God's turmoil holds a mirror to our own opportunity to control our indignation at having been slighted or to exercise self-restraint in such circumstances. Throughout the Tanak, we see God sometimes exercising righteous indignation and sometimes exercising gracious mercy as noted in Chapter 1.

I think that the poet has two messages for us, one when we identify with ill-behaved Israel and one when we identify with God. As God-resistant Israel the message to us is that we bring opprobrium on ourselves by bad choices. As Israel accommodates the dominant culture, the poet urges us to lift our eyes from fitting in with the prevailing ethos and to consider our moral wellbeing as the true foundation of a good, I would say joyous, life. Although this psalm enters the conscience through miserable circumstance-generated suffering, and relief at its overcoming, its deeper grammar presses the reader to self-examination that can result in a change of heart and behavior. When we look at this psalm through God's eyes, we see a parent dealing with a teenager who is heading in the wrong direction, coming face-to-face with the challenge of discipline. How to discipline with judicious restraint? How to guide others effectively? How to correct helpfully, without damaging the fundamental trust between parent and child that is so essential for the child to receive the discipline as an expression of love; and not only maintain the relationship but enhance it?

Psalm 107

While Psalm 106 admonishes Israel to self-examination that it may flourish, Psalm 107 is perhaps more theologically interesting because it addresses a broader public on how to live wisely, although liturgically speaking, of course, Israel was the audience for both Psalms. This poem neither mentions Israel nor refers to any events in Israel's history. Rather, it has four vignettes of people who are suffering in different circumstances, encouraging all of them to expect divine rescue whatever their circumstance, in the hope of bringing them to God.

I think that this psalm targets non-Israelites (despite the Israelite implication of verse 11) or at least aims to inform Israel about God's concern for all people. This is partly because the poet does not scold, but encourages, as would be appropriate for outsiders. The universal scope of the poem is also evident in its highly stylized form. Two formulaic messages appear in each of the four vignettes and are separated by one—or in one case, two—intervening verses; in each case repeating both messages four times. The first message (repeated using slightly different wording) is that people are rescued because, "They cried to the Lord in their trouble," and he responded lovingly (107: 6, 13, 19, 28). The message is that God pays attention to those who call upon him. The second message is repeated each time without word variation: "Let them thank the Lord for his steadfast love, for his wonderful works to humankind" (107: 8, 15, 21, 31). The message is that how one responds to being rescued matters.

God's loving-kindness is attested in specific experiences of rescue attributed to him. He is a safety net for those who call upon him in trouble and they should be grateful. The four miserable situations are 1) being trapped in the desert, 2) being incarcerated and consigned to hard labor, 3) suffering serious illness, and 4) being endangered at sea. Of these, the first and fourth do not attribute any misdeeds to the sufferers, although the poet holds God responsible for the storm at sea that has the seamen at their wits' end. Only the second and third circumstances are associated with wrongdoing. The incarcerated are held presumably on warranted charges, having rebelled against God (Ps 107:11) and sinful ways led to the serious illness that some people now experience (v. 17). In the case of the incarcerated, they have clearly brought their suffering on themselves by bad behavior. In the case of at least some medical sufferers, injury and illness are the result of poor choices involving risky behavior.

It is noteworthy that no consistent underlying cause powers these sufferings. The poet is not interested in scolding people or exhorting repentance, but simply in advising them how to live well given life's precariousness. The point seems to be that God's loving-kindness extends both to those who suffer for no apparent reason, as well as those whose suffering is self-inflicted.

In terms of theology's gift to Positive Psychology I find two takeaways here. One is a wise rule-of-life, a posture toward life that crosses time and culture. Ask for help when needed and if and when it comes, go out of your way to say "thank you," so that the helper is reinforced in helping behavior. Asking for help is not easy for everyone because it implies a lack of self-sufficiency that some will perceive as a form of weakness.

A second takeaway has to do with the type of circumstance that has led to suffering. It does not matter to God whether the untoward circumstance is the result of random events or from bad or foolish behavior. Both types of sufferers receive a loving response from God. Here, unlike the message of Psalm 106, grace is offered without exacting any price whatsoever. Scolding is not recommended. There is only truly and freely-given help offered to strangers, be they trapped by natural forces or entrapped by their own missteps. In the latter case, there is no shaming, no punishment, only care that perhaps speaks louder than any sermon, scolding, or exhortation could. One is reminded of Jesus protecting the adulterous woman in John 8. The hope of that story is to spur self-reflection on those who would hypocritically condemn another without being accountable for their own behavior. It is a striking message in a patriarchal culture.

Spiritual Misery and Joy

Having looked at how two psalms seek to stimulate self-examination, I now turn to two short psalms that consider spiritually-based anxiety resulting from disordered relationships. Psalms 4 and 32 illustrate the collapse and repair of relationships. Although they do not "face each other" as Psalms 106 and 107 do, they are alike in making the inward turn that Augustine taught us. They both examine the distress caused by disrupted or disordered relationships and the pleasure that results from their repair. To anticipate the discussion just a bit, Psalm 4 considers disrupted interpersonal relationships, while Psalm 32 considers a disordered relationship with oneself and with God, giving us a good spread of relationship types. Let us consider Psalm 4.

Psalm 4

Psalm 4 is a lament that cries to God for rescue from an unspecified situation in which the speaker (in my judgment) feels dishonored. It illustrates what I believe is the basic situation behind many if not most of the lament Psalms. That situation is identified by the Psalter's introduction, Psalm 1, as the struggle of the righteous to bear up under the taunts and scoffing of the wicked; where the righteous represent Israelites/Jews loyal to their ancestral faith and the wicked represent idolatrous Israelites/Jews who have strayed from that faith—as clearly stated in Psalms 78 and, as we just saw, Psalm 106.

What should be mutually supportive relationships among sisters and brothers joyfully worshiping God together, have quite fallen apart. In reading these psalms I see Israel as religiously divided and it seems to the psalmists that disloyal Israelites have the upper hand, perhaps in several ways. Laments of this type speak prophetically on God's behalf to two ends. One is to urge other loyalists who experience ridicule and isolation to hold fast to their loyalty to God and to their willingness to speak out against religious disloyalty that turns to pagan deities. The other is to chastise those who have gone astray and bring them home. The speakers have taken on a difficult homeland missionary assignment. Psalm 69, and a snippet of Psalm 119, identify this situation precisely.

> Zeal for your house has consumed me; the insults of those who insult you have fallen on me.
>
> When I humbled my soul with fasting, they insulted me for doing so.
>
> When I made sackcloth my clothing, I became a byword to them.
>
> I am the subject of gossip for those who sit in the gate, and the drunkards make songs about me. (Ps 69:9–12)

> My eyes shed streams of tears because your law is not kept.
>
> My zeal consumes me because my foes forget your words. (Ps 119: 136, 139)

Psalm 4 is as ambiguous as it is ambivalent. Assuming that there is one speaker in this poem, he turns toward and from different addressees abruptly, creating a sense of confusion in the reader. The lamenter first addresses God (v. 1), then turns immediately to disloyal Israelites both to censure them and to speak to those who might be open to the speaker's guidance in repairing the fractured relationship (vv. 2–6). Finally, he returns to address God, with words of praise meant to be overheard by those inclined to repair the alienation plaguing Israel (vv. 7, 8). The hurried nature of these changes creates a frenzied atmosphere in eight brief verses.

The poem opens with a call for God to attend to the speaker's suffering in this difficult mission. He expects a response because God has done so previously and this has encouraged him to ask again (v. 1). Yet the very next verse is confusing. It turns from addressing God to addressing people, scolding them for their acts of defaming. Just who is being defamed, however, is ambiguous. It could be God or it could be the speaker who is crying to God for relief from precisely that situation. I believe that the dishonored one of the second verse is best appreciated as being about both the complainant and God, because shaming the missionary shames God.[4] Here, the cry to God, and the exasperated scolding of the disloyal, form an entryway for the poet's approach to healing the breach in Israel that occupies the rest of the psalm.

The missionary presents his counsel for healing as trustworthy because he is sure that God will answer him as he has previously. His claim to God's reliability constitutes his "street cred." It could also be that the lament Psalms that follow this pattern are part of an *Atheismusstreit* taking place in Israel at that time. Perhaps the debate is between those who do not see evidence of God's loyalty to the covenant with Israel, and as a result defect to other gods, and those who doggedly cling to the view that God is "there" and rescues those loyal to him. In the latter case, God's rescue of the complainants from their current distress would constitute important evidence for the argument that those who have been disloyal should return to the fold.

With this background, I suggest that our loyalist missionary gathers the strength to address those who are spiritually sensitive enough to be disturbed by the breach of relationship within Israel, and whose consciences and ancestral ties are awake enough to tend to God's demand for loyalty. The second half of this psalm offers a way to repair this disrupted relationship within Israel. Although he denounces the disloyal in verse 2, our missionary now changes his posture toward them at verse 4. Rather than continuing to scold the disloyal as simply resistant, he enters their mindset, sympathetically recognizing that their conscience keeps them awake at night. He believes that their apostasy bothers them and he invites them to reflect thoughtfully on whether the bad times that have beset the community are not a response to religious disloyalty (v. 4). Our loyalist missionary will not give up on those from whom he is alienated, believing that with him his adversaries hope that God will smile upon Israel again (v. 6). The way to that repair is, of course, to return to Israelite worship and to trust God (v. 5). In the final two verses of this psalm our loyalist missionary turns back to address God, using himself as a model for a restful night's sleep and

4. Identifying the one shamed as the speaker also explains his suffering, enables the rest of the poem to flow more smoothly, and is more in keeping with the standard style of the lament psalms.

a deep sense of security (v. 8). Returning to God will calm their disturbed consciences and create more joy than money can buy (v. 7).

Here is an instance of the Christian admonition to self-examination that locates confidence and safety in personal conviction and behavior, not in material circumstances. Self-examination is the path to healing breaches of personal integrity but also of disrupted interpersonal relationships that scar the community, and that should also scar the conscience if one is in place. Self-confidence comes not from self-sufficiency but from healing the community's divisions.

Psalm 32

While Psalm 4 laments Israel's spiritual inconstancy, Psalm 32 is a soliloquy that uses one person's experience of inner joy to instruct others that they might know it too. It is among seven psalms that Cassiodorus identified as penitential in the sixth century. The speaker acknowledges that his misery is self-inflicted and that he was tormented by self-recrimination for his sin until he confessed. Simply confessing enabled him to feel forgiven and that relieved his distress.

Psalm 32 is staccatoed into sections by three appearances of that elusive separator *selah*. I follow that leading. The psalmist announces his theme at the outset. Happiness is the exaltation that comes from being forgiven (vv. 1–2). Here is the leitmotif of Protestantism identified in chapter 1. The poet then moves on to tell his story (vv. 3–5). Bottling up iniquity condemned by God was quite debilitating (vv. 3–4) while confession was cathartic and brought relief (v. 5).[5]

At this point, the confessor pulls himself up to his full moral height, to use his experience of cleansing to advise others, just as the poet in Psalm 4 had done. Those mature enough to learn from the sad experience of others should now mind his words (v. 6). Those who have succumbed to the lure of iniquity (perhaps idolatry) can rid themselves of guilt (vv. 3, 4), by not hiding it from themselves in the grip of self-deception, but by confessing it to God. That will deliver them from the distress that harasses them and turn their anxiety into glad songs of deliverance (v. 7).

---

5. Because of abuses some have abandoned the practice of private auricular confession of sin, putting a general public confession into the Eucharistic liturgy instead. While an understandable move, the opportunity for unburdening oneself to another, indeed to a relative stranger has been lost.

The remainder of the Psalm instructs the poet's hearers based on his experience. Sin, he says, is powered by that stubborn demon *superbia* that so smoothly rears its ugly head day by day. The psalmist likens such obstinacy to being a horse or a mule that must be harnessed and bridled to go the right way (v. 9). Yet how rarely are this demon's victims able to recognize him, so clothed is he in comfortable garb. Identifying him, let alone vanquishing him through sincere repentance, is an act of strength that joyfully and gladly celebrates the rare feat of self-mastery. Vanquishing self-deception by self-mastery is beautiful to watch, yet more delicious to taste. Luke's Jesus puts it thus: "there will be more joy in heaven over one sinner who repents than over ninety-nine righteous persons who need no repentance" (15:7). The penitent's hard-won power enables him to count himself triumphantly among those who have paid a price to stand among Israel's faithful righteous.

While Christian theology has often spoken of such experiences as repairing damaged relationships with God, we do well to keep in mind that earnest confession of sin also repairs the damaged self. Simply recognizing that one is damaged and unable to act from one's best self is a gift of divine grace. Moving from dejection to hope when one can envision and desire to become one's best self is yet a further step forward.

Saint Teresa of Avila (1515–82) symbolized this journey of the soul though architectural imagery, to lead us from spiritual exile into the interior castle of the self that stands as a resplendent diamond waiting to be "entered." Its six apartments bespeak different levels of divine grace, most of which will not be experienced by us. I made it to the third apartment.

Those who have emerged from exile from themselves to reflect upon their inner life, have crossed the moat surrounding the interior castle and passed through the well-guarded entry gate into the interior castle, and are lodged in the first apartment. Here the soul finds itself in a large dark tunnel where the light is far away. Yet pressing toward the light, the penitent seeker enters the second apartment of the luminous castle of the soul, where self-awareness is stronger and the grace of Christ is more attractive.[6] Although St Teresa urges us beyond self-repair and toward union with God, Psalm 32 sets us down in what I take to be the more accessible, yet still challenging domain of the second apartment of the interior castle, where self-repair commences.

---

6. Teresa, *Interior Castle*.

While repair of one's relationship with God and repair of one's relationship with oneself would more than adequately validate the importance of this Psalm, there is yet one further theme to which the poet opens the door, though he does not walk through it. Psalm 32 appreciates the purgative power of confession but does not pursue the other side of the experience: the power held by the one who extends forgiveness. Christian theology has generally assumed that it is God who extends forgiveness and has neglected the horizontal application of the virtue. Yet in daily life everyone is sinned against and has the power to forgive, or to withhold this prize and delay its timing. Here is a test of spiritual maturity.

The Jewish tradition, acutely aware of the opportunity that extending forgiveness provides to self-repair, devotes a full month of every year to the opportunity both to petition those whom one has harmed, and to grant forgiveness to the family, friends, and acquaintances one may have been harmed by during the past year. The month of Ellul, leading up to the Days of Awe, Rosh Hashanah and Yom Kippur, is marked by the daily recitation of Psalm 27 that petitions God for shelter, teaching, and protection from harm. During this month each person is urged to contact all whom s/he has harmed in the past year and ask forgiveness. Should one's petition be spurned, one is to ask twice more, thus providing ample opportunity for a softening of heart by those whom one has hurt. If there is no softening one takes one's petition to God, leaving the person to continue nursing their pain. It is a strenuous spiritual discipline. Going directly to God to ask forgiveness for behavior that has harmed other people is not an option. Horizontal relationships must be repaired for the vertical relationship to be made whole.

Mustering the courage to approach those against whom one has sinned, and on the other hand marshaling the generosity of spirit to grant forgiveness, calls for the highest levels of personal maturity and civility. Asking members of the community to actually comply with these injunctions, makes for a spiritually demanding month every year.[7] It might be appropriate for Christians as a Lenten discipline.

This strenuous annual discipline is challenging, for who has not offended and been offended in any given year? One must simultaneously ramp up the courage to seek forgiveness from some, while being challenged to extend it to others, in order both to heal personally and to heal the community. Psalm 32 does not move in this direction but its theme of

7. Ellul generally falls in the Gregorian month of August into September.

forgiveness invites reflection on the ability of forgiveness to heal, not only the sinner but also the person who is able to grant this vaunted gift by letting go. Being both an agent and recipient of healing, even if one begins clumsily and is guided by a spiritual friend, is foundational to the maintenance and repair of healthy communities. To practice such discipline annually may well be training for human excellence and the flourishing of the societies to which we contribute.

CONCLUSION

I have suggested that one gift theology brings to Positive Psychology is the entrée into our interior castle, where self-examination in light of realities larger than those determining immediate identity and wellbeing, may speak to the spiritual integrity of life that its theology deems crucial for living well. The psalms enable us to confront the inner life's divided loves that rend our hearts, as disclosed to us by Augustine, the first great psychologist. The characters and circumstances populating the psalms can speak to our demons, ghosts, trolls, and hobgoblins, as they struggle for ascendency. Precisely in their most vexing moments these beloved poems function as lifeguards blowing their whistles when we swim out too far or veer into rocky water. They implore us to live wisely.

The texts light the way to a flourishing life, with God out in front, followed by those who suffer both physically and psychologically. Readers are invited to construe themselves through the personae of the various characters: God, the sufferers, their opponents, and their friends, where self-reflection lights the way. They also invite us to see ourselves in terms of the various relationships that the poets depict—the supplicant in relation to God, God in relation to the supplicant, and the supplicant in relation to his foes. The same is true for the horizontal relationships that the poems portray. We come to know ourselves through these various angles of vision, to gain distance on our inclinations, choices, and reactions and so to envision ourselves through larger frames of reference. That is, despite the negative feelings, experiences, and environments that the psalms plunge us into, they offer us freedom from myopic self-appraisals that can close in on us if we do not acknowledge that we need help from beyond ourselves. Meditating on the psalm takes us into ourselves by taking us out of ourselves.

That God is a central character in the psalter, and that the human characters in the poems are focused on that centrality, need not dissuade those psychologists with whom the techniques of secular mindfulness are popular. Mindfulness is a meditation technique with many forebears. It is found for instance in Theravada and other schools of Buddhist *anapanasati* (attention to breathing). The Christian analogue, hesychasm, might also be explored in this connection. In psychology, perhaps strongly in Positive Psychology, mindfulness is a technique for staying focused on the present moment. It is undoubtedly helpful in some circumstances, but it is limited by the fact that it focuses on the individual self in the present and does not encourage self-examination. Meditation on the psalms as I have offered it, is a quite different therapeutic technique, because the poems create a safe space through which the pray-er can try on the situations, relationships, stresses, and challenges faced by the characters. This provides an opportunity to filter one's own experience through their defeats, triumphs, and wisdom. In this Christian form of meditation, the characters go ahead of us as a sort of yellow-brick-road, leading to the Oz of self-knowledge that enables one to return home content.

I hope that this chapter functions as an invitation to psychologists who might otherwise shy away from religious texts and ideas, to appreciate the therapeutic and strengthening potential of ancient biblical poetry. Classics are classics for a reason and the psalms are perhaps the classic of classics. Many psalms are morally and socially daunting in our day. They are not easily digested, nor can we claim to understand them. Yet neither can we put them down. So wisdom holds true—go and drink from this fountain.

REFERENCES

Athanasius. "Letter to Marcellinus." In *The Classics of Western Spirituality*, edited by Robert C. Gregg, 101–47. New York: Paulist, 1980.

Key, Katty, and Claire Shipman. *Confidence Code: Science and Art of Self-Assurance— What Women Should Know.* New York: HarperCollins, 2014.

Nussbaum, Martha Craven. *Upheavals of Thought: The Intelligence of Emotions.* Cambridge: Cambridge University Press, 2001.

Roberts, Robert Campbell. *Emotions: An Essay in aid of Moral Psychology.* Cambridge: Cambridge University Press, 2003.

———. *Spiritual Emotions: A Psychology of Christian Virtues.* Grand Rapids: Eerdmans, 2007.

Solomon, Robert C. *The Passions.* Garden City: Doubleday, 1976.

Teresa of Avila. *The Interior Castle.* Translated by Kieran Kavanaugh and Otilio Rodriguez. Classics of Western Spirituality. New York: Paulist, 1979.

Chapter 3

An Introduction to Positive Psychology, Positive Education, and Wellbeing

MATHEW A. WHITE

INTRODUCTION

Unless I see the nail marks in his hands and put my finger where the nails were, and put my hand into his side, I will not believe." . . . Then Jesus said to Thomas, "Put your finger here; see my hands. Reach out your hand and put it into my side. Stop doubting and believe." Thomas said to him, "My Lord and my God!" Then Jesus told him, "Because you have seen me, you have believed. . . (John 20:25–29)

THIS CHAPTER PROVIDES THE reader with an introduction to the foundation of Positive Psychology, positive education, and wellbeing. It acts as an introduction to the science. To grasp fully the origins of Positive Psychology it is important to consider the culture and context of the movement.

Given psychology is concerned with the scientific study of human kind and its functions—a Positive Psychology as its title suggests does have a series of underlying assumptions about the growth and reach of psychology in general. In their study of self-identified mentally ill Christians ($n = 85$) Standford and McAlister claim the church dismissed the diagnoses of a significantly large number of the participants (41.2 percent). Furthermore, they contend, "clergy, not psychologists or other mental health professionals, are the most common source of help sought in times of psychological distress."[1] This study raises some questions for clergy and theologians alike on the relationship between theology and psychology. In her recent commentary on this study, Greta Wells expands Standford and McAlister's analysis, contending, "while clergy often claim that their role is predominantly one of spiritual support, the statistical reality of mental illness suggests that they cannot afford to forgo training in this area. This is not only a matter of providing good pastoral care—but also often of meeting their duty of care obligations."[2]

THEOLOGY AND POSITIVE PSYCHOLOGY: TWO SIDES TO THE SAME PROBLEM?

Listening to discussions about theology and Positive Psychology the black cat analogy often comes to mind:

> Philosophy is like being in a dark room and looking for a black cat. Metaphysics is like being in a dark room and looking for a black cat that isn't there. Science is like being in a dark room and looking for a switch. The light will reveal a cat if there is one. Theology is like being in a dark room, looking for a black cat that isn't there, and shouting "I found it!"[3]

Theologians have long been concerned with psychology. From Thomas Aquinas to Miroslav Volf they have considered how and if the two disciplines might, or might not, contribute to each other. Some theologians have resolved this question by separating the two fields entirely. This position

---

1. Stanford and McAlister, "Perceptions."

2. Wells, "Pastoral Care."

3. There are many variations of this truism. Its exact origin is hotly disputed. It has been attributed to Charles Darwin, the English Judge Lord Bowen, and philosopher and "father" of psychology William James. However, the source is unknown.

was also adopted by many psychologists who assert that theology has very little insight into an empirical view of humanity.

Why Does It Matter?

This separation comes from the underlying assumptions between and across what science and faith tell us. Other perspectives are not so clear cut.[4] St Thomas the Apostle's skepticism has always resonated with me. His probing questions and reflections on Jesus' answers show the significant depth of his emerging faith when he says "Lord, we don't know where you are going, so how can we know the way?" in John's Gospel (11:16; 14:5; 20:24–29). So can theologians learn anything about faith, hope, and love from psychologists? There is little doubt that psychology has much to say and many insights into how individuals, groups, and institutions behave. Martin Seligman claims that "psychology after World War II became a science of healing" as it "concentrated on repairing damage using a disease model of human functioning."[5]

When surveying achievements in knowledge and understanding, it is impossible not to recognize the advancements made by psychology. Before the launch of Positive Psychology, psychologists focused on curing mental illness, making everyone's lives more productive and meaningful, and identifying high talent. Seligman claims two events changed psychology. From 1946, the year of the foundation of the American Veterans Administration, thousands of psychologists were able to dedicate their lives to treating mental illness, leading to "clinical" psychology and the development of the National Institute of Mental Health, which was founded using a pathology-based model. Seligman also identified that, despite advances in psychology and treatment, "The most recent data show that there is more than ten times as much serious depression now as four decades ago. Worse, depression is now a disorder of the early teenage years rather than a disorder that starts in middle age, a situation that comprises the single largest change in the modern demographics of mental illness. And that, I believe, is the major paradox of the late twentieth century."[6]

The advances in the therapy of mental illness are undeniable, with many disorders becoming known, understood, and treatable. However,

4. McCall et al., "Comparison."
5. Seligman, "Positive Psychology," 3.
6. Seligman, "The President's Address," 560.

Seligman argues that the central mission of psychology—to help all people better themselves—was lost. Instead, the empirical lens of psychology moved towards a disease-based model.

As Seligman notes, psychology's "almost exclusive attention to pathology neglected the idea of a fulfilled individual and thriving community, and it ignored the possibility that building strength is the most potent weapon in the arsenal of therapy." Positive Psychology has launched a movement within the science of psychology to act as a catalyst by challenging clinicians' preoccupation with "repairing the worst things in life to also building the best qualities in life."

The Context—Mental Ill-Health

One of the significant ethical challenges of the twenty-first century has been the rise of mental ill-health and stress facing young people in particular. Shockingly, The Hon Sussan Ley MP, the Australian Federal Minister for Health, noted in August 2015, "About one in 13 teenagers (aged 12 to 17) contemplated suicide—the equivalent of 128,000 youth—with one in twenty reportedly making a plan to take their own life and one in forty attempting it."

Professor Julio Licinio from the South Australian Health and Medical Research Institute (SAHMRI) has called for a "war" on mental illnesses with the same intensity as a war on cancer. There is growing evidence there is a rise in mental illness and that psychiatric disorders represent a substantial burden to the world.

In an Australian context, "depression represents the largest cause of nonfatal disease burden" and "suicide, which is in most cases an outcome of depression, is the third cause of fatal disease burden in Australian men." One in four Australians will experience mental illness requiring intervention between the ages of sixteen and twenty-four years. For boys' and men's mental health, this statistic is worse. How this presents in society itself varies.

As Waters summarizes, Tucci et al.'s online study of 600 Australians (aged ten to fourteen years) revealed that 46 percent of respondents did not feel confident or secure in themselves; 54 percent were worried about not fitting in; and 40 percent felt they were not performing well enough.[7] The estimated economic and social impact of this on society is huge.

7. Waters, "Review."

The Australian Bureau of Statistics highlights, "suicide rates remain high, with suicide now the foremost cause of death in fifteen to twenty-four year olds."[8] I work at an Anglican boys' school, St Peter's College, where we have instigated a whole-school approach to wellbeing. Our strategies and programs are aligned with the recommendations of organizations like Young and Well CRC, BeyondBlue, MindMatters, KidsMatters, and The Black Dog Institute.

The World Health Organization predicts that there will be a global crisis in wellbeing where, by 2030, depression will be the leading burden of disease, and that one person will commit suicide every forty seconds—more than all the yearly victims of wars and natural disasters (WHO, 2011). Something needs to be done and Positive Psychology has much to offer this challenge.

At first glance, the study of psychology and theology appear opposite fields of inquiry. Certainly, from a methodological perspective, this is true. However, what could each learn in dialogue with the other?

Theology is the study of the nature of God and religious belief. Within psychology and theology, there are various areas of specialization. For instance, from a Christian theological perspective, there are some subcategories that focus on the Bible, God, and Jesus. Psychology is the study of behavior and the mind. Within psychology, topics include abnormal psychology, cognitive psychology, clinical psychology, and organizational psychology. So although theology and psychology do appear to be considering vastly different fields of inquiry they share a mutual interest in the area of human nature: what does it mean to be human? Hence each discipline examines some similar topics, such as love, hope, joy, optimism, strengths, compassion, and gratitude. Yet a tension remains, in that psychology is secular and theology is religious. At the heart of this tension is the creative space between knowledge, understanding, and belief.[9]

DEFINING POSITIVE PSYCHOLOGY

I am sure the average reader picking up this book will be surprised to see chapters considering the links between and across theology and psychology. Just as Positive Psychology is a clarion call on psychology to refocus scientific energy, I think that this book's contents are timely given the

8. Robertson et al., *How Did We Score?* 10.

9. McCall et al., "Comparison."

increased interest in Positive Psychology in particular, and what it can do to help us to move individuals, groups, and institutions towards a more flourishing life.[10]

Over the past fifteen years a number of criticisms have been leveled at Positive Psychology. Critics have claimed that it is overly American, positive thinking, paternalistic, simplistic, quasi-science, over-reaching in its claims, a phase, or a jingoistic trend.[11] Many of these points are entirely justified as maverick providers jump on the Positive Psychology bus and shout the benefits from the rooftop. In addition to advocacy for reform in education in particular, what the field truly needs at this point in its developments is the serious reflection and robust discussion to help it grow to a new level of scientific inquiry.[12]

As defined by Gable and Haidt, Positive Psychology is the study of "the conditions and processes that contribute to the flourishing or optimal functioning of people, groups, and institutions."[13] Whereas traditional psychology focuses on approaches that focus on the reduction of negative factors, Positive Psychology focuses on approaches that build positive factors. Alex Linley, the founder of the Centre for Applied Positive Psychology in the United Kingdom, notes a common misunderstanding—that Positive Psychology and its practitioners are just as interested in determining the factors that stop people from flourishing as they are in understanding those that enable it.[14]

Positive psychologists specialize in scientific knowledge in order to understand human flourishing.[15] Positive Psychology focuses on how to build a flourishing life. It is more concerned with helping individuals and communities to grow, rather than focusing on pathology—or disease. As a science Positive Psychology is a systematic study of the structure and behavior of human interaction through observation and experiment. The University of Michigan psychologist Christopher Peterson defined Positive Psychology as "the scientific study of what goes right in life, from birth to death and all the stops in-between."[16]

10. Seligman and Csikszentmihalyi, *Positive Psychology*.

11. Lazarus, "Legs?"

12. Kristjánsson, "Ten Myths"; White, "Why Won't it Stick?"

13. Gable and Haidt, "What (and Why)?" 104.

14. Linley et al., "Positive Psychology."

15. Huppert, "Psychological Well-Being."

16. Peterson, *Primer*, 4.

The objectives of Positive Psychology have been clearly noted by Martin Seligman and Mihaly Csikszentmihalyi, two of the world's most influential psychologists of the past fifty years.[17] Seligman and Csikszentmihalyi initially defined Positive Psychology as early as 1997 and this was later described by Gable and Haidt as the "conditions and processes that contribute to the flourishing or optimal functioning of people, groups, and institutions. It is a field of science that underlines the importance of moral virtues and character strengths that enable individuals and groups to thrive and lead a fulfilling life."[18]

When Martin Seligman was elected president of the American Psychological Association (by the largest vote in history) he called on fellow psychologists in his 1998 Presidential Address to tackle two urgent areas:

1. Ethnic conflict: the twentieth century's shameful legacy.

2. A "Positive Psychology"; that is, a reoriented science that emphasizes the understanding and building of the most positive qualities of an individual: optimism, courage, work ethic, futuremindedness, interpersonal skill, the capacity for pleasure and insight, and social responsibility.

In this bold address, Seligman claimed that "since the end of World War II, psychology has moved too far away from its original roots, which were to make the lives of all people more fulfilling and productive, and too much toward the important, but not all-important, area of curing mental illness."[19] The result was the creation of the American and Canadian Psychological Association Task Force of Ethno-political Warfare.

Seligman and Csikszentmihalyi were concerned with what they considered were psychology's limitations.[20] Seligman and Csikszentmihalyi contended that psychology was over-reliant on a pathology model, which focuses on what goes wrong in lives and how damage can be repaired. They called for a Positive Psychology focusing on the topics of what goes right in life, including emotions such as love, joy, hope, optimism, meaning, and purpose, with the same empirical rigor that is applied to the study of topics such as hate, disgust, depression, anxiety, and fear.

17. Seligman and Csikszentmihalyi, "Positive Psychology."
18. Gable and Haidt, "What (and Why)?" 110.
19. Seligman, "The President's Address," 559.
20. Seligman and Csikszentmihalyi, "Positive Psychology."

In Seligman's Presidential address he noted, "Entering a new millennium, we face a historical choice. Standing alone on the pinnacle of economic and political leadership, the United States can continue to increase its material wealth while ignoring the human needs of our people and the people on the rest of the planet."[21]

Figure 1: Individual, Institutions and Positive Psychology

As the world turned its mind to the new millennium in 2000, Martin Seligman and Mihaly Csikszentmihalyi officially launched the field in the "millennial edition" of *American Psychologist*.[22] This publication included fifteen articles written by over thirty of the world's leading psychologists discussing such issues as what enables happiness, the effects of autonomy and self-regulation, how optimism and hope affect health, what constitutes wisdom, and how talent and creativity come to fruition. There was also examination of the tensions captured in Figure 1: Individual, Institutions and Positive Psychology.

The call for a Positive Psychology movement was a step forward in the science, where Seligman challenged his peers to "articulate a vision of the good life that is empirically sound and, at the same time, understandable and attractive. We can show the world what actions lead to wellbeing, to positive individuals, to flourishing communities, and to a just society."[23]

Christopher Peterson joined Martin Seligman and Mihaly Csikszentmihalyi to develop much of the foundational theories and approaches

21. Seligman, "The President's Address," 560.
22. Seligman and Csikszentmihalyi, "Positive Psychology."
23. Seligman, "The President's Address," 560.

supported by many of the world's preeminent philosophers, psychologists, and ethicists. Seligman hoped that this project would reflect "the idea that human greatness occurs not only in the realm of achievement, but that genius can also come into play in mastering human relationships, assuming moral responsibility, engaging in spirituality, and viewing life as a work of art."[24]

Seligman argues the focus of Positive Psychology considers three areas:

- Positive experiences: joy, meaning, hope, happiness, optimism, love
- Positive traits: strengths of character and psychological resilience
- Positive institutions: family, schools, political systems (democracy)[25]

In his concluding remarks as President of the American Psychological Association, Seligman said, "We have misplaced our original and greater mandate to make life better for all people—not just the mentally ill. I, therefore, call on our profession and our science to take up this mandate once again as we enter the next millennium."[26]

Initially, the field of Positive Psychology explores positive subjective experiences.[27] It revolves around individual's subjective emotional perspective at particular points in time. For example:

- Wellbeing and satisfaction (past)
- Flow, joy, the sensual pleasures, and happiness (present)
- Optimism, hope, and faith (future)

The field has focused on the individual's level of experience: love, courage, perseverance, and forgiveness. At the group level, it has been about developing civic virtue and institutions that promote good citizenship and altruism. More recently, Martin Seligman et al.[28] and Chandra Sripada et al.[29] have coined the term "prospecting psychology—or possible futures," which challenges underlying assumptions about what it means to

24. Ibid.

25. Seligman, "Positive Psychology."

26. Quotation from Martin Seligman's concluding speech as President of the American Psychological Association.

27. Seligman, "Positive Psychology," 3–5.

28. Seligman et al., "Navigating."

29. Sripada et al., "Reply."

be "free," as well as "free will" within mental disorders. The aim is to "highlight the important theoretical differences between the emerging future-oriented perspective versus previous "driven by the past" or "reflexive" perspectives" summarized in Figure 2: Positive Psychology and Time.[30]

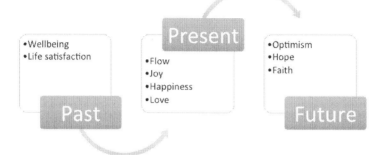

Figure 2: Positive Psychology and Time

What Positive Psychology is Not

A common misunderstanding about Positive Psychology is that it is positive thinking. As a science, it describes what empirical evidence suggests about the benefits of Positive Psychology approaches. A common mistake by some critics is to claim that "it is all about thinking positive." These individuals have failed to engage the scientific literature in the field.

Positive Psychology does not:

- Claim to be a short cut about realizing your dreams
- Claim individuals will become new persons
- Ignore negative and catastrophic events
- Promote blind optimism in the face of adversity
- Argue that you can have it all
- Claim that it is "easy" to be positive
- Tell anyone how to live their lives

30. Ibid., 151.

Limitations

Not without its critics within psychology and beyond, the field of Positive Psychology needs balanced discussions.[31] It can be a divisive science and dismissed as a distraction from far bigger issues. It has stepped on the toes of philosophers and theologians. However, far from dismissing these disciplines, some positive psychologists are open to discourse between and across the fields of Positive Psychology and theology in particular.[32]

Many psychologists take offence at generalizations positive psychologists make about their overt focus on welfare, pain, suffering, and depression. At worst, Positive Psychology can appear to present a binary view of the world. You are either positive, or you are negative. You are either too negative about being negative or not positive enough. At its worst, Positive Psychology can be misrepresented and appear gauche, crass, ineffective, or an oversimplification of happy-ology.

Positive psychologists often see Abraham Maslow and Carl Roger's "humanistic psychology" as unscientific and too subjective, despite being a forerunner to Positive Psychology. Csikszentmihalyi, Park, Peterson, and Seligman reject humanistic psychology as the realm of self-help and mindless happiness.

There is a significant difference between positive psychologists and humanistic psychologists in their research methods. The foundations of Positive Psychology are found in the process of a quantitative scientist: hypothesis, statistical tests, testing, validation, and large samples.

Some of the criticisms of Positive Psychology include:

- Positive psychologists can oversimplify and imply that psychology is purely negative
- There is over-claiming of results
- There is overemphasis on self-reports or data collection
- There is no single overarching theory or framework in Positive Psychology
- There is an overreliance on western socio-economic systems and values

31. Lazarus, "Legs?"
32. McCall et al., "Comparison"; White, "Why Won't it Stick?"

- The field is Eurocentric and focused on western conceptualizations of happiness and flourishing

BEFORE OR BEYOND SELIGMAN? DESCRIBING AND DEFINING WELLBEING

In general wellbeing can be understood to be when people are feeling good and function well. There are many ways to describe and define wellbeing. For example, the work of Dodge et al. summarizes many of the major advances from a psychological perceptive,[33] while Ryff and Keyes highlight an "absence of theory-based formulations of wellbeing,"[34] with "blurred and overly broad definitions of wellbeing."[35] Another perspective is that of Diener and Suh, who note that:

> subjective wellbeing consists of three interrelated components: life satisfaction, pleasant affect, and unpleasant affect. Affect refers to pleasant and unpleasant moods and emotions, whereas life satisfaction refers to a cognitive sense of satisfaction with life.[36]

White and Murray have discussed wellbeing in the context of building a positive institution; McCall, Waters, and White outline a definition when making comparison between theological Christian approaches to wisdom and Peterson and Seligman's classification of character strengths and virtues. Waters, White, Wang, and Murray propose an approach when considering the unique complexities of leading whole-school change; Alford and White examine wellbeing in the context of evolving traditional approaches to school psychology to create Positive Schools Psychology; and Kern, Waters, Adler, and White consider an array of definitions when measuring whole school wellbeing in students and staff.[37] The World Health Organization defined quality of life as:

> an individual's perception of their position in life in the context of the culture and value systems in which they live and in relation

33. Dodge et al., "Challenge."
34. Ryff and Keyes, "Structure," 719–20.
35. Forgeard et al., "Doing the Right Thing," 81.
36. Diener and Suh, "Measuring Quality of Life," 200.
37. White and Murray, "Future Directions"; McCall et al., "Comparison"; Waters et al., "Leading"; Alford and White, "Positive School Psychology"; and Kern et al., "Assessing," respectively.

to their goals, expectations, standards and concerns. It is a broad ranging concept affected in a complex way by the person's physical health, psychological state, personal beliefs, social relationships and their relationship to salient features of their environment.[38]

Increasingly wellbeing is understood as one of the primary goals of Positive Psychology. A measure of wellbeing is human flourishing. Nevertheless, wellbeing is far more than the absence of illness (an orthodox definition from the World Health Organization). It is possible for people and communities to be functioning but not flourishing. Felicia Huppert of Cambridge University argues that psychological wellbeing is about lives going well. It is the combination of "feeling good and functioning effectively."[39]

Wellbeing frameworks in schools are informed by Positive Psychology, the "scientific study of what goes right in life, from birth to death and all stops in between."[40] Positive Psychology was launched in 2000 as a field of study and is now the fastest growing area in psychology. The theory was expanded by Seligman's much-discussed multidimensional "PERMA" model of flourishing, which argues that wellbeing consists of positive emotions, engagement, relationships, meaning, and accomplishment.[41]

DEFINING POSITIVE EDUCATION

The majority of pastoral care structures in schools were developed in the 1920s. In the twenty-first century, this is no longer adequate. There are two approaches to wellbeing: reactive (welfare) and proactive (wellbeing). The reactive model is out of date. The wellbeing strategy at St Peter's College is a proactive approach to mental health and is linked to our existing pastoral care models at the school.[42]

What is positive education? Positive education is the way that we deliver wellbeing programs. It is an approach to education for both traditional skills and character development. It is an umbrella term used to describe scientifically validated programs from Positive Psychology that have an impact on student wellbeing. Positive education interventions in schools have three similar approaches. They focus on building positive factors,

38. World Health Organization, "Global Burden."
39. Huppert, "Psychological Well-being," 137.
40. Peterson quoted in White and Murray, "Building."
41. Seligman, *Flourish*.
42. Furlong et al., *Handbook*.

rather than simply ameliorate negative ones. They are implemented within schools rather than clubs or societies, and they are evaluated using valid and reliable research designs and measures.[43]

Positive education has had various definitions.[44] Lord O'Shaughnessy and Emily Larson claim positive education as a paradigm shift in educational approach, where education traditionally focuses on academic accomplishment only, and argue that it is an approach to education and wellbeing.[45] White defines it as a blend of evidence-based learning from the science of Positive Psychology and best practices in learning and teaching.[46]

It is often used as a common umbrella term that is easily misunderstood or confused with thinking positively. Positive education describes scientifically validated programs from Positive Psychology, taught in schools, that have an impact on student wellbeing. Therefore I argue that positive education is the way in which schools deliver a wellbeing framework. It is an approach to education including both traditional skills and character development.[47] From an empirical lens, there has been substantial growth in the field. Melbourne University researchers Reuben Rusk and Lea Waters' biblio-metric analysis of the field claims that it appears to touch all aspects of human endeavor, including arts, business, economics, education, geography, health, human resources, humanities, literature, medical sciences, music, organizational scholarship, philosophy, and theology.[48]

The world's leading universities, Harvard, Cambridge, Stanford, Oxford, Imperial College, University of Pennsylvania, University of Melbourne, Ecole Normale Superieure–Paris, and Tsinghua University in China, all have courses and academics focusing on Positive Psychology research. As I have summarized below,[49] recent findings by Gregory Park from the University of Pennsylvania revealed the following benefits of teaching wellbeing:

43. Seligman et al., "Positive Education"; Waters, "Review"; Waters et al., "Leading."

44. Seligman et al., "Positive Education"; White and Waters, "Case Study"; White, "Evidence-based Whole School Strategy."

45. O'Shaughnessy and Larson, "Work Hard."

46. White, "Positive Education"; "Evidence-based Whole School Strategy"; and "Why Won't it Stick?"

47. Seligman et al., "Positive Education"; Seligman, *Flourish.*

48. Rusk and Waters, "Tracing."

49. White, "Positive Education."

- Using one's signature strengths in a new way increased happiness and decreased depression for six months.

- Self-control predicted high school grades, absences, and at-home study habits better than IQ.

- Self-control predicted homework completion, classroom conduct, and report card grades in a longitudinal study of over 500 middle school students.

- Individuals' levels of grit—perseverance for long-term goals—predicted several forms of academically-related achievement, including grades at top US universities, retention in elite military academy classes, and ranking in a national spelling competition.

- Character strengths of the mind (e.g., self-regulation, perseverance, love of learning) were predictive of school success.

- The character strengths of perseverance, love, gratitude, and hope predicted academic achievement in middle school students and college students.

- Changes in a student's self-control predicted changes in his/her school grades for six months.

- Self-control predicted childhood health.

- A study of children progressing into adolescence found that self-control was an important protective factor against becoming overweight.

- A recent meta-analysis of 213 school-based universal positive education or social emotional learning (SEL) programs, involving over 250,000 students, concluded that these interventions had positive effects across a range of outcomes.

CONCLUSIONS AND FUTURE DIRECTIONS

The most common source of help sought in times of psychological distress is clergy, not psychologists or other mental health professionals.[50] This raises questions for clergy and theologians alike on the relationship between theology and psychology, and prompts the suggestion that if clergy were a common source of encouragement/inspiration/knowledge of how

---

50. Stanford and McAlister, "Perceptions," 144.

to establish positive healthy relationships, then a dialogue between theologians/clergy and positive psychologists may discover new insights into wellbeing. Personally, I can understand St Thomas the Apostle when he states: "Unless I see the nail marks in his hands and put my finger where the nails were, and put my hand into his side, I will not believe" (John 20:24–29). The reality is that the future is one paved with more mental ill-health for many people and there is a unique opportunity for positive psychologists and theologians to collaborate to grow a new field. We all have a choice in how we shall move towards this future. It requires substantial creativity and cross-disciplinary collaboration and this book is a step towards a better tomorrow.

REFERENCES

Alford, Zoë, and Mathew A. White. "Positive School Psychology." In *Evidence Based Approaches to Positive Education in Schools: Implementing a Strategic Framework for Well-being in Schools,* edited by Mathew A. White et al., 93–109. Netherlands: Springer, 2015.

Diener, Ed, and Eunkook Suh. "Measuring Quality of Life: Economic, Social, and Subjective Indicators." *Social Indicators Research* 40 (1997) 189–216.

Dodge, Rachel, et al. "The Challenge of Defining Wellbeing." *International Journal of Wellbeing* 2 (2012) 222–35.

Forgeard, Marie J. C., et al. "Doing the Right Thing: Measuring Well-being for Public Policy." *International Journal of Wellbeing* 1 (2011) 79–106.

Froh, Jeffrey J., and Acacia C. Parks, eds. *Activities for Teaching Positive Psychology: A Guide for Instructors.* Washington: American Psychological Association, 2012.

Furlong, Michael J., et al., eds. *Handbook of Positive Psychology in Schools.* 2nd ed. Hoboken: Taylor and Francis, 2009.

Gable, Shelly L., and Jonathan Haidt. "What (and Why) is Positive Psychology?" *Review of General Psychology* 9 (2005) 103–10.

Huppert, Felicia A. "Psychological Well-being: Evidence Regarding its Causes and Consequences." *Applied Psychology: Health and Well-Being* 1 (2009) 137–64.

Kern, Margaret L., et al. "Assessing Employee Wellbeing in Schools Using a Multifaceted Approach: Associations with Physical Health, Life Satisfaction, and Professional Thriving." *Psychology* 6 (2014) 500–13.

———. "Measuring Whole School Well-being in Students and Staff." In *Evidence-based Approaches to Positive Education in Schools: Implementing a Strategic Framework for Well-being in Schools,* edited by Mathew A. White et al., 65–91. Netherlands: Springer, 2015.

Kristjánsson, Kristján. "Ten Myths About Character, Virtue and Virtue Education—Plus Three Well-Founded Misgivings." *British Journal Of Educational Studies* 61 (2013) 269–87.

Lazarus, Richard S. "Does the Positive Psychology Movement Have Legs?" *Psychological Inquiry* 14 (2003) 93–109.

Linley, P. Alex, et al. "Positive Psychology: Past, Present, and (Possible) Future." *The Journal of Positive Psychology* 1 (2006) 3–16.

McCall, Theo, et al. "A Comparison Between Theological Christian Approaches to Wisdom and Peterson and Seligman's Classification of Character Strengths and Virtues." In *Evidence Based Approaches to Positive Education Schools: Implementing a Strategic Framework for Well-being in Schools,* edited by Mathew A. White et al., 27–41. The Netherlands: Springer, 2015.

Mitchell, Joanna, et al. "Positive Psychology and the Internet: A Mental Health Opportunity." *E-Journal Of Applied Psychology* 6 (2010) 30–41.

O'Shaughnessy, James, and Emily Larson. "Work Hard, Be Nice." *Positive Psychology News*, December 10, 2014. Online: http:// positivepsychologynews.com/news/ james-oshaughnessy-and-emily-larson/ 2014121030526.

Peterson, Christopher. *A Primer in Positive Psychology* New York: Oxford University Press, 2006.

Robertson, Sebastian, et al. *How Did We Score? Engaging Young People in the Development of a National Report Card on Mental Health and Suicide Prevention.* Melbourne: Young and Well Cooperative Research Centre and Batyr Australia Limited, 2013.

Rusk, Reuben D., and Lea E. Waters. "Tracing the Size, Reach, Impact, and Breadth of Positive Psychology." *Journal of Positive Psychology* 8 (2013) 207–21.

Ryff, Carol D., and Corey L. M. Keyes. "The Structure of Psychological Well-being Revisited." *Journal of Personality and Social Psychology* 69 (1995) 719–27.

Seligman, Martin E. P. *Flourish: A Visionary New Understanding of Happiness and Well-being.* New York: Atria, 2013.

———. "Positive Psychology, Positive Prevention and Positive Therapy." In *Oxford Handbook of Positive Psychology*, edited by C. R. Snyder et al., 3–9. New York: Oxford University Press, 2005.

———. "The President's Address (Annual Report)." *American Psychologist* 54 (1999) 559–62.

Seligman, Martin E. P., and Mihaly Csikszentmihalyi. "Positive Psychology: An Introduction." *American Psychologist* 55 (2000) 5–14.

Seligman, Martin E. P., et al. "Navigating Into the Future or Driven by the Past." *Perspectives On Psychological Science* 8 (2013) 119–41.

———. "Positive Education: Positive Psychology and Classroom Interventions." *Oxford Review of Education* 35 (2009) 293–311.

Sripada, Chandra, et al. "Reply to Comments." *Perspectives On Psychological Science* 8 (2013) 151–54.

Stanford, Matthew S., and Kandace R. McAlister. "Perceptions of Serious Mental Illness in the Local Church." *Journal Of Religion, Disability and Health* 12 (2008) 144–53.

Waters, Lea. "A Review of School-based Positive Psychology Interventions." *The Australian Educational And Developmental Psychologist* 28 (2011) 75.

———. "Why Positive Education?" *TLN Journal* 22 (2015) 16.

Waters, Lea, and Mathew A. White. "Strengths-based Approach in the Classroom and Staffroom. In *Evidence-based Approaches to Positive Education in Schools: Implementing a Strategic Framework for Well-being in Schools*, edited by Mathew A. White et al., 111–33. Netherlands: Springer, 2015.

Waters, Lea, et al. "Leading Whole-School Change." In *Evidence Based Approaches to Positive Education in Schools: Implementing a Strategic Framework for Well-being in Schools,* edited by Mathew A. White et al., 43–63. Netherlands: Springer, 2015.

————. "Toward the Creation of a Positive Institution St Peter's College, Adelaide, Australia." *AI Practitioner* 14 (2012) 60–65.

Wells, Greta. "Pastoral Care and the Complexity of Mental Illness in Pentecostal and Evangelical Churches." *ABC Religion and Ethics*, October 9, 2015. Online: http://www.abc.net.au/religion /articles/2015/10/09/4328908.htm.

White, Mathew A. "An Evidence-based Whole School Strategy to Positive Education." In: *Better than OK: Helping Young People to Flourish at School and Beyond*, edited by H. Street et al., 194–98. Perth: Fremantle, 2014.

————. "Positive Education at Geelong Grammar School." In *The Oxford Handbook of Happiness*, edited by Susan A. David et al., 657–70. Oxford University Press, 2013.

————. "Why Won't it Stick? Positive Psychology and Positive Education." *Psychology Of Well-Being: Theory, Research and Practice* 6 (2016) 1.

White, Mathew A., and Simon Murray. "Building a Positive Institution." *Evidence Based Approaches to Positive Education: Implementing a Strategic Framework for Well-being in Schools*, edited by Mathew A. White et al., 1–26. Netherlands: Springer, 2015.

————., eds. *Evidence-based Approaches to Positive Education: Implementing a Strategic Framework for Well-being in Schools*. Dordrecht: Springer, 2015.

————. "Well-being as Freedom: Future Directions in Well-being." In *Evidence-based Approaches to Positive Education in Schools: Implementing a Strategic Framework for Well-being in Schools*, edited by Mathew A. White et al., 167–75. Netherlands: Springer, 2015.

White, Mathew A., et al., "Student Leadership, Well-Being and Service: Integrating Appreciative Inquiry, Strengths and Leadership." In *Evidence-based Approaches to Positive Education in Schools: Implementing a Strategic Framework for Well-being in Schools*, edited by Mathew A. White et al., 151–65. Netherlands: Springer, 2015.

White, Mathew A., and Lea Waters. "A Case Study of 'The Good School': Examples of the Use of Peterson's Strengths-based Approach with Students." *Journal of Positive Psychology* 10 (2015) 69–76.

World Health Organization. "Global Burden of Mental Disorders and the Need for a Comprehensive, Coordinated Response from Health and Social Sectors at the Country Level." Geneva: World Health Organization, 2011.

————. "Measuring Quality of Life." Geneva: World Health Organization, 1997.

Biblical Perspectives

Chapter 4

"And God Saw it was Good"

The Creation of Wellbeing and the Wellbeing of Creation

MATTHEW P. ANSTEY

GENESIS 1 IS A love story—Creation is a love story.

But it is an understated love, a shy love, disclosed along the way, a love only known when encountered.

God, the Thoughtful One, appears in Genesis 1 without a history, without a biography; no bragging heralds this One's devoted shaping of words and worlds.

God the Artisan makes everything that is, heaven and earth. There is nothing that God does not make.

And then God pauses. The Thoughtful One lingers, as Spirit hovering over chaotic waters. God is at home in the disorder, in the yet-to-be-formed places. The watery chaos is the dormant rumblings of the world waiting to be brought graciously to abundance.

The Softly Spoken One then speaks, "Let there be light."

The music begins, the song of creation.[1] God says to Job: "Where were you when I laid the foundation of the earth? . . . when the morning stars sang together and all the heavenly beings shouted for joy?"[2]

This music is continuously unfolded by grace and without necessity by the love of the Father, Son, and Spirit, eternally communing in shared joy and delight.

And so the Softly Spoken One weaves creation threads on the loom of a seven day week, a deep and profound metaphorical structure of beginnings and middles and ends, seasons and rhythms.

Day One is wrought of spoken light; it is bathed in luminosity, a radiance of pure goodness, separated from darkness so that day and night might alternate as the world's metronome, evening and morning, evening and morning, evening and morning.

Day Two is a Sky-making Day, a Sky given to separate water from water, above from below.

Day Two then gives to *Day Three* the waters below the Sky, to be separated further into Land and Sea.

And God sees the goodness of all these places: Light, Sky, Land, and Sea.

But Day Three is not finished. God says, "Let the earth bring forth vegetation." I have granted you your place. Now you can give of yourself, by bringing forth plants and trees, and they in turn can share their seed and fruit. Giving spawns more giving. God creates spaces which in turn create life.

From Day Three onwards, the world partakes in its own creation.

By granting such reproductive potential to the world, God, as pure love, does not insist on getting God's own way.[3]

So Days One–Three progress through the creation of Light, Sky, Land and Sea. And from here, Days Four–Six receive these gifted spaces of Days One–Three and fill each in turn with its indigenous members.

In medieval exegesis Days One–Three were called *opus distinctionis*, "the work of separation" and Days Four–Six were called *opus ornatus*, "the work of embellishment."[4]

---

1. An analogy that came to be known as *musica mundana* or *harmonia mundi*. I am indebted to Hart, *Beauty of the Infinite*, 275 for the elaboration of this idea.

2. Job 38:4, 7.

3. First Corinthians 13:5, "Love does not insist on its own way."

4. Middleton, *Liberating Image*, 76 n. 89.

Day Four receives the Light space and fills it with sun and moon and quasars, supernovas and shooting stars. These lights bestow their own gift, for they determine days and months and years. The simple rhythm of morning and evening is overlaid with the syncopated bossa nova of tides and years, winter and summer, spring and autumn.

Day Five receives the Sea space and God populates it with swarming creatures, plankton and sea snakes, coral and starfish. The Thoughtful One then fills the Sky space with flying creatures, kestrels and hawks, finches and nightingales.

Day Six receives the Earth space, dappled by the gift of fruitful vegetation, and God fills it with animals galore, rhinos and echidnas, llamas and water buffalos.

And then, *a paradox at creation's zenith*. God, the One with no image, gives God's image to humankind. Humans are on the "frontier"—the *methorios* in patristic language—between the physical and spiritual, "the priesthood of creation that unites earth to heaven."[5]

Humans are blessed and released to thrive and permeate the world.

After all is created, God says to humankind, "Look! I *give* you everything."

Creation is through and through sheer gift, a dress rehearsal, one might say, for the gift of Christ's *kenosis*.

The Softly Spoken One, having declared all of creation *very* good, then rests on *Day Seven*, and listens in on the ongoing melodies of a world fully prepared to sing God's song forever.

Amen and Amen!

༅

In telling the story of Genesis 1 in this way, I hope to imitate the creative potency of the original Hebrew itself, but also establish a conversational space in which *theological* reflection on the narrative is first and foremost; rather than the all-too-common and utterly erroneous practice of *scientific* reflection on the narrative, which is "an epic adventure in missing the point."[6] To ask about the science of Genesis is like asking, "What color is the note C?" It is an error of categorization.

So, to the task at hand, namely, theological reflection on the text.

---

5. Hart, *Doors of the Sea*, 63.

6. Smith, *Whose Afraid of Postmodernism?* 74 n. 17, though said in relation to something entirely different.

I want to unpack the phrase I used in my retelling of Genesis above: "a paradox at creation's zenith. God, the image-less One gives God's image to humankind." I wish to take this in a somewhat different direction than is found in traditional commentaries on Genesis. What I would like to do is to give serious and proper consideration to the text itself as the primary source for providing the content for construing humankind as *imago dei*, the image of God. Namely, to be the image of God means first and foremost to be like the God of Genesis 1.

Hence we must first unpack who this God is in Genesis 1, *prior* to unpacking who this creature is who is in God's image. That is, *theology grounds anthropology*. And in stating it this way, I am foreshadowing my basic objection to Positive Psychology *al a* Seligman, for whom *psychology grounds anthropology*. But more on this later.

First, back to God. Who is this God that we are to imitate? Genesis 1 is remarkable in recording over *twenty-five* different activities God does in creating.[7] Together they divide into three groups: *speaking, acting,* and *resting.*

GOD SPEAKS

Let's consider God's speaking, which occurs in five different ways.

The first and most common speech act in Genesis 1 is the *let there be*: let there be light, let them grow, let them fly, let them look after each other.[8]

God lets everything find its own way and place and vocation. How contrasting with our words, "Let me do it! Let me take over!" But God speaks energizing life into creation—*Let creation thrive! Let world create as well!* God lets go and does not "dominate" the world, as Moltmann was known to say.

---

7. Creating v. 1, lingering v. 2, speaking v. 3, let there be light v. 3, seeing the good v. 4, separating v. 4, naming v. 5, let there be a space v. 6, making v. 7, let it be gathered v. 9, let it be seen v. 9, let the earth sprout v. 11, let there be lights... as signs v. 14, making lights to govern v. 16, setting in place v. 17, let the water swarm v. 20, let them fly v. 20, blessing v. 22, be fruitful! v. 22, multiply! v. 22, fill! v. 22, let the earth bring forth v. 24, let them rule v. 26, subdue! v. 28, look! v. 29, giving v. 29, finishing 2:2, resting 2:2, sanctifying (making holy) 2:3.

8. Or govern, or superintend, administer, rule.

The second way God speaks is to *name,* thereby granting identity. God names the day, night, sky, earth, seas. God names humanity as bearers of God's image, *male* and *female,* perfectly equal.[9]

The third way God speaks is to *command.* "Be fruitful! Multiply! Fill the place! Manage it!"[10] These commands say that life is a project. They promote our life and our giving of life to others.

The fourth way God speaks is to *draw attention.* In verse 29 God says to humanity *Look!*—God invites the listener to pay attention to our context, to what is before us, a good world pregnant with hope and possibility. *Look!* This centers human life on our particular context, our materiality and subjectivity.

This fifth and final way God speaks is the *declaration*—"I give you everything. I have withheld nothing." God is unfailingly generous.

GOD ACTS

Let's now consider God's actions, which complement at every point God's words. These can be grouped in three ways. The first group of activities is the most obvious: God creates, makes, separates, and sets in place.[11] *God works to maximize the creative work of others.* God creates the environment where life arises naturally. These actions by God correspond to the speaking of *let there be* and *naming.*

The second activity is *seeing the good*—seven times the story declares that God sees the good. Each particular thing is seen as delightful, as interesting and important in its own right. Seeing the good corresponds to God's exclamation of *Look!*—see the goodness all around you, despite the distortions of sin.

The third activity is *blessing*—God blesses. This corresponds to God's commands[12] to *be fruitful, multiply, manage,* whereby God calls creation to live out its life abundantly and responsibly. That is, to bless is to reveal the true nature of something, to show someone who they are and who they are called to become.

---

9. A radical statement in the context not only of the Ancient Near East, but even in the context of the Old Testament writings.

10. Verses 22 and 28.

11. Verse 17: "And God *set* them in the expanse [space] of the heavens to give light on the earth."

12. In vv. 22 and 28 God blesses and this is followed by the imperatives.

The call to "manage" creation, or subdue, or master it, has received a much-needed critique, but I suggest these be directed towards the *mis*management done in the name of God, and not the call to good management. Think of the "beneficent mastery" of nature: clothing, food, sanitation, housing, healthcare, business, and of course, education!

GOD RESTS

Finally, God rests. Not as an interruption to an otherwise busy schedule, but as the natural endpoint to God's working and speaking. Even this dimension, however, is layered, composed of four activities: finishing, sanctifying, blessing, and resting.

INTEGRATION AND VOCATION

So we can see that God's activities cohere perfectly with God's speech.[13] Thus to be made in God's image means to pursue a way of living in which all our speech and activity and rest intertwine in a flawless integrity.

In imitation of God, we come to participate in "let others be fruitful," "let others flourish," because love delights in the particular beauty of the other in and of itself. It shapes not only a way of seeing the world but an integrated way of being, with the seamless interweaving of speech, activity, and rest. David Bentley Hart writes, "Beauty is the beginning and end of all true knowledge: really to know anything, one must first love, and having known, one must finally delight; only this corresponds to the trinitarian love and delight that creates."[14]

And what is vital in this construal of the human person, is that it is a *vocation*, a *project*, it has a direction, namely, to flourish, to be fruitful, to participate in the creation as co-creators and caretakers. In other words, the image of God is both gift and vocation. Thus, the *imago dei* entails the *missio dei*, the yearning of God for the wholeness of all. In theological language: creation itself is eschatological, or better still, *the protological is the eschatological.*

13. The declarative "I give you" is perhaps therefore best analyzed as a performative, which is a speech act that *performs* what it says (e.g., "I baptize you"). That is, no activity is tied to "I give you" because the speech *is* the activity of giving.

14. Hart, *Beauty of the Infinite,* 132. "Truth is ultimately aesthetic, . . . a unity of form and message, having no separable essence or content for dialectic to pry loose."

Now, I cannot claim originality in this. In as early as the third century, Origen suggested that the repetition in Hebrew, "in our image, after our likeness" indicates that we *are* God's image and we are also *to become* God's image.[15]

POSITIVE THEOLOGY

So, let's take stock. We have pondered afresh, I hope, the creation narrative of Genesis 1, and then lingered over the intricate and rich portrayal of the God of this story and the implications for us as made in the image of this God. Where then does Positive Psychology fit into this?

For me, Positive Psychology is a gift, at so many levels. First, it provides evidence-based analysis of the human condition and the condition in which humans flourish. It quantifies, measures, and analyzes the variables that maximize wellbeing, qualitative factors notwithstanding.

Secondly, it provides a spur, a prod, a challenge to theologians, especially Protestant theologians, whose trademark dialectic is one of *difference* between humankind and God, as opposed to Catholic theologians whose dialectic is one of *similarity*. For too many Protestants, theology commences in Genesis 3, The Fall—without exception rendered in Capital Letters!—and *grace* is understood as a response to sin, rather than sin as a wounding of grace. To put it bluntly, the Incarnation is God's *reaction* to Adam and Eve's misdemeanor, rather than the intention of God from all eternity to be in full communion with God's creation.

Thirdly, it provides an apparent neutral vocabulary for conversation on the human project, neutral with respect to any particular religious tradition.

The neutrality, however, I suggest is naïve and comes at too high a price, and this neutrality is ultimately unsustainable. When pushed, *those with* religious beliefs would argue that psychology rests upon theological a priori, as I have above, and *those without* would argue, when pushed, that it rests on a-theological a priori. Epistemology, however much vaunted as foundational, always rests on ontology. It rests ultimately not on *science*, but on a *set of beliefs*. We cannot escape the issue of human beliefs about the ultimate origin, purpose, and destiny of the world, even if those beliefs are that there are none, or none knowable.

---

15. I am indebted to Cotter's commentary on Genesis for pointing this out.

But debating this point takes us in a different direction from that in which I wish to head. Rather, I'd like to outline what Positive Psychology would look like if given theological, and here I would mean Christian theological, foundations. What some would call Positive Theology.

First, we would argue that the very notion of human wellbeing is *intrinsic* to the human project, because it is grounded in the wellbeing of creation, and the creation of wellbeing by God.

Second, we would assert that human wellbeing is fundamentally a *gift*. It is God-given and God-shaped, resting on the belief that humans are *imago dei*. The very *being* that is called to flourish is no less than the image of God.

Third, we see from our reading of Genesis 1 that human wellbeing is intrinsically *interpersonal and relational*. The command is "Be fruitful and multiply."

Let's reflect on this for a moment. In order for the multiplying to lead to fruitfulness and wellbeing, the multiplying requires love, and the love requires trust and respect and equality of the sexes. This love requires the ability to make promises and vows, to commit to one another in faithfulness and care. Hence it requires covenant. For the one born into this community, there must be identity and hence remembrance and hence story. And so on and so forth.

I am concerned that Positive Psychology, if theological foundations are absent, too easily becomes individualistic. Even when it promotes good relationships, I cannot but sense that it is still within the envelope of utilitarianism, that in caring for you, you will care for me. The theological notion is however, in caring for you, I am caring for God's image. Full stop.

Fourth, we see that from Genesis 1 human flourishing is intrinsically *interdependent with the created world*. The sun and moon give days and seasons. The days and seasons allow trees to be fruitful. The fruit feeds the animals and birds and humans. Hence the humans emerge on Day Six, not Days One–Five, into a world upon which they depend and "over" which they have a sacred stewardship, though we might wish now to say "with which" rather than "over which."

Now, to take this *scientifically* and to ask for instance, "But don't the animals sometimes eat the humans?" is wrong-headed. Rather, theologically, we must take this to indicate the *utter dependence of human wellbeing on environmental wellbeing*.

Fifthly, these notions of relationship and environmental interdependence entail *ethical obligations*, and hence, economic and political constraints.

But it is these wider implications and contexts and entailments of the notion of human wellbeing that I find lacking (at times) in Positive Psychology. It is the theological grounding of human wellbeing in *God's* wellbeing and God's creation that I find is unavoidable as a Christian theologian engaged in thinking Christianly about such matters. Or as I said above, theology grounds psychology.

Finally, I also said above that *the protological is the eschatological.* The first word, the word of creation, is the last word.[16] Human wellbeing is hence not an end in itself, but a means to an end, and that end for Christians is understood as friendship with God. Again, let us think of Genesis 3 prior to The Fall, a garden in which humans and God walked together in the cool of the day.

It is telling that the great touchstones of the Christian story are set in gardens; the garden of Eden and creation, the garden of Gethsemane and crucifixion, the garden of the empty tomb and resurrection, with these haunting words from John's gospel:

> Jesus said to her, "Woman, why are you weeping? Whom are you looking for?" Supposing him to be *the gardener*, she said to him, "Sir, if you have carried him away, tell me where you have laid him, and I will take him away." (John 20:15 NRSV)

The garden is portrayed in the very last chapter of Revelation, "Then the angel showed me the river of the water of life, bright as crystal, flowing from the throne of God and of the Lamb through the middle of the street of the city. On either side of the river is the tree of life with its twelve kinds of fruit, producing its fruit each month; and the leaves of the tree are for the healing of the nations" (Rev 22:1–2 NRSV).

So by placing theology as the ground for psychology, we come to view *the basis* of human wellbeing as deriving from the divine wellbeing and *the project* of human wellbeing as being bound up with the wellbeing of the whole creation, and *the goal* of wellbeing as communion with the divine itself.

The Scriptures abound with this notion of God as the ground of human wellbeing:

16. Let me put this another way: we have no fear of the last judgment, because the world *begins* in judgment. "And God saw all that God had made and it was very good."

"Be holy, because I the Lord your God am holy" (Lev 19:2 NRSV).

"We love, because God first loved us" (1 John 4:19 NRSV).

Or, in modern parlance, "We flourish, because God flourishes."[17]

REFERENCES

Anstey, Matthew P. "29th July: Proper 12: Ephesians 3:14–21." *Expository Times* 123 (2012) 452–54.

Cotter, David W. *Genesis: Studies in Hebrew Poetry and Narrative*. Collegeville: Michael Glazier, 2003.

Hart, David Bentley. *The Beauty of the Infinite: The Aesthetics of Christian Truth*. Grand Rapids: Eerdmans, 2003.

———. *The Doors of the Sea*. Grand Rapids: Eerdmans, 2005.

Middleton, J. Richard. *The Liberating Image: The* Imago Dei *in Genesis 1*. Grand Rapids: Brazos, 2005.

Smith, James K. A. *Who's Afraid of Postmodernism? Taking Derrida, Lyotard and Foucault to Church*. Baker, 2006.

17. For a critique of Positive Psychology from a Christological angle, albeit in homiletical style, see Anstey, "29th July: Proper 12."

Chapter 5

Shalom, Gospel and the Mission of God

Tim Harris

I AM RELATIVELY NEW to Positive Psychology, but have been exploring notions of *shalom* and blessing from a biblical theology perspective for some time. In encountering the key insights advocated by exponents of Positive Psychology, the points of connection are significant, and the possibility of bringing the two lines of research into some level of alignment are indeed promising.

A number of contributors from the theological side of the fence have identified a potential tension between recognition of flawed human nature that cannot be underestimated, and the positive attributes in a healthy human character to be nurtured through Positive Psychology. Both perspectives are of course inevitably caricatured, and the biblical corpus in its various genres gives testimony to both dimensions, so identifying such a tension is far from novel.

My proposal, however, is to broaden the foundation upon which a biblical theology of flourishing may be grounded. While the fallen humanity in need of redemption trajectory can claim much biblical warrant, a greater dynamic can be identified in/as moving from chaos and disorder through to harmony and the flourishing of creation, via the ministrations of humanity created in the image and likeness of God. Flourishing throughout creation is tied of necessity to the calling of humanity to enter into the missional purposes of God.

Christopher J. H. Wright, in his significant volume *The Mission of God: Unlocking the Bible's Grand Narrative,* makes a deceptively simple but profound observation: "The God revealed in the Scriptures is personal, purposeful, and goal-orientated."[1] That is to say, life grounded in God is purposeful, comes with an inherent dynamic of potential and development, and has a goal.

While it is our contention that a creational understanding of the *missio Dei*[2] establishes the essential parameters of God's purposes, a second critical purpose co-exists within this framework, and is essential to the fulfillment and realization of God's wider purposes. The mission of God in providing redemption may be considered the heart of God's purposes, consistently identified in terms of issuing from God's love, grace, and faithfulness.

Such affirmations reflect the classic tension in identifying the *missio Dei.* Do we conceive it as including the totality of God's activities, in which case anything and everything that comes with the creation and sustaining of the cosmos is included? Every facet of life then expresses God's mission. It is all encompassing and we conceive God at work in every minute molecule and event of creation.

Or, while acknowledging the foregoing, do we limit the *missio Dei* more specifically to the work of redemption? That is surely the great burden of scriptural narrative and predominant from Genesis 3 onwards.

My response is to point to the importance of distinguishing the means from the *telos.* As noted above, salvation is not the goal or *telos* of the mission of God, but the critical means to that *telos.*

---

1. Wright continues: "The opening account of creation portrays God working toward a goal, completing it with satisfaction and resting, content with the result," (*Mission of God*, 63). Similarly, Gunton contends that creation "cannot finally be understood without its directedness to an end, because it has to be understood as God's project, a project in which he freely and graciously involves us, his personal creation," (*Triune Creator*, 88).

2. This term designates the sending of God, and is more broadly understood as the mission of God as revealed through activities of the Trinity, both distinctively and collectively (known more technically as an intra-trinitarian movement of God). For a concise but well-informed introduction to the history and theology underlying this term, see Van Gelder and Zscheile, *Missional Church,* 29–40.

Any understanding of God's mission that overlooks God's redemptive purposes neglects the diagnosis not only of the human condition (as in Rom 1:18–30), but the travails of creation no less (Rom 8:20–23). By the same measure, an emphasis on the mission of God in terms of salvation, without reference to the goal of the flourishing of God's developing creational purposes, strips the biblical narrative of its essential reference point and direction.[3]

Put simply, a biblical understanding of *shalom* needs to hold together both God's creational and salvific purposes, not as equal themes, but as one (redemption) within the other (the dynamic from creation to new creation). As we explore below, creation is not a static state of perfection before humanity messed it up, but an ongoing project awaiting fuller realization, extension and fruitfulness. The calling of humanity in the image and likeness of God (Gen 1:26–28) relates both to participating in the creational mission and purposes of God, and the unique capacity to do so.

"Flourishing in faith" is a promising way to express a potential integration of Positive Psychology with theology. However, this has theological integrity only if such flourishing has the breadth of *shalom* construed as both the flourishing of God's creative purposes and potential on the one hand, and the wholeness of salvation understood in personal, communal, and renewed creational terms on the other.

This contribution is very much by way of offering a bare sketch of the themes of *shalom* and blessing as they feature and develop through the overarching biblical narrative. More detailed treatment would be possible at many points, but I have intentionally kept my focus on the bigger picture and thematic development.

THE CREATIONAL DYNAMIC: FROM CHAOS AND DISORDER TO WHOLENESS AND FLOURISHING

The Bible is a seriously realistic book. It recognizes the realities of the messiness of life and that experientially all is far from right. There is a darkness that is part and parcel of the world as we encounter it. Battles on an epic scale with powers and forces of chaos and disorder were a widespread and central motif in a culturally widespread range of Ancient Near Eastern

---

3. At this point I part company with Goldingay, *Old Testament Theology I*, 126–28 who views creation in more complete, non-continuing terms. For a contrary view, (of which I am persuaded), see Fretheim, *God and the World*, especially 38–42.

traditions, identified explicitly in Canaanite, Babylonian, and Egyptian legends. It is important to note how clearly the motifs feature.

In the Canaanite context, *Ba'al* was initially something of an upstart and minor deity amongst the senior gods. But he eventually and notably conquered *Yam*, the god of the depths and the source of all chaos, and as a result was elevated in status amongst the Canaanite pantheon, rewarded with a temple and state of rest. *Ba'al* was honored and worshiped as the god who triumphed over chaos.[4]

In very similar terms, further to the East, Babylonian traditions as conveyed in *Enuma Elish* (with underlying influences from Sumerian mythology), *Marduk* was ascendant over *Tiamat*, and was likewise renowned for calming the turbulent waters and subduing the forces of chaos. The focus in this narrative lies not with the creation of humans, but in the elevation of *Marduk* as a supreme god as reflected in his great Temple in Babylon, and Babylon as the supreme city in the cosmos.

Just as profound are the Egyptian creation traditions. Here, earthen forms of hills and mounds arise out of Nun, the primeval watery abyss. As summarized by Rikki Watts, "Creation emerges from the deep, the darkness, the formlessness and emptiness, and the wind."[5] Chaos is personified, and as represented in the Ogdoad of Hermopolitas. Four pairs of male and female primeval deities embody various spheres of chaotic powers: *Nun* and *Naunet* (primordial water and the sky above), *Heh* and *Hehet* (infinite space and formlessness), *Kek* and *Keket* (darkness), and *Amun* and *Amaunet* (invisibility).

My reason in drawing attention to this background of chaotic motifs identified throughout the Ancient Near East is to underscore the cosmological and theological significance of these features in the Genesis accounts. They are more than flourishes in imagery or literary artistry. They make a significant statement about the character and direction of God's creative purposes. Creation is depicted as an ongoing project in which order is imposed on chaos and the creation of male and female in the image and likeness of God features not only as the crowning element of creation, but more significantly to share and employ the dominion of God over the

---

4. Note, for example, the Ba'al Epic: "Message of Aliyn Ba'al, word of the Mightiest Hero: Withdraw war from the earth, set upon the land love, pour forth peace in the midst of the earth, increase love in the midst of the fields, spare thy rod, put back thy sword," (Tablet V, section 6; translation in Cassuto, *Anath*).

5. Watts, "On the Edge," 139.

rest of creation, extending the triumph of order over chaos in the process of filling the earth.

The two biblical creation accounts of Genesis 1 and 2 are written with a clear awareness of such legends and make profound statements against such a backdrop, both polemically and more positively in expressing a fundamental belief upon which the faith of Israel stands.

Right from the opening verses of the Bible, this darkness is acknowledged:

> Now the earth was total chaos, and darkness covered the deep and the Wind of God hovered over the waters. (Gen 1:2a, Wenham.)[6]

Such darkness is not elaborated, but evokes something threatening and menacing, and which has not been fully eradicated. We continue to live in an imperfect world where "darkness hovers over the deep." However, the very next words provide the basis for belief and hope that runs throughout the Bible and indeed become stronger and stronger as the biblical narrative progresses. To be truly "flourishing" is to be flourishing in faith, hope, and love. One of the most precious contributions from bringing theology and Positive Psychology into conversation and interaction is that the notion of "flourishing" is located within the context of a wider narrative that provides meaning, purpose, and hope to our experience of life.

God acts to bring light and order, and changes the environment of darkness to one of security and order. While Genesis 1 speaks of a defining narrative of creation, the wider biblical canvas points to this being an ongoing process,[7] continuing in our own experience. The final "word" of Genesis 1 ("it was very good," 1:31) indicates that creation was (and is) both aesthetically beautiful and "good for purpose," but it does not indicate that creation is perfect, nor a static state of being. It continues to be developed, with the goals of bringing forth fruit and "flourishing." The creation narrative reflects a dynamic from chaos and disorder to wholeness and flourishing.

With a number of other interpreters, I take the reference to being made in the image of God (1:28) in the sense of receiving vice-regal authority (the exercise of delegated authority on behalf of a sovereign), essentially designating the role and responsibility that is uniquely given to humanity.

---

6. Despite the simplicity of most translations, there is some complexity in just how the opening verses of Genesis are construed. Without going into the various syntactical options, I have chosen to go with the translation offered by Wenham, *Genesis 1–15*, 4.

7. See especially Fretheim, *God and the World*, 38–42.

To be created in the likeness of God enables the functional dimension to be fulfilled, a secondary feature with a more ontological sense.

The verses that immediately follow explicate this functional sense of being in the image of God. The phrase "let them have dominion" is no license to lord it over creation according to whim, but rather a manifestation of the blessing of God (1:28) to "be fruitful, to multiply, and to fill the earth and subdue it." Again, we need to pay careful attention to the sense of this. The filling and subduing is to participate in the ongoing creative process of addressing a world that still needs to be brought to order and subdued.

There are two further indicators as to what this involves. One is the reference to "rest" as the goal of creation as realized in the final day, day seven. In Ancient Near Eastern reference, rest is the outcome of triumph over chaotic forces. In the first creation account, it is the *telos* of creation: its goal and endpoint. This reference to rest at the conclusion of this first account is relatively brief, but it receives more extensive attention in later passages, where it comes to embody the whole notion of *shalom* as the fullness of all that creation was intended to be (most clearly as delineated in Psalm 132, amongst other passages).

God speaks ten times in the first creation account. Put simply, God's *word* brings order out of chaos. The active word of God is set against a prevailing darkness and transforms darkness. The exact nature of such darkness is unclear, but it is no benign state of affairs. In the most elemental terms, darkness is everything that is not light, that is, not of God—or as Gordon Wenham puts it, it is "anti-God."

There are clearly patterns that give expression to God's activities in Genesis 1:

- "and God said" (10x—vv. 3, 6, 9, 11, 14, 20, 24, 26, 28, 29)
- "let there be. . ." (8x—or equivalent; vv. 3, 6, 9, 11, 14, 20, 24, 26)
- "and it was so" (7x—vv. 3, 7, 9, 11, 15, 24, 30)
- "and God made/created" (7x—or similar; vv. 4, 7, 11, 16, 21, 25, 27)
- "and God saw that 'x' was good" (7x—vv. 4, 10, 12, 18, 21, 25, 31)

Furthermore, there are various declarations that represent the establishing of boundaries and the introduction of order:

"there was evening and there was morning" (vv. 5, 8, 13, 19, 23, 31), followed by the designation of each day as "first," "second" and so on (vv. 5, 8, 13, 19, 23, 31; 2.2)

While the genre of Genesis 1 is not poetic as such, it is notable that a number of the distinctive phrases fall in patterns of seven. To the numerically attuned Hebrews, this is indicative of completeness and something uniquely of God.

For our purposes it is especially important to note references to God naming or blessing (vv. 5, 8, 10, 22, 28). Blessings are not just a sign of God's favor or expression of grace. More specifically, they are an outworking of God's creational purposes and a realization of all that creation was intended to become.

The second creation account in Genesis 2 introduces an evocative scene that conveys God's purposes in creation, both as it was established, and no less in terms of what it is intended to become—creation is a project, a work in progress. An indicator of the commission and responsibilities given to the human race comes with reading the second creation account in parallel to the first. There are numerous points of connection, but we should especially note the indicators that 2:15 is an elaboration on the mandate given in 1:28. The key verbs in 2:15 specify the "earth creature's" responsibilities in the garden: to "till" the garden and to "guard" it. There is work to be done and the flourishing of creation is tied to humanity's commission to live out what it means to be in the image and likeness of God.

THREADS AND MOTIFS IN THE BIBLICAL NARRATIVE

As the Old Testament narrative progresses, a cluster of terms is used to describe this state: The Sabbath "rest" realized as the goal of creation; the flourishing of the garden, the sanctuary "home" that comes through being in the dwelling place of God, the abundance and fruitfulness bursting forth in and through the garden. One word in particular conveys this state of affairs, a rich Hebrew word that needs a whole cluster of English words to even begin to capture what is being conveyed: *shalom*. The notion of *shalom* is well summed up by the quote from Cornelius Plantinga:

> The webbing together of God, humans, and all creation in justice, fulfillment, and delight is what the Hebrew prophets call *shalom*. We call it peace but it means far more than mere peace of mind or a cease-fire between enemies. In the Bible, *shalom* means *universal flourishing, wholeness and delight*—a rich state of affairs in which natural needs are satisfied and natural gifts fruitfully employed, a

state of affairs that inspires joyful wonder as its Creator and Savior opens doors and welcomes the creatures in whom he delights. *Shalom*, in other words, is the way things ought to be.[8]

While drawing on the expansion of the garden and temple motifs, the sense of purpose and intent is distinctive in Genesis 2. The expansion of the garden is a continuation of the creation process, and one in which the man and the woman are to put into effect their divine calling as God's image and do so through the employment of the aptitudes and capabilities that comes with being created in the likeness of God.

Jumping ahead to Genesis 12, the promises given to Abraham are well recognized as programmatic for God's missional mandate, and the greater purpose in the blessing of all nations is signaled from the outset. Of particular interest for our study is the parallel between the promises to Abraham and the creational mandate to be fruitful and fill the earth. Just as with the creation accounts, God's blessings are indicative not just of God's favor, but constitute the endpoint or *telos* of the great creation project. The experience of such blessings is the fulfillment of all that creation was and is intended to be.

Christopher Wright's translation captures this nuance well:

> And YHWH said to Abram,
> Get yourself up and go
> from your land, and from your kindred, and from your father's house,
> to the land I will show you.
> And I will make you into a great nation;
> and I will bless you;
> and I will make your name great.
> And be a blessing.
> And I will bless those who bless you;
> whereas the one who belittles you I will curse;
> and in you will be blessed all kindred groups on the earth.
> And Abram went just as YHWH said to him.[9]

As Wright observes, the "mission of God will be to preserve and maximize the blessing that is in the multiplication and spread of the nations while removing the blight of human sin and arrogance represented

8 Plantinga, *Not the Way*, 10.

9. Wright, *Mission of God*, 200.

by Babel . . . a process that will ultimately include all nations in the scope of its blessing."[10]

The "promised land," the goal of the journey out of slavery (the "exodus") and through the wilderness, the realization of the land promised to Abraham and Sarah and their descendants, is expressed in terms of being a "sanctuary" (Exod 15:17). This sanctuary is further depicted in terms of an Edenic garden realizing its potential for fruitfulness, health, and abundance. As the tabernacle is introduced and established in the second half of Exodus, we see in the furnishings, ornaments, color schemes, and especially the architectural layout a symbolic representation of the "holy of holies," a place of ultimate sanctuary in the presence of YHWH, located at the center of the community of God's people, and through them available to all nations and peoples.[11]

The well-known priestly blessing drawn from Num 6:24–26 sets the blessing from God in parallel to the quality of *shalom* received from God. In Deuteronomy, the land about to be entered is similarly described in Edenic-type terms (Deut 7:7–9), and the prophets use *shalom* as descriptive of redemptive hope (e.g., Isa 32:17; 48:18; 53:5; 60:17). Much more could be said of such themes in both Deuteronomic and prophetic traditions, but the focus of the remainder of this chapter will move to New Testament appropriation of *shalom*-related concepts.

SHALOM, GREETING, AND MISSIONAL PROCLAMATION

By the time of the New Testament period, *shalom* had become the primary Jewish form of greeting (welcome and farewell).[12] Within the synoptic traditions, this is reflected in the sending of the Twelve in Matt 10:12–13, where the mission is expressed in terms of expressing a greeting to the house upon arrival, followed by a bestowal of peace (*eirenē*), which may be withdrawn if the welcome is not forthcoming. A similar instruction is given to the seventy-two in Luke 10:5–6:

---

10. Ibid., 202.

11. For a detailed and convincing treatment of the symbolic significance of the tabernacle and Temple, see Beale, *Temple*.

12. Often expressed in the Hebrew phrase *shalom aleichem* ("peace be upon you"), with the response expressed in reverse *aleichem shalom* ("to you, may there be peace").

> Whatever house you enter, first say, "Peace to this house!" And if anyone is there who shares in peace, your peace will rest on that person; but if not, it will return to you.[13]

This constitutes more than social niceties. The greeting of peace is a proclamation of the presence of the kingdom of God (and further manifested through healings, Luke 10:9). The realization of the kingdom of God drawing near is synonymous with the experience of *shalom*.

This is similarly picked up in Paul's variation in his greetings "grace and peace," becoming his short hand for the gospel itself. The "peace" here ("*eirenē*") is very much an expression of the fullness and breadth of *shalom*, and is a direct appropriation of the *shalom* motif. Variations on the characteristic "Grace to you and peace from God our Father and the Lord Jesus Christ" (Rom 1:7) not only echo Greek and Hebrew greetings, they interweave two profound theological terms that are foundational to Paul's articulation of the gospel.

Thus, Paul describes Christ himself as "our peace," with the very real outworking of the breaking down of barriers otherwise separating Israelites on the one hand, and aliens and strangers on the other (Eph 2:12–15). The result is "one new humanity in place of the two, thus making peace." While clearly a cessation of hostilities is now possible through Christ's work on the cross, such peace may also be understood as the realization of the gathering from all nations of a united people of God. A healthy and harmonious community is similarly a manifestation of God's *shalom*. Thus Christ

> came and proclaimed peace to you who were far off and peace to those who were near; for through him both of us have access in one Spirit to the Father. So then you are no longer strangers and aliens, but you are citizens with the saints and also members of the household of God (Eph 2:17–19).

"Preaching peace" is the realization of *shalom* through Christ and the Spirit, now manifest in the community of the church.

13. Unless indicated otherwise, all translations in this chapter are from the New Revised Standard Version Bible, copyright © 1989 National Council of the Churches of Christ in the United States of America. Used by permission. All rights reserved worldwide.

SHALOM AND THE GOSPEL OF SALVATION

The language of salvation/being saved/healed (*soteria/sōzō*) also has significant overlap with *shalom* (conceptually and theologically), and in the Synoptic Gospels includes social, mental, psychological, and spiritual healing—very much in a holistic sense (thus avoiding a body/soul dualism). Around one third of the content of the synoptic Gospels details the outworking of "*soteria*" in the form of healings[14] (understood in a wide semantic range)—this is what *shalom* looks like as a foretaste of the fullness of the kingdom. The realm of heaven breaks into earthly experience, anticipating the new creation in which heaven and earth become one (Rev 21:1–5).

A helpful window into the multilayered dimensions of salvation can be found in Zechariah's prophecy (Luke 1:67–79). Such salvation embraces personal assurance, and especially forgiveness of sins (Luke 1:76), yet is also a communal work of God through the house of David (Luke 1:69). It involves salvation from the activities of enemies, deliverance from fear, and, perhaps most profoundly, the coming of "light to those who sit in darkness and in the shadow of death, to guide our feet into the way of peace" (Luke 1:79).

Viewed in such terms, *shalom* is nothing less than the realization of the creational hope where God's light overwhelms the "anti-god" darkness (Gen 1:2; John 1:5), and a fullness of peace, vitality, and life ensues. In the gospel imagination, the future fullness of the creation project is breaking into the present. Salvation brings together both redemption and creational fulfillment, at once restoring a right relationship with God and establishing a flourishing world characterized by justice, righteousness, and harmony.

SHALOM AND RESURRECTION LIFE

The work of the cross and resurrection also relates to the work of God in Christ establishing peace: "Therefore since we are justified by faith, we have peace with God through our Lord Jesus Christ, through whom we have obtained access to this grace in which we stand. . ." (Rom 5:1–2a).[15] Similarly, we may understand the "first fruits" of the resurrection as expressed in 1 Cor 15:23 as an all-encompassing reality—all creation is redeemed to

---

14. For the identification of healings in terms of salvation within the gospel traditions, see especially Twelftree, *Jesus the Miracle Worker*.

15. For the work of the cross as achieving shalom, see Cole, *God the Peacemaker*.

become all it was and is intended to be. The "new creation" motif here is tied to the prophetic vision of *shalom* being realized through the kingdom of God.

It is also in the context of affirming a resurrection hope in redefining and transforming the experience of affliction, frailty, and mortality that Paul asserts the "in Christ" outworking of a new creation: "everything old has passed away; see, everything has become new!" (2 Cor 5:17). Again we find forgiveness of sin, reconciliation, transformation, renewal, and righteousness combining to constitute a *kairos* opportunity, the "day of salvation" in the present "now" moment (2 Cor 6:1–2).

Lest we construe these exhortations in overly abstract terms, the manifestation of such renewal is to be reflected in very real terms within the communal life of God's people: "live in peace; and the God of love and peace will be with you" (2 Cor 13:11), for in this the Corinthian church may personally and communally "become perfect" (2 Cor 13:9); in other words, to flourish.

In John's Gospel the motif of "life" is similarly tied to a quality of life now breaking into the present order through Jesus (John 10:10: "I came that they may have life, and have it abundantly"), and is also expressed through the language of "peace." This theme, again located against a backdrop of light prevailing over darkness,[16] reaches a profound climax in the post-resurrection commissioning recounted in John 20:19–26. In terms evoking the communal resurrection prophesied in Ezekiel 37, and in like measure adopting a heightened expression of a *shalom* greeting and farewell, Jesus breathed upon the disciples, accompanied by the emphatic "Peace be with you."

Similar connections can be made with references to God's provision of a quality of life in terms of "rest" (Matt 11:28). In the same vein, the movement of the people of God towards a state of "rest" is characterized in relation to the journey towards the promised land, reflecting the abundance associated with Eden (Heb 4:1–11, picking up a range of Old Testament allusions and motifs).

---

16. John 1:5–9; 12:35–36. John notably casts significant events and encounters with reference to daylight or darkness: e.g., 13:30 "and it was night" following the departure of Judas Iscariot; compare also 21:3–4.

SHALOM, THE GOSPEL,
AND RENEWAL OF THE MIND

Returning to Paul, the quality of *shalom*-peace is a distinctive attribute of experiencing the mind of Christ. The notion of "mind" is much wider than our limited post-enlightenment limitation of mind to rational capacities. In the world of St. Paul such "thinking" conveys much deeper senses of intellect, desires, emotions, ambitions, and will, combining to produce an "attitude of mind."

It is in this sense that Paul highlights in Philippians 4 what it means to be drawn into the "mindset" of Jesus. The path to true joy and the absence of anxiety is found in thinking as Christ does. *Shalom*, hearts, mind, and the gospel converge:

> And the peace of God, which surpasses all understanding, will guard your hearts and your minds in Christ Jesus.
>
> Finally, beloved, whatever is true, whatever is honorable, whatever is just, whatever is pure, whatever is pleasing, whatever is commendable, if there is any excellence and if there is anything worthy of praise, think about these things. Keep on doing the things that you have learned and received and heard and seen in me, and the God of peace will be with you. (Phil 4:7–9)

The "peace of God" (v. 4) and the "God of peace" (v. 9) provide more than a pleasing stylistic symmetry. Just as the Jewish greetings "God be with you" and "*shalom* be with you" are effectively synonymous, so the identification of the peace of God with a distinctive quality of God summarize the goal of creation and redemption.

The same interweaving of rich gospel motifs is found in Romans as well. As Paul elaborates his understanding of the "gospel as the power of God for salvation . . ." (Rom 1:16), he goes deeper than outlining an indictment sheet as descriptive of the human condition (all are guilty of sin), and explores the nature of the mindset that has led to this state of being rightly considered deserving of the judgment of God (1:21: "for though they knew God, they did not honor him as God or give thanks to him, but they became futile in their thinking, and their senseless minds were darkened.") Actions resulting from this flawed mindset bring a grim prognosis: it is a dead end (1:32), and no way to experience the fullness of life.

Paul's account of the gospel that addresses such a dire state takes us to the work of Christ upon the cross (Rom 3:24–25), and only in and through that is assurance of forgiveness, redemption, righteousness and reconciliation with the God of life attained. Yet the gospel does not stop at this point. Amongst an array of gospel treasures, notions of freedom from tyranny and a new expression of being human, touch on profound changes in both human experience and potential for growth (both personally and communally).

However, the unique game-changer is still to take center stage in Paul's narrative. Like a dancer waiting in the wings, the Holy Spirit leaps into full view in Romans 8, and the gospel as the power of God for salvation addresses what Positive Psychology aspires to, yet struggles to attain: transformation of the mind. Deeper than assurance of forgiveness, the Spirit relocates the object of the heart and mind towards all that is life-giving has the potential to flourish:

> For those who live according to the flesh set their minds on the things of the flesh, but those who live according to the Spirit set their minds on the things of the Spirit. To set the mind on the flesh is death, but to set the mind on the Spirit is life and peace. (Rom 8:5–6).

As these motifs continue in Paul's explication of the gospel, the first two verses in Romans 12 see a stunning reversal of the state of human experience outlined in Romans 1, the heart of which is conveyed in the much quoted terminology of transformation of the mind. The futile and senseless mind of Romans 1 is transformed into a mind that "may discern what is the will of God—what is good and acceptable and perfect."

Grace and peace. An abundance of grace and a quality of *shalom-*peace summarize the gospel as affirmed across the New Testament. If we are to be true to the scope of the biblical narrative, then the mission of God is understood as the bringing of order out of chaos, of light prevailing over darkness, and in the fulfillment of the creation project manifest in the flourishing of all creation. Within this wider working of God, and into which all humanity is called to participate, the mission of God in redemption in Christ and through the Spirit brings personal and global salvation, wholeness and healing to all creation.

CONCLUSION

This chapter has provided a portrait of dynamics of order, wholeness, flour-ishing, and *shalom* throughout the biblical narrative. Notwithstanding the necessary brevity, the potential for a broader theological movement to be identified has profound convergence of themes with Positive Psychology.

Yet where might a deeper dialogue between biblical theology and Positive Psychology take us? Clearly there is much in common that would benefit from closer examination, but what of essential differences? From the perspective of biblical theology, I would ask whether Positive Psychol-ogy contemplates a transformation of mindset or worldview? The biblical narrative identifies vitality and holistic health in necessary relation to the provision of life itself from a creator God. The metaphorical DNA of life is located in the grace of God. "For from him and through him and to him are all things" (Rom 11:36). To seek life and to flourish as a human is futile if unrelated to living in a right relationship with the God who alone gives life.

By the same token, we might ask whether the holistic vision of Positive Psychology provides a salutary corrective to a dualist understanding of sal-vation, the separation of body and soul from mind and spirit? Salvation is all too often reduced to matters of the soul, without reference to the broader notions of human existence in a more integrated sense. A deeper dialogue between biblical theology and Positive Psychology has the potential to be of significant benefit in both directions, and this chapter has identified key theological motifs that may provide a focus bringing greater convergence, as well as clarifying distinctive features of the respective perspectives.

REFERENCES

Beale, G. K. *The Temple and the Church's Mission: A Biblical Theology of the Dwelling Place of God*. Downers Grove: IVP, 2004.

Cassuto, Umberto. *The Goddess Anath. Canaanite Epics of the Patriarchal Age*. Jerusalem: Magnes, 1951.

Cole, Graham. *God the Peacemaker: How the Atonement Brings Shalom*. Downers Grove: IVP, 2009.

Fretheim, Terrence. *God and the World in the Old Testament: A Relational Theology of Creation*. Nashville: Abingdon, 2005.

Goldingay, John. *Old Testament Theology I: Israel's Gospel*. Downers Grove: IVP, 2003.

Gunton, Colin E. *The Triune Creator: A Historical and Systematic Study*. Grand Rapids: Eerdmans, 1998.

Plantinga, Cornelius. *Not the Way it's Supposed to Be: A Breviary of Sin*. Grand Rapids: Eerdmans, 1995.

Twelftree, Graham. *Jesus the Miracle Worker: A Historical and Theological Study.* Downers Grove: IVP, 1999.

Van Gelder, Craig, and Dwight J. Zscheile. *The Missional Church in Perspective: Mapping Trends and Shaping the Conversation.* Grand Rapids: Baker, 2011.

Watts, Rikki E. "On the Edge of the Millennium: Making Sense of Genesis 1." In *Living in the Lamblight: Christianity and Contemporary Challenges to the Gospel,* edited by Hans Boersma. Vancouver: Regent College, 2001.

Wenham, Gordon. *Genesis 1–15.* Waco: Word, 1987.

Wright, Christopher J. H. *The Mission of God: Unlocking the Bible's Grand Narrative.* Downers Grove: IVP, 2006.

Chapter 6

Mary-Theotókos

Fulfillment of God's Grace and Embodiment of Virtues—A Strengths-Based Reading

MATHEW A. WHITE

INTRODUCTION

I REMEMBER BEING AT a dinner with Martin Seligman and colleagues at St Peter's College in Adelaide, where he posed a challenging question: "Is it possible to have a Christianity without the Cross?"[1] Listening to the conversation that followed, I was struck that no-one appeared to consider the role that Mary, Mother of God, had played. Naïvely, I asked, "How is it possible to have this conversation without reflection on the role of Mary, Mother of God? She is the Mother of God and was at the base of the Cross. It is in considering Mary that we must come to some truth about Christ."

---

1. For an overview of Seligman's published views on the topic see Seligman, "God comes at the end"; Yaden et al., *Being Called.*

My colleagues were rather surprised and this led to a lively discussion about Mary's strengths. I declare from the outset I am not a theologian, or a psychologist. What follows is an exploration of two fields of inquiry and the question: "Is it possible to have a deeper understanding of Mary by integrating Peterson and Seligman's language of virtues and character strengths?"

The Millennium—A Turning Point in Theology and Psychology?

As the world focused on the new millennium in 2000, people's minds were drawn to the past and pulled into the future. Thankfully, the Y2K bug, widely predicted to destroy all computer systems around the world, did not happen, and we seemed to move from one century to the next with little difficulty.

During that year, there were a number of significant events in both religious and scientific communities around the world. In Rome, the pope declared it the year of the Great Jubilee. The four Jubilee Doors across Rome were opened and there were special Vespers celebrated at St Peter's Basilica. At an ecumenical gathering on January 18, 2000, Pope John Paul II opened the final of the four Holy Doors at St Paul Outside the Walls and prayed for the world. In an act of Christian unity, the Archbishop of Canterbury, the Rt Rev and the Rt Hon the Lord Carey of Clifton and Patriarch Athanasios spontaneously knelt with the pope in prayer, side by side.

In the scientific community, the millennial edition of American Psychologist was published in 2000 and edited by Martin Seligman and Mihaly Csikszentmihalyi.[2] In this highly influential edition the field of Positive Psychology was launched and the journal dedicated itself to related topics from some of the world's leading psychologists. While Abraham Maslow first coined the phrase "Positive Psychology" in the 1950s, the term is more recently associated with developments in the psychological field in the mid-1990s, launched by Martin Seligman in his American Psychological Association's (APA) Presidential Address in 1998. Later that year in an editorial he concluded, "it is equally important to explore how building on human strengths can help make 'normal' people stronger and more productive as well as making high human potential actual."[3]

2. Seligman and Csikszentmihalyi, "Positive Psychology."
3. Seligman, "Building Human Strength," 1.

POSITIVE PSYCHOLOGY AND THEOLOGY?

As outlined by Reuben Rusk and Lea Waters from the University of Melbourne, Positive Psychology has grown over the past fifteen years and it now appears that it will touch nearly all aspects of scientific inquiry; education, business, government, policy, and law.[4] It can seem that there are ideological turf wars between theology and positive psychology. This perspective encourages a separation of each discipline rather than exploring what each could learn from the other.

Seligman's stance was highlighted in 2014 with a thought-provoking reflection on God in the first edition of the journal *Spirituality in Clinical Practice*:

> I confess that I don't read the theology literature, and when I come across the theological speculations written by graying scientists, I suspect the loss of gray cells. I have wavered between the comfortable certainty of atheism and the gnawing doubts of agnosticism my entire life, but I have intimations of a God for those of us who are long on evidence and short on revelation and for those of us who are long on hope but short on faith.[5]

This stance appears to be developing into the start of a rich dialogue between the two approaches. It is clear to theologians and psychologists that the disciplines of theology and psychology do not automatically go hand in glove. As noted previously by McCall, Waters, and White, "for a handful of theologians, advances in contemporary psychology are grounded in the secular world and diminish the charism of God's grace as they live the exhortation in 1 Peter 3:15."[6]

As I write this chapter, I can hear some of my less sympathetic readers asking, "What could a chapter on a strengths-based reading of Mary possibly tell us that Marian theology hasn't achieved already?" Alex Abecina notes, "Christian psychologists, ethicists, and theologians have actively sought to bring Positive Psychology and theology into constructive dialogue."[7] This chapter contributes to this dialogue. It is an exploration between and across theology and Positive Psychology and concludes with a close reading of the strengths and virtues present within the Magnificat, the Song of Mary.

4. Rusk and Waters, "Tracing."
5. Seligman, "God Comes at the End," 67.
6. McCall, et al., "Comparison," 27.
7. Abecina, "Whose Virtues?"

From the outset, I invite you to embrace the possibility that theology and Positive Psychology can learn from each other. Indeed, they can enrich each other, and as Ellen Charry argues, they can participate in an exchange of cognitive and spiritual gifts. So, consider this chapter as my meditation on these two systems of thought rather than a justification for the interaction of Positive Psychology and theology.[8]

This chapter will be about an application of Christian Positive Psychology. I have adopted Charry's definition where "Christian Psychology embraces those disciplines that speak of the soul (thus the etymology of 'psychology') from within Christianity, encouraging a transdisciplinary dialogue." In "Positive Theology: An Exploration in Theological Psychology and Positive Psychology," Charry claims that Christian theological psychology has been preoccupied with the topics of sin and helplessness.[9]

Very little has been written about love from this particular viewpoint. I recognize the lack of theoretical models from which one could approach the integration of psychological strengths into a discussion of theological text. In this chapter, I advocate for the adoption of a strengths-based narrative approach using an empirical framework adopted from Positive Psychology. I commence by exploring the theoretical limitations of Positive Psychology, defining positive education, and summarizing Peterson and Seligman's strengths and virtues classification. Peterson and Seligman's classification will form the framework for a strengths-based interpretation of the Song of Mary from Luke 1:46–55.

LIMITATIONS OF THIS APPROACH

Theology is the systematic study of the nature of God or religious belief, whereas psychology is the study of the science of the mind or of mental states and processes. Positive psychologists challenge us to consider individual and community wellbeing or flourishing as a major goal. Moreover, this definition of Positive Psychology is based on individuals and communities demonstrating that they have measurable characteristics that are more than just the absence of illness. Since 2009, the field of positive education has grown in many schools—some faith-based, others not.[10]

8. Charry, "Positive Theology," 284.

9. Ibid.

10. For a comprehensive list of schools integrating positive education refer to the International Positive Education Network and the Positive Education Schools Association.

Considering the growth of interest in preventative mental health strategies in schools, Alex Abecina reflects, "The technical vocabulary of the movement has been quickly adopted as a norm for speaking of Australian student wellbeing. For instance, Christian schools across the country have begun to opt for 'wellbeing' as a replacement for what has traditionally been called 'pastoral care.'" Abecina's comments do have some validity, but a degree of skepticism is warranted.[11] I have also been surprised how quickly many schools claim that they are adopting some form of wellbeing program. School leaders are engaging with the challenging rates of anxiety and depression in youth. It would be unusual if school communities did not sit up, take notice, and respond. But there is not the evidence to suggest an increased interest in wellbeing is simply the result of Positive Psychology muscling into areas where theology has traditionally been the focus.

For example, contemporary recommendations from the National Coalition Against Bullying—key mental health providers in Australia including BeyondBlue, The Black Dog Institute, and The Young and Well CRC—all stress the significance of adopting whole-school approaches to wellbeing.[12] Together with Simon Murray, I have surveyed and documented the growth of positive education and its empirical roots within positive psychological interventions. Positive education is based on the established discipline of Positive Psychology and underpinned by theories and empirical research in this field. It aims to develop the wellbeing, flourishing, and optimal functioning of children, teenagers, and students as well as parents and educational institutions.[13]

Lea Waters and I have outlined the limitations of positive and character education, highlighting the work of Benninga et al., who argue that school courses can be used to "form the character of the young through experiences affecting their attitudes, knowledge, and behaviors."[14] The character education movement seeks to ensure that a student's academic abilities are developed in unison with his/her character, and that attention is given to the promotion of virtuous behaviors such as respect, fairness, civility, tolerance, fortitude, self-discipline, effort, and perseverance.[15]

---

11 Abecina, "Whose Virtues?"

12. White and Murray, "Building."

13. Ibid.

14. Benninga et al., "Character."

15. Berkowitz and Bier, "What Works in Chracter Education"; Lickona, "The Return of Charater Education."

WHAT ARE THE BENEFITS OF THIS APPROACH?

Alex Abecina claims, "Christian schools ought to gladly welcome the language of virtue, character, and flourishing that underpins Positive Psychology" as a means to articulate and engage a wider audience in theological discussions.[16] Christopher Peterson defined Positive Psychology as "the scientific study of what goes right in life, from birth to death and all stops in between." This definition has been enriched by Jacolyn Norrish and Diane Vella-Brodrick, Australian psychologists who argue that "positive psychology contributes a comprehensive approach to mental health by adding investigation of positive emotions and human strengths to existing knowledge of mental illness and dysfunction."[17]

A goal of Positive Psychology is to enrich the traditional deficit-based or disease model of psychology, with its focus on repairing the negatives in life, by promoting the positives. In general, research in Positive Psychology has focused on the scientific study of:

- Positive emotions: hope, joy, trust, comfort
- Positive traits: loyalty, leadership, modesty, and gratitude
- Positive institutions: family, community, schools, and democracy

It is from the perspective of the third area, positive institutions, that I will explore the integration of character strengths in Mary's Song. To do this, I will adopt what Theo McCall has termed a Christian Positive Psychology: recognizing a number of points of contact between the biblical understanding of topics such as strengths, love, and wisdom; and Positive Psychology.[18] I concur with Professor Charry's reflection on her study of Positive Psychology, stating:

> I read positive psychology to see if it can help theology have a more balanced view of human psychology than a strong Augustinianism seems to permit. I seek to articulate theologically warranted strengths that Christians can rely on for the sake of their own flourishing and that of the societies to which they contribute.[19]

16. Abecina, "Whose Virtues?"
17. Norrish and Vella-Brodrick, "Positive Psychology."
18. McCall et al., "Comparison," 27.
19. Charry, "Interview."

My subjective experience in discussions about these concepts with theologians and psychologists is that there is a possibility for rich dialogue about meaning, virtue, and strengths, that deepens our understanding of the topic of faith and religiosity.

DEFINING CHARACTER STRENGTHS AND VIRTUES

Within psychology, defining virtue and strengths is a problematic area. A number of theoretical challenges emerge when we are asked to describe the virtues and strengths within a text of any kind (religious or secular). Since its publication in 2004, the Peterson and Seligman's *Character Strengths and Virtues: A Handbook and Classification* has been widely recognized a seminal text in Positive Psychology. Often critics of Peterson and Seligman's classification claim that it is derivative, and there is a gap between theory and application in educational and therapeutic settings.

However, it is one of the most widely adopted classifications. The framework is useful because it provides teachers and students with a language to discuss what is good about the people within the school and the school culture at large. Within the six virtues, there are twenty-four subordinate, empirically measurable, character strengths: Humanity (love, kindness, and social intelligence), Wisdom and Knowledge (creativity, curiosity, judgment, love of learning, and perspective), Temperance (forgiveness, self-regulation, prudence, and humility), Transcendence (hope, humor, gratitude, spirituality, and appreciation of beauty and excellence), Justice (leadership, fairness, and citizenship), and Courage (zest, bravery, perseverance, and honesty).

If we are to adopt a Positive Psychology approach to theology, then a combination of a theoretically informed and evidence-based positive theology framework is required. Here, we can turn to the scientific framework and research done by Christopher Peterson and Martin Seligman on universal human character strengths and virtues.[20] Peterson and Seligman's framework identifies six overarching virtues and twenty-four character strengths. Peterson and Seligman's theory has been tested empirically, and it has been found to be positively related to wellbeing outcomes in youth samples. For example, in a cross-sectional study conducted with middle school students in the United States of America, Park and Peterson found

---

20. Peterson and Seligman, *Character Strengths.*

that the character strengths of persistence, honesty, prudence, and love were negatively correlated with aggression, anxiety, and depression.[21]

MARY, MOTHER OF GOD

Mary has always held a particular place of veneration in the Christian tradition and as a paragon of the virtues. She is the Mother of God [*Theotókos*].[22] Across denominations, veneration of Mary varies. In Pope John Paul II's Encyclical Redemptoris Mater, on the Blessed Virgin Mary in the Life of the Pilgrim Church, he notes:

> The Mother of the Redeemer has a precise place in the plan of salvation, for "when the time had fully come, God sent forth his Son, born of woman, born under the law, to redeem those who were under the law, so that we might receive adoption as sons. And because you are sons, God has sent the Spirit of his Son into our hearts, crying, 'Abba! Father!'" (Gal 4:4–6).[23]

In the Catholic Church, Mary, as "full of Grace" [*kecharitoméne*], is one of the dogmas of faith including the Immaculate Conception and her Assumption. The veneration of Mary within the Church is well documented in art, poetry, prayer, iconography, and music. Central to this is Luke's portrayal of Mary in his Gospel.[24]

In particular, where the angel Gabriel selects Mary as God's handmaiden. It is a natural evolution of Christology to see Jesus and Mary, son and mother, as both the redeemer and the redeemed. "The followers of Christ still strive to increase in holiness by conquering sin, and so they raise their eyes to Mary, who shines forth to the whole community of the elect as a model of the virtues."[25]

I have long been attracted to the role that Mary, the mother of God, plays in the life of the Church. I think my personal engagement in the topic commenced as a child, when I was trying to work out how everyone fitted together in the story. Mary held a particular place of devotion for my Mother's family. On occasion, often under duress, sets of the Rosary were

21. Park and Peterson, "Positive Psychology."
22. Vatican II, "Lumen Gentium."
23. Ibid.
24. Ibid.
25. Bunson, *Guide to the Church*, 121.

prayed—I believe that my understanding of the virtue of courage and the strengths of bravery and perseverance was formed from these prayers.

Images of Mary were common—they were traditional portrayals of her as the Mother of the infant Christ. Images of Mary were present throughout my Christian education. I often thought about what Mary might have been thinking during the Annunciation and her pain in the pieta. So, my understanding of Christ as the redeemer has been shaped by my reflection on Mary as the redeemed.

However, it was being a chorister, learning the various settings of the Magnificat (Song of Mary, Luke 1:46–55), that helped me to know and understand Mary's holiness and her role as the realization of the Church. John Paul II tells us that the "Annunciation, therefore, is the revelation of the mystery of the Incarnation at the very beginning of its fulfillment on earth." The musical settings that first helped me to meditate on Mary, "Full of Grace," include majestic settings by English composers such as Stanford and Howells and earlier works by Palestrina and others. It has long interested me how each composer expresses Mary's strengths, courage, and awe in her opening lines.

> My soul proclaims the greatness of the Lord, my spirit rejoices in God my Savior; for he has looked with favor on his lowly servant. (Luke 1:46–48)

What has long fascinated me about Mary's Song and her vocation and life is found in her unyielding dedication as an instrument of God's will. For me, it is both awesome and terrifying. What, if anything, can a strengths-based reading of Mary's life and devotion do to strengthen my understanding of her supplication to God's grace?

I am sure many theologians would consider a strengths-based analysis of Mary's Song unconventional. I know that several psychologists would consider it unorthodox. From the outset of this analysis, I would like to stress this chapter is theoretical in nature and is an exploration of the application of a framework. What interests me in this approach is twofold: can the language of character strengths enrich my knowledge and understanding of Luke 1:46–55; and can it enable me to be able to reflect more deeply on the miracle of Mary's circumstance?

A CHARACTER STRENGTHS-BASED ANALYSIS OF THE SONG OF MARY

It is the anticipation and promise of God's mercy that is sustained throughout Mary's Song, which captures the magnitude of her story. As Peterson and Seligman contend, if strengths are to be put into action—that is, if they are done or acted out—before we can consider the strengths identified by Mary throughout the Magnificat, it is necessary to consider the grammatical tenses she uses overall.

Why the Magnificat?

Mary as Theotókos is the counterpoint to John's description of Christ as the "Word . . . made flesh."[26] It is by starting with the grammatical tenses that our understanding of how Mary positions her own experience will be formed. From this, we will be able to understand "our" role as the reader through "her" experience at the Annunciation. We are truly present with her at that moment. We can truly grasp the energy of the strengths and values she describes throughout the text. This claim is supported by the use of tenses in the Book of Common Prayer version of the Magnificat.[27]

During the Annunciation, it is evident that as Mary experiences the thoughts, feelings, and emotions of the event, she places herself at the center of a point in time, place, and history. For example, the narrative structure of her Song commences in the present tense as she states, "My soul doth magnify the Lord," using the present plural, and then the immediate past in the phrase "and my spirit hath rejoiced in God my Savior." She then looks deep into the future without end; "For behold, from henceforth: all generations shall call me blessed." She then moves back to her experience in the present tense: "For he that is mighty hath magnified me," and again to the past, present, and future.[28]

A series of empathic statements leaves no room for ambiguity around God's previous authority: "He hath shewed strength" and "hath scattered the proud." The Song then effortlessly moves into the present tense. Cardinal Joseph Ratzinger, eventually called to be Pope Benedict XVI, argues, "It is necessary to go back to Mary if we want to return to that 'truth about

26. John 1:14.

27. Luke 1:46–55.

28. Ibid.

Jesus Christ', 'truth about the Church', and 'truth about man.'"[29] The strengths that readily come to mind when reading the Magnificat for the first time are Mary's gratitude, open-mindedness, and curiosity as she seeks to make sense, from her perspective, of the events that take place; the joy that God has chosen her to conceive the Christ-child.

Her Song is declared predominantly in the present tense. As we read the Magnificat, we are with Mary in the moment she learns she is the instrument of God's will. The opening verse of her Song is startling, filled with energy and bravery, and she starts to consider the emotion and reason of this miraculous event. When I consider the opening sentence of the Magnificat, I hear a woman who is gripped with courage, using the pronoun "my" as the determiner of the sentence.

This deep exhortation highlights Mary's voice as being one of bravery at the enormity of God's grace that has been granted to her. Her soul and her spirit leap towards the all-encompassing love of the Lord, her redeemer, as she "proclaims what has happened." Mary's interpretation of God's gift to her is to recognize the underlying theme of justice. This role was granted to her and her leadership within the Jewish people; to bear the Son of God. She expresses it in these stunning lines:

> My soul proclaims the greatness of the Lord, my spirit rejoices in
> God my Savior; for he has looked with favor on his lowly servant.
> (Luke 1:46–48)

The paradox found in the tone of Mary's reflection is apparent to the reader. Her humility is coupled with strength and it is clear she calls on the strength of self-regulation to maintain her integrity through her awesome lines of reflection. The weight of God's love does not crush her. Instead it is apparent that it gives her body and soul the strength to see her calling. The movement of the Song propels the reader forward. Not only into the immediate future but into the present, where the reader is the interior of Mary's psychological reflection of her role. She states:

> From this day, all generations will call me blessed:
> the Almighty has done great things for me,
> and holy is his Name. (Luke 1:48–49)

The emphatic tone of Mary's declaration, "From this day," unequivocally highlights the significance of her role. Her words fly up. Mary is with us and we are with her in this moment of personal revelation and calling

---

29. Miravalle, *Mariology*, xxi.

to her ministry as the redeemed. Mary's gratitude for God's intervention in her life is deeply personal.[30]

The enormity and space of God's love are implied by Mary's reflection—the height of the Almighty and the lowliness of Mary create a sense of God's infinity in the reader's mind as she says, "the Almighty has done great things for me." When first considering this line, I always considered that Mary was a reflection on the annunciation alone. However, it is clear from the plural of "things" that she is considering her relationship with God before this event. It is apparent that Mary sees God's intervention as one linked with the virtues of humanity and his actions, which encompasses his love and kindness, not only to her but also to future generations.

Mary's tone moves from being the deeply intimate and personal "my," to then considering God's place within her life in the third-person singular pronoun "He," which places him at the center of generations into the future (including the reader) who will call her blessed. I invite you to reflect with me on Mary's choice of diction: "blessed," "Almighty," "great things," and "holy."

These words are a paradox and yet they coalesce in imagery as her soul flies up towards God and as her feet touch the ground. Her reflection on this serves to worship God's Name, as it manifests the virtue of transcendence.

As Mary's words fly up with her "soul" in the first lines, the direction of her vocabulary considers the expanse of God's character; "He," praised for his mercy, compassion, and willingness to forgive those who know and understand the enormity of his role. I have always found these lines perplexing. Christ as the "word incarnate"[31] and who will be the redeemer's vehicle is representative of God's love for his people, whereas Mary recounts the fear of God and then the scattering of those who are disobedient, saying

> He has mercy on those who fear him
> in every generation. (Luke 1:50)

The dichotomy that is expressed in Mary's description of God over these verses enables the reader to consider the paradox of God, both as a source of his love for humankind and as the all-powerful and omnipotent ruler. However, Mary's rationalization of the event is as much about the God of the Old Testament as it is about the miracle of the moment. Mary

---

30. As I was writing this Chapter I was teaching *Hamlet* to my senior class. I am reminded of the imagery used by Claudius as he repents saying, My words fly up, my thoughts remain below, Hamlet (III, iii, 100–103).

31. John 1:14.

understands her place in God's plan. Her description of God's strength is masculine and aggressive, as she states,

> He has shown the strength of his arm,
> he has scattered the proud in their conceit. (Luke 1:51)

She expands her reflection of God's place:

> He has cast down the mighty from their thrones,
> and has lifted up the lowly. (Luke 1:52)

After Mary has considered the virtue of Justice, her thoughts move "down" to the "lowly" and he "has lifted [them] up." She is no longer simply "proclaiming" her "soul." It is evident that this a turning point for Mary's realization of the enormity of the event that has taken place. She sees humility and modesty in God as he fills "the hungry with good things." In Mary's comparison of the "lowly" and the "rich," his "servant Israel" appears to provide a template for the strengths demonstrated by good discipleship. She logically reflects:

> He has filled the hungry with good things,
> and the rich he has sent away empty. (Luke 1:53)

And then Mary also remembers God's agreement for the chosen people of Israel, which stretches back to Abraham. Her reflection, like the enormity of God's grace, captures his place as the Alpha and Omega in the "promise he made to our fathers, to Abraham and his children forever." The imagery chosen by Mary throughout the Magnificat strongly references the Old Testament. Mary's vision concludes by capturing her open-mindedness to the future role she will play in the unfolding events of the Christ-child's life.

> He has come to the help of his servant Israel,
> for he has remembered his promise of mercy,
> the promise he made to our fathers,
> to Abraham and his children for ever. (Luke 1:54–55)

It is in these concluding lines of verse that Mary considers God's virtue of temperance with his "promise of mercy"—and that she is paradoxically God's highly favored lady to bring his mercy into the world.

CONCLUSIONS

Mary's prophetic words captured in the Magnificat are a source of rich reflection as Theotókos. In this chapter, I have chosen to reflect on the virtues and character strengths of Mary, Mother of God, as noted in the Magnificat. I outlined a short overview of the theoretical framework underpinning Christopher Peterson and Martin Seligman's strengths-based classification. I then applied this systematically to an analysis of the diction and imagery throughout her Song. From this, it is evident that a richer interpretation of the relationship between God the father, Mary, and her son can be discovered.

REFERENCES

Abecina, Alex. "Whose Virtues? Which Character Strengths? Positive Psychology in Christian Schools." Ethos: Centre for Christianity and Society, 2014.

Charry, Ellen. "Interview: Turning Theology from Pathology to Strength." Regent College, 2014.

Benninga, Jacques S., et al. "Character and Academics: What Good Schools do." *Phi Delta Kappan* 87 (2006) 448–52.

Berkowitz, Marvin W., and Melinda C. Bier. "What Works in Character Education." *Journal of Research in Character Education* 5 (2007) 29–48.

Bunson, Matthew, ed. *The Catholic Almanac's Guide to the Church.* Huntington, IN: Our Sunday Visitor Publishing Division, 2009.

Charry, Ellen T. *God and the Art of Happiness.* Grand Rapids: Eerdmans, 2010.

———. "Positive Theology: An Exploration in Theological Psychology and Positive Psychology." *Journal Of Psychology And Christianity* 4 (2011) 284.

Charry, Ellen T., and Eric L. Johnson. "Interview with Ellen T. Charry: Towards a Christian Positive Psychology." *Edification: The Transdisciplinary Journal of Christian Psychology* 5 (2011) 61–68.

Green, Susie, et al. "Positive Education: Creating Flourishing Students, Staff and Schools." *InPysch* 33 (2011) 16–17.

Lickona, Thomas. "The Return of Character Education." *Educational Leadership* 51:3 (1993) 6–11.

McCall, Theo, et al. "A Comparison Between Theological Christian Approaches to Wisdom and Peterson and Seligman's Classification of Character Strengths and Virtues." *Evidence Based Approaches to Positive Education in Schools: Implementing a Strategic Framework for Well-being in Schools,* edited by Mathew A. White et al., 27–41. Netherlands: Springer, 2015.

Miravalle, Mark, *Mariology: A Guide for Priests, Deacons, Seminarians, and Consecrated Persons.* Queenship, 2008.

Norrish, Jacolyn M., and Dianne A. Vella-Brodrick. "Positive Psychology and Adolescents: Where are we now? Where to from here?" *Australian Psychologist* 44 (2009) 270–78.

Park, Nansook, and Christopher Peterson. "Positive Psychology and Character Strengths: Application to Strengths-based School Counselling." *Professional School Counselling* 12 (2008) 85–92.

Peterson, Christopher, and Martin E. P. Seligman. *Character Strengths and Virtues: A Handbook and Classification*. New York: Oxford University Press, 2004.

Rusk, Reuben D., and Lea Waters. "Tracing the Size, Reach, Impact, and Breadth of Positive Psychology." *Journal of Positive Psychology* 8 (2013) 207–21.

Second Vatican Ecumenical Council, Dogmatic Constitution on the Church Lumen Gentium, 52 and the whole of Chapter VIII, entitled "The Role of the Blessed Virgin."

Seligman, Martin E. P. "Building Human Strength: Psychology's Forgotten Mission." *APA Monitor* 29:1 (1998) http://www.apa.org/monitor/jan98/pres.html.

———. "God Comes at the End." *Spirituality In Clinical Practice* 1 (2014) 67–70.

Seligman, Martin E. P., and Mihaly Csikszentmihalyi. "Positive Psychology: An Introduction." *American Psychologist* 55 (2000) 5–14.

Vatican II. "Lumen Gentium." In *Dogmatic Constitution on the Church*. "Chapter VIII: The Blessed Virgin Mary, Mother of God in the Mystery of Christ and the Church." Promulgated by Paul VI on November 21, 1964.

White, Mathew A., and Simon Murray, eds. "Building a Positive Institution." *Evidence Based Approaches to Positive Education: Implementing a Strategic Framework for Well-being in Schools*, edited by Mathew A. White et al., 1–26. Netherlands: Springer, 2015.

———. *Evidence-based Approaches to Positive Education: Implementing a Strategic Framework for Well-being in Schools*. Dordrecht: Springer, 2015.

Yaden, David B., et al., eds. *Being Called: Scientific, Secular, and Sacred Perspectives*. Santa Barbara: Praeger, 2015.

Theological Perspectives

Chapter 7

Drawn into the Inner Life of the Trinity

A Dialogue between Theology and Positive Psychology

Theo D. McCall

INTRODUCTION

In the late twentieth century a new approach within psychology emerged, named "Positive Psychology." This movement has the deliberate aim of moving away from a deficit-based approach to one based on learned optimism. At the turn of the twenty-first century, Martin Seligman and Mihaly Csikszentmihalyi asserted that, since World War II, psychology had concentrated on "repairing damage within a disease model of human functioning."[1] These two leading psychologists and academics led the discipline of psychology in a different direction, focusing on building positive qualities. For those psychologists who have embraced it, this movement

1. Seligman and Csikszentmihalyi, "Positive Psychology," 5.

has been a radical development in both academic publications and clinical work. The shift in emphasis has allowed a new branch of psychology to flourish, with publications in the field increasing exponentially.

CONNECTIONS

There is an immediate and obvious parallel with Christian theology. If we were to change Seligman and Csikszentmihalyi's words slightly, we might say that Christian theology since Augustine of Hippo has concentrated on "repairing *weakness* within a *sin* model of human functioning." In the twenty-first century, were we to attempt a (very) brief summary of the history of doctrinal theology, as it pertains to salvation and the doctrine of justification, it would reveal a significant, almost overwhelming, focus on the cross. From Augustine, to Anselm, and then Calvin, and as Ellen Charry points out elsewhere in this volume, much of Christian theology has maintained that all persons are fundamentally flawed. There is nothing that we as human beings can do to bring about our own salvation—we depend utterly on God's grace. The Reformation in particular has left an indelible mark on the emphasis of Christian theology, as writers explore themes of salvation, particularly the atonement. Luther's interpretation of the book of Romans, "Justification by faith *alone*," has become a non-negotiable statement of faith, certainly for churches in the Protestant tradition. The notion that we might somehow balance faith and works, as the letter to James suggests, has become unacceptable if we are talking about the doctrine of the atonement. In other words, salvation and sanctification (the believer increasing in holiness or the spiritual life) have become separated. The believer cannot participate in his or her salvation—he or she may *respond* with a life of good works, but such actions in no way contribute to his or her salvation.

Interestingly, and somewhat in contradiction to later theological movements, there appear to have been few, if any, artistic presentations of the cross in the very early Church. The catacombs under Rome contain no such pictures. We might speculate that the early Christian artists felt that the resurrection was the more appropriate focus of their artistic endeavors, or that the horror of the reality of the cross was too overwhelming to represent. Despite the New Testament focusing both on a theology of the cross and the resurrection, and not drawing a false distinction between them, this focus was not reflected in the new movement's art for the first few centuries. Of course later centuries would more than make up for this.

As a result of theologians and positive psychologists engaging in dialogue, the question has emerged, "Is there a place for a new theology, or a spiritual psychology, using contributions from both traditions?" In the context of questions of salvation and sanctification, with an acknowledgement of the questions Positive Psychology might pose of Christian theology about these themes, this paper will look at the notion of believers being drawn into the inner life of the Trinity. This will serve as a model for reconciling some of the apparent contradictions between a positive psychological approach to wellbeing and theological notions of justification. I will suggest that, far from being a hindrance to the development of a "positive theology," an exploration of our entering into the suffering of Christ will draw us most powerfully into the inner life of the Trinity and thus into a state of spiritual wellbeing.

THE ATONEMENT

The letter to the Hebrews, written principally to encourage Jewish Christians in the faith and to explore theology in a Jewish context, is explicit in its notions of the atonement and salvation. It will serve as a starting point for examining a theology of salvation. Within the context of the First Century Jewish sacrificial system at the Temple, the letter to the Hebrews asserts that in offering himself once and for all, Jesus Christ has replaced the older system of sacrifices. The role of the high priests in the Jewish sacrificial system was to offer gifts and sacrifices for sin, both their own sins and those of the people.[2] The writer then states that these earthly rites had their place in purifying the "sketches of the heavenly things" but that Christ entered heaven itself on our behalf.[3] There is no need for sacrifices to continue to be offered, as was the annual custom of the high priest at the Passover, because in the person of Christ the ultimate sacrifice has been made in a single offering.

As a side note, despite its clear references to the Jewish sacrificial system, it is interesting to observe that the letter to the Hebrews doesn't in fact use the word "atonement," nor indeed does any New Testament book. Nevertheless, phrases such as "having been offered once to bear the sins of many" and "Christ had offered for all time a single sacrifice for sin,"[4] have

2. Hebrews 5:1; 9:7.
3. Hebrews 9:23–24.
4. Hebrews 9:28; 10:10.

been explained using the language of atonement. Theologians have debated and argued precisely what the atonement might mean for many centuries. Colin Gunton gives one of the most succinct summaries of the debate.[5] Notions have ranged from the extreme "penal substitutionary theory," in which Jesus quite literally takes our place on the cross, to gentler understandings, such as the idea that *human beings* were the ones who needed to see justice for our sins.[6]

The penal substitutionary theory is the "hardest" of the doctrines of the atonement, in the sense that it emphasizes God's righteousness and holiness far more than God's mercy and love. In order to satisfy God's holiness, a sacrifice had to be made. If Jesus had not taken our place, then it would have fallen to us to pay for our sins in order to satisfy God's holiness and wrath. It needs to be stated that most academic theologians who argue for this understanding of the atonement do not have a simplistic notion of God's holiness—God is not an angry tyrant who rages against his creatures simply because he can. Rather, in this model, God is understood to be absolutely holy. It depends on a notion of God that is pure, undefiled, and utterly righteous.

Other models of the atonement have an emphasis more on God's love and understanding and less emphasis on satisfying God's righteousness. The model in the letter to the Hebrews, for example, is far less specific. The use of the word "for" in such phrases as "the offering of the body of Jesus Christ once for all" reveals that Christ replaces the sacrificial system of the Temple, to be sure, but the language is less absolute than that used in the penal substitutionary theory.

There is, however, no escaping the legacy of the Reformation. Human beings cannot participate in their salvation, if we follow that tradition and make an absolute separation between the doctrine of salvation and the believer's sanctification.

Does this mean a rejection of the cross, at least as Christians have traditionally interpreted its meaning? In other words, is there a new approach in combination with Positive Psychology?

---

5. Gunton, *Actuality.*

6. Ian Mackay, unpublished comments.

SALVATION AND SANCTIFICATION

In practical terms very few, if any, practicing Christians today would completely ignore the contribution their faith might make to the betterment of the world and themselves. Whether they always act on it is another matter, but the separation between salvation and life in the Spirit (sanctification) is far less absolute in the daily life of the Christian than the theology we have explored above. Indeed, many churches, certainly in the Western tradition, have a significant focus on good works. There are also literally hundreds of Christian programs, thousands and thousands if you include unpublished and locally based ones, with a focus on improving the spiritual life of the believer and/or his or her local church. Rick Warren's *The Purpose Driven Life* is a widely used example and it has great reach into evangelical churches across the English-speaking world. Technically, such programs may not be understood by the authors to be Pelagian—in the sense of the believers' good works being the cause of their salvation—and indeed will often have statements of "salvation by faith alone" or similar somewhere in the material. But in practical terms the aim is for the spiritual, emotional (and often physical) life of the believer to be improved.

A change of emphasis is needed. For Christians a total rejection of a theology of the cross would be a bridge too far. A focus purely on the resurrection and the life of the Spirit would be to ignore significant parts of the New Testament and deny much of the rich history of theology. Nonetheless, there is a much wider audience being missed by Christian theology when it makes a separation between the doctrine of salvation and the believer's sanctification. To reach this wider audience, and to make an impact in people's lives in a spiritual sense, a different emphasis may be needed. This may be thought of as being very similar to Positive Psychology's impact in shifting the emphasis in psychology from deficit-based to a more positive approach.

Theology already has the tools to contribute to this greater project. This chapter will concentrate on just one theological notion and explore how it might align with Positive Psychology.

DRAWN INTO THE LIFE OF THE TRINITY

Although not unique to theology, the concept of "'self-transcendence" has been explored by theologians as a way of understanding the process of sanctification. The emphasis within theology has been on the understanding that God begins this process, which reaches a climax in the person of Jesus Christ, who draws everyone else into the journey, if they are open to it. Yet this journey of self-transcendence towards something greater than oneself is unique to each person.

Through the person of Christ, the believer is drawn to undertake a very *personal* journey, which culminates in the person being drawn into the life of God the Holy Trinity. Salvation then is not simply an abstract notion of "being saved," with no more significant involvement on the part of the individual than the admittedly profound action of saying "Yes." Rather, salvation is profoundly and intimately connected to the process of sanctification. The call to "continual conversion," to use Benedict's terminology, means that the individual believer is constantly choosing to be drawn further and further into the extraordinary experience of the mutual self-giving life of the Trinity.

The three persons of the Trinity exist in a state of *perichoresis*, mutual indwelling, in which they coexist in a state of mutual self-giving and loving. It is important to note that the doctrine of trinitarian perichoresis both emphasizes the unity of the Godhead and allows for the distinctiveness of the three divine persons. Neither the unity nor the individuality of the divine persons is compromised. The dangers of both tri-theism and modalism are equally avoided. In other words, as Jürgen Moltmann puts it, the "doctrine of perichoresis combines the threeness and the oneness without reducing the threeness to the oneness or the oneness to the threeness."[7] The uniqueness of the three persons of the Trinity is retained, yet they exist not only in relationship to one another but "in one another" as the Johannine statements reveal.[8]

Crucially, the doctrine of perichoresis is self-evidently not a static understanding of God. John Damascene's doctrine emphasizes an eternal life process, which "takes place in the triune God through the exchange of energies."[9] Not only, then, do the persons of the Trinity dwell within one another, they also bring an energy to the divine life through the very process of the circulatory relationships within the Trinity. It is this very energetic process, which is never static, that brings about the unity of the three persons. Through this dance of energy, the three persons become one

---

7. Moltmann, *History*, 86.

8. Ibid.

9. Moltmann, *Trinity*, 174.

and yet the personal differences are not abolished. The living fellowship of the three persons, who relate to one another and exist in one another, allows both unity and differences to exist.

For Moltmann, influenced by his German evangelicalism, his reading of German philosophy, but also his reading of patristic and Orthodox theologians, the concept of perichoresis means all sense of any subordinationism within the Trinity is avoided.[10] Thus the Father is understood properly as the origin of the Godhead, but only as this relates to the constitution of the Trinity, not as it relates to the divine life. The three persons are equal. Significantly, they do not simply exist and live in one another, they also bring one another to shine in the divine glory. The glory of God, in other words, glows in perfect form through the very interaction of the persons of the Trinity. It is the perichoretic dance of the three which makes manifest the divine glory.

This perichoretic understanding of the Trinity provides both a model for our human relations and an invitation to enter into relationship with the persons of the Trinity. It is an understanding of God that inspires us to live in mutual relationship with one another, recognizing our differences and aspiring to be one in Christ. It is also an understanding of God that allows us to retain our unique identity as individual persons, even as we are drawn into the life of the Trinity. Elizabeth Johnson describes the perichoretic movement of the three persons of the Trinity as "an exuberant movement of equal relations" which is "an excellent model for human interaction in freedom and other regards."[11] Indeed it is such a model and has quite a practical application in the way human beings relate to one another.

The Trinity is transformative for those who enter into that relationship. Salvation and sanctification lie in communion with God. Human beings are accepted into the life of the Trinity. In Moltmann's earlier work on the Trinity, he envisages this occurring finally and completely in the eschatological kingdom of glory.[12] In his later work Moltmann seems to allow for salvation to occur in this life. Salvation then "consists in the gracious acceptance of the creature in communion with God,"[13] yet this union in not just an external one. Moltmann describes this union with God as one which:

10. Ibid., 175.

11. Johnson, *She Who Is*, 221.

12. Moltmann, *Trinity*, 213.

13. Moltmann, *History*, 87.

takes place by the Son accepting human beings into his relationship with the Father and making them children, sons and daughters, of the Father. It takes place by the Holy Spirit accepting human beings into his relationship with the Son and the Father and letting them participate in his eternal love and his eternal song of praise.[14]

The life of the Trinity is therefore open and inviting—the Trinity is not closed. Salvation lies in creation "being accepted into the cycle of divine relationship and the mutual indwellings of the Father, the Son and the Spirit."[15] Both salvation and sanctification are found in the believer, and indeed the whole of creation, participating in the divine dance.[16] The intimacy of relationship with the divine, described metaphorically as being lost in the narrative of Genesis 3, is restored. As Charry has noted previously, this is something explored by Augustine, albeit with his somewhat negative view of human sin and its inevitability lurking in the background. Augustine saw human beings as being changed by God into what he intended us to be. We can be perfected by God's "goodness, wisdom, and truth." We are actually healed by God, through the work of Christ in the Incarnation. We are healed as we journey into God, a journey that "is made possible by the triune God."[17]

SALVATION: HUMAN OR DIVINE?

To return to the Reformation, the notion of causality has been of interest to theologians for centuries as it pertains to salvation and sanctification. In other words, putting it perhaps too simply, is salvation given or earned? A related question concerns the origin of sanctification, namely whether this journey towards the life of the Trinity begins with grace freely given, or whether it begins with the individual's longing for something greater. However, this is something of a false dichotomy, which presupposes an absolute and abiding separation between the human and the divine.

In one sense there must be a separation between the Creator and the creature. The Eastern Orthodox tradition, which maintains that God is an absolute mystery and that the Creator and the creature must not, and indeed cannot, be subsumed ontologically, is instructive here. If we accept

14. Ibid.

15. Ibid.

16. See also McCall, *Greenie's Guide*, 131–32.

17. Charry, *Art of Happiness*, 61.

the tradition that God is the Creator, then the Creator and the creature will always be separate. There will always be an ontological separation. The creature can never be of one *substance* with the divine Creator.

That said, the very notion of sanctification is that we are drawn into the perichoretic life of the Trinity. We participate in the divine. Although there may always remain an ontological separation between God and us, the *relational* separation has been overcome through the person and work of Christ and life in the Spirit. In other words, there may be an ontological separation, but not a functional one: the believer is drawn into the very life of the Trinity.

Thus, we can argue that in an absolute, transcendent sense, all actions begin with God, especially the gift of grace to respond to God's call to us. Yet, in a functional and relational sense, our part is crucial. Our spirit responds to the Spirit of God and vice versa: the Spirit responds to our cries. To put it in less oppositional terms, our spirit and the Spirit of God respond to each other, growing closer and more intimate, as the believer is more and more absorbed in the perichoretic dance of the Trinity. As St Paul puts it:

> When we cry "Abba! Father!" it is that very Spirit bearing witness with our spirit that we are children of God, and if children, then heirs, heirs of God and joint heirs with Christ—if, in fact, we suffer with him so that we may also be glorified with him.[18]

There is no salvation or sanctification unless we respond to God's call. Our participation is fundamental. The question of causation becomes far less relevant than the manner of our participation. Duncan Reid makes a helpful observation on this very issue when discussing the relationship between the doctrine of grace, as explored in the West by such theologians as Karl Barth, and the doctrine of divine energies, as used by theologians such as Georges Florovsky in the East. Reid notes that salvation has both an objective and a subjective side. The objective side of salvation is the sanctification of the whole of human nature, which occurs as a result of Christ's objective work on the cross. The subjective side is "the sanctification of the wills of particular human beings through grace."[19] Objectively, our human nature is saved through the death and resurrection of Christ. However, our will is not automatically saved, because this would be "an act of violence on

18. Romans 8:15b–17.
19. Reid, *Energies*, 64.

the part of grace."[20] Rather, God seeks our participation and cooperation and through this co-working with God, we are able to ascend to the divine nature. Another way of expressing this is to suggest that redemption occurs through the objective actions of Christ on the cross and in the resurrection. Sanctification occurs through the outworking of the Spirit in the lives of human beings, who respond to the invitation of grace. In other words, we can tap into God's presence. When we read about the Christian mystics who had powerful experiences of God's transcending presence, or study the works of Russian Orthodox writers talking about God's energies flowing around us, there is an invitation to experience God's creative energies in our lives. Sanctification frees us for participation in the divine nature. Grace, or the uncreated energies to use the rediscovered Eastern orthodox doctrine, is an invitation to participate. There is nothing automatic about our salvation as it pertains to our participation in the divine nature. There is nothing predestined about it in that sense.

Interestingly, and importantly for our discussion of the links with Positive Psychology, the invitation to participate is described in language that would be familiar to those interested in the new movement within psychology. For the eastern Orthodox, including Florovsky's colleague and fellow Orthodox theologian, Vladimir Lossky, the doctrine of salvation remains incomplete if it is simply redemption *from*. "The *positive* (my emphasis) element of sanctification or deification is needed for its completion."[21] Lossky is suggesting that salvation is only made manifest in individual human beings through a constant effort on their part. There is no force or necessity on the part of God's grace, rather the human being responds to God's grace (the uncreated energies) and cooperates with God's will. Human beings are not simply passive observers in the great act of salvation; they must be positive, active participants in the process of sanctification.

Other language used to describe this process of aligning our wills with that of God is the language of being in love. In collaborating with God's will, we give ourselves in love to God. We love God with all our heart, soul, mind, and strength and commit to love our neighbors as ourselves. We become intimate with the divine. We allow ourselves to be "filled with the all-fulfilling presence we commonly name, 'God', the ultimate reality in which we live and move and have our being."[22]

20. Ibid.

21. Ibid., 65.

22. Kelly, *Trinity*, 153.

Thus the distinction between salvation and sanctification becomes far less significant than our participation in the life of the Trinity. Indeed, the issue of the cause of salvation, that is the question of "faith and works" as it pertains to *how* we are saved, becomes an interesting and curious historical debate.

More significantly though, removing the functional distinction between salvation and sanctification allows a deeper theological acceptance of such movements as Positive Psychology. Seen in trinitarian terms, the *cause* of salvation becomes less important than the *fact* that we are invited to participate in the life of the Trinity.

CONCLUSION

None of this is to suggest that Positive Psychology somehow replaces the Christian journey of sanctification or that the grace of Christ is subsumed by the science of psychology. Yet, within the Christian journey of sanctification, within the process of self-transcendence, there is always room for helpful spiritual disciplines and constructive programs. Positive Psychology, with its significant basis in science and growing evidence in scientific literature, may be one such program.

Within this context, then, Positive Psychology can be seen as one very practical way for Christians to participate in this process of self-transcendence. The tools and the mindset of Positive Psychology can be seen as helpful additions to the Christian's search for a closer relationship with the divine, noting too that the focus of positive psychology is not simply on the self. There is a significant focus on the other, particularly through service and gratitude.

Of course the invitation to make this journey into the life of the Trinity need not be seen as contradictory to the notions of salvation and sanctification explored in such biblical books as the letter to the Hebrews, which I have referenced. Indeed, the writer of the letter invites the reader on such a journey, within the context of a rich theology of salvation:

> Therefore, my friends, since we have confidence to enter the sanctuary by the blood of Jesus, by the new and living way that he opened for us through the curtain (that is, through his flesh), and since we have a great priest over the house of God, let us approach with a true heart in full assurance of faith, with our hearts

sprinkled clean from an evil conscience and our bodies washed with pure water.[23]

The invitation to enter the sanctuary is an invitation to enter into the inner life of the Trinity.

REFERENCES

Charry, Ellen. *God and the Art of Happiness*. Grand Rapids: Eerdmans, 2010.

Gunton, Colin. *The Actuality of the Atonement: A Study of Metaphor, Rationality and the Christian Tradition*. London: T. & T. Clark, 1988.

Johnson, Elizabeth. *She Who Is: The Mystery of God in Feminist Theological Discourse*. New York: Crossroad, 1996.

Kelly, Anthony. *The Trinity of Love: A Theology of the Christian God*. Wilmington: Michael Glazier, 1989.

McCall, Theo. *The Greenie's Guide to the End of the World: Ecology and Eschatology*. Adelaide: ATF, 2011.

Moltmann, Jürgen. *History and the Triune God: Contributions to Trinitarian Theology*. London: SCM, 1991.

———. *The Trinity and the Kingdom of God: The Doctrine of God*. London: SCM, 1981.

Reid, Duncan. *Energies of the Spirit: Trinitarian Models in Eastern Orthodoxy and Western Theology*. Atlanta: Scholars, 1997.

Seligman, Martin E. P., and Mihaly Csikszentmihalyi. "Positive Psychology: An Introduction." *American Psychologist* 55 (2000) 5–14.

23. Hebrews 10:19–22.

Chapter 8

Gratitude

A Theological and Psychological Dialogue

CARLA FORD AND ANDREW FORD

INTRODUCTION

GRATITUDE, A CHRISTIAN VIRTUE and central tenet within Christian theology, is being lauded as a panacea for wellbeing within Positive Psychology. A myriad of studies have been conducted and the results are impressive. Gratitude has been shown to increase wellbeing, both physically and mentally, and those who practice gratitude consistently report a range of benefits: stronger immune systems; lower blood pressure; better, more refreshing sleep; lower levels of stress and depression; higher levels of positive emotions; more energy; and more optimism and happiness. In addition, they are more generous and compassionate and have stronger relationships.

Although traditionally a topic of inquiry within the disciplines of philosophy and theology, interest from sociology and psychology has seen the number of publications referring to gratitude increase exponentially over the last twenty years. It seems that Positive Psychology is catching up with what Christians have known for two millennia—gratitude is important.

BIBLICAL GRATITUDE

The Bible contains instruction on, and examples of, thanksgiving to God. Sacrifices of thanksgiving were offered in the Old Testament (Lev 7:12–15; 2 Chron 29:31; Ps 50:23) and priests were allocated to represent and facilitate the people in giving thanks to God (1 Chron 16:4, 41; 2 Chron 20:21). Thanksgiving and gratitude to God are prevalent within the Psalms: "O Lord my God, I will give you thanks for ever" (Ps 30:12) and "I will praise you, O Lord, with all my heart" (Ps 9:1). Throughout the gospels Jesus models the practice of gratitude by giving thanks to God (Matt 11:25; 15:36; Mark 14:23; John 11:41). Pauline theology is rich in both expressions of thankfulness and instruction regarding gratitude: "And whatever you do, whether in word or deed, do it all in the name of the Lord Jesus, giving thanks to God the Father, through him" (Col 3:17). Biblical gratitude always appears to be attributed directly, and indirectly, to God, as in 1 Thess 1:2, "We always thank God for all of you."

The life and death of Jesus Christ is viewed as the highest expression of God's love and benevolence to humanity (Phil 2:6–8; 1 John 3:16). The English words "grateful" and "grace" share the same derivative *gratus* from the Latin, meaning thankful and pleasing. The eminent theologian Karl Barth wrote, "Grace and gratitude belong together like heaven and earth. Grace evokes gratitude like the voice an echo. . . . As far as man is concerned there can be no question of anything but gratitude"[1] and this acknowledgement forms a deep part of Christian worship.

Unsurprisingly, Positive Psychology studies have found a strong correlation between religiousness and gratitude. When participants of one proto-type study were asked to list the characteristics or attributes they associate with prayer, "thanking" was frequently mentioned, second only to "God."[2] Individuals who spend time praying, reading the Bible and cultivating a relationship with God, tend to be more grateful in everyday life.

1. Barth, *Church Dogmatics*, 42.
2. Lambert et al., "Prototype Analysis."

POSITIVE PSYCHOLOGY'S UNDERSTANDING OF GRATITUDE

Gratitude is complex and has been conceptualized in a number of different ways within Positive Psychology. Robert Emmons and Michael McCullough, leading researchers in the area of gratitude, have described gratitude as an attitude, an emotion, a personality trait, a habit, a moral virtue and a coping response.[3] Positive Psychology has analyzed gratitude, dissecting and scrutinizing the various components in order to understand its complexities.

There is a difference between gratitude as a state (a temporary emotion) and as a trait (a consistent personality attribute), yet recent insights from neurobiology show that states, traits and moods all concern activation of the same neural circuits. This means that those with a disposition towards gratitude (trait) will experience more frequent and intense states of gratitude, whilst those who practice gratitude (state) may eventually find their disposition changing.

Positive Psychology, as a science, has developed three main scales to measure levels and types of gratitude. An analysis of the questions posed in these scales point towards eight distinct, but related, concepts:

1. An individual's perception of how often and how deeply gratitude is experienced, (expressed in terms such as "I have so much in life to be thankful for").

2. An appreciation of others (I'm really thankful for friends and family).

3. An appreciation of what an individual has (I reflect on how fortunate I am to have basic things in life like food, clothing, and shelter).

4. Feelings of awe (When I see natural beauty like Niagara Falls, I feel like a child who is awestruck).

5. Behaviors designed to express gratitude (I say "please" and "thank you" to indicate my appreciation).

6. Stopping and focusing on positive aspects in the present moment (I think it's really important to "stop and smell the roses").

7. Appreciation arising from the understanding that nothing is permanent (Thinking about dying reminds me to live every day to the fullest).

3. Emmons and McCullough, "Counting Blessings," 377.

8. An appreciation of one's own life in comparison with someone worse off (When I see someone less fortunate than myself, I realize how lucky I am).[4]

As a result of this analysis, Wood and colleagues conceptualized trait gratitude as involving a life orientation towards noticing and appreciating the positive in life.

ELEMENTS OF GRATITUDE

In psychological literature, gratitude has widely been defined with reference to the presence of a benefactor, a benefit, and a benefit appraisal.

External Benefactor—Or Not

Some researchers conceptualize gratitude as an emotion that occurs after receiving a positive outcome from a benefactor. This triadic understanding of gratitude requires 1) a beneficiary, 2) a benefit, and 3) a benefactor to whom the beneficiary is grateful. The emotion that results from this interpersonal exchange has been referred to as "benefit-triggered gratitude," or "agentic gratitude," and research has shown that the level of gratitude experienced depends on one's perception of the cost, intention and altruistic nature of the benefit. We've probably all received a gift at Christmas that could have been for anybody in the family, and we have perhaps not been as appreciative as we were of a carefully selected or expensive gift. When the recipient of a benefit (the beneficiary) perceives the benefactor as being thoughtful and responsive to their needs, it can lead to increased levels of gratitude and a higher quality relationship, for both parties.

An in-depth review of publications from psychology, sociology, and philosophy revealed two related but possibly distinct constructs—gratitude and gratefulness—whereby gratefulness is perceived as similar to gratitude in terms of benefit appraisal, but differs in that there is no perceived agent or benefactor. For example, it may include a sense of wonder and universal gratitude, such as a peak experience in the solitude of a mountain top. This dyadic understanding of gratitude (beneficiary + benefit) has been called "generalized gratitude" or "non-agentic gratitude," whilst some have referred to it as gratefulness.

4. Wood et al., "Gratitude," 890–905.

Theological Objection

As discussed in the opening chapter, the science of psychology is based on the belief that human behavior can be explained without resorting to spiritual or transcendent explanations. In its simplest form the philosophy that underpins psychology, naturalism, is often defined as an understanding of the world without God. This obviously leads to tensions and disagreements between the fields of Positive Psychology and theology.

The suggestion that gratitude exists without a benefactor is incompatible with a Christian worldview. During the Anglican Eucharist service, the congregation declare, "Yours, Lord, is the greatness, the power, the glory, the splendor, and the majesty; for everything in heaven and on earth is yours. All things come from you, and of your own do we give you," and Col 1:15–17 makes it clear that God is the creator and sustainer of life and that all things originate from him. God is intricately involved in all of life, regardless of people's awareness or acknowledgment of his presence.

Positive Psychology may interpret phrases such as "I have a very good life" and "I am fortunate to be me" as measures of non-agentic gratitude, but when viewed through a Christian lens, these items can still be attributed to an agent; God. Some researchers have suggested that gratitude occurs in two stages. Firstly, people recognize that they have experienced a positive outcome, which causes happiness. And secondly, this happiness is attributed to an external source and labeled as gratitude. This theory seems to align more with a Judeo-Christian worldview, in which the positive emotion induced through experiencing a glorious sunset, whilst having no immediate benefactor, is attributed to God, as creator.

There has been a call within Positive Psychology for further research to explore the extent to which the experience and expression of generalized gratitude may relate to views of God. In their proto-type analysis of gratitude, Lambert, Graham and Fincham found that although almost half of the participants considered generalized gratitude as an important component of their concept of gratitude, God still appeared as a subtheme within these narratives.[5] With over 84 percent of the world's population (5.8 billion people) identifying with a religious group (Pew Research Center, 2012), exploring all aspects of religiousness/spirituality and how it relates to human flourishing is imperative.

---

5. Lambert et al., "Prototype Analysis."

Benefit Appraisal

Benefit appraisal is the notion that a real situation is more favorable than the alternatives. As human beings, we are constantly comparing and assessing ourselves, and our situation, against other alternatives, past, present, or even expected future, and this often influences how we think, feel, and act. For example, we may take our previous circumstances into consideration (I'm glad our noisy neighbors moved away), compare our current situation with a negative outcome of what could have been (at least no-one was seriously injured in the accident), view the situation against what was expected (I didn't think I would get such a large bonus), or compare our own situation with that of a third party (I'm so thankful that I'm not a refugee). Benefit appraisal spans a wide range of subjects, such as our circumstances; our relationships; our possessions; how we perceive qualities such as peace and happiness; events or experiences; sensations such as warmth; and opportunities such as education. In addition, someone else's actions or motivations may cause a benefit appraisal, either in a specific way (e.g., I'm grateful that Bob made my lunch today) or more vaguely (e.g., I'm grateful that people are willing to be farmers).[6]

Theological Objection

From a Christian perspective, a person can feel and express gratitude to God without being the recipient of a specific gift. The fact that God is God elicits thanksgiving and gratitude from his people. 1 Chron 16:25 declares, "Great is the Lord, and most worthy of praise," whilst the psalmist exhorts the people to give thanks to God for his goodness (Ps 136:1). The theologian C. H. Spurgeon remarked, "he is the Giver of all good . . . the source of good, the good of all good, the sustainer of good."[7] Separating God from his goodness is a redundant notion, as is separating the gift from the giver. Giving thanks to God for who he is, is arguably distinct from benefit-triggered and generalized gratitude, and was referred to as "gracious gratitude" by the seventeenth-century theologian, Jonathan Edwards.[8]

As the research surrounding gratitude continues to grow, it is becoming apparent that the layperson's definitions and understandings of gratitude

---

6. Rusk et al. *Gratitude or Gratefulness?*

7. Spurgeon, "Psalm 136."

8. Edwards, *Treatise.*

are broader than those currently being used by researchers. Participants in a 2009[9] study listed characteristics that came to mind when they heard the word gratitude, resulting in fifty-two gratitude features, more than commonly utilized in research. The use of more qualitative methodology, and drilling down into more complex concepts such as indebtedness and gratitude, as well as felt and expressed gratitude, may help to deepen our understanding of this complex concept.

Children of God and the Abundant Life

In the opening chapter of this book, Ellen Charry writes, "God wants us to flourish [and] is genuinely distressed when we languish." In much the same way parents and teachers want the children in their care to flourish. In keeping with this desire they give their children "requests" (which are actually commands in disguise), only to be met with "why?" Of course, the immediate answer may be "because I said so," and yet behind the command lies wisdom and a desire to see the child safe, happy, and successful.

As a child grows and develops, the adult may share the reasoning behind an instruction. In the same way, God urges us to give thanks, which as believers, we do without necessarily knowing why. Positive Psychology, in observing and analyzing gratitude, has highlighted many positive outcomes associated with giving thanks, and can perhaps give some insight as to why God has given this instruction. In John 10:10, Jesus says, "I have come that you might have abundant life," and it could be argued the findings of Positive Psychology illustrate some of that abundance.

BENEFITS OF GRATITUDE

When asked which commandments were the most important, Jesus answered, "Love God and Love your neighbor as yourself" (Mark 12:30–31). The benefits of gratitude are well documented and plentiful, but Positive Psychology's primary focus has been on the "loving self" part of the command, with more recent studies beginning to look at "loving your neighbor." Physical benefits were revealed in an analysis of almost 1000 Swiss adults, where higher levels of dispositional (trait) gratitude correlated with

9. Lambert et al., "Prototype Analysis."

better self-reported physical health.[10] Psychological benefits were demonstrated in a 2003 study, showing that those who consciously focused on and documented what they were grateful for, were more optimistic.[11] Social benefits are discussed in more detail below.

Positive Psychology has shown there are many positive relational outcomes associated with the practice of gratitude, including benefits to the beneficiary, the initial benefactor and the wider community. Researchers have suggested the experience of gratitude, and the actions it stimulates, build and strengthen social bonds and friendships. In one study, 2000 Swiss children were asked how they would respond if someone gave them something they had always wanted. Whilst many of the children spoke of repaying the action in some way, many imagined doing things that would connect them more closely with the benefactor, such as sharing an activity together or offering friendship or faithfulness.

A number of studies support the idea that people who have been grateful for receiving a benefit are more likely to act pro-socially towards the benefactor, and in some instances, towards other people in ensuing interactions. Not only do grateful individuals demonstrate more positive mental states (e.g., optimistic, enthusiastic, and motivated), they are also more helpful, caring, and generous towards others.[12] McCullough et al. refer to this "pay-it-forward" idea as a moral motivator. In addition, gratitude can act as a reinforcer of moral behavior.[13] When a beneficiary expresses gratitude, the benefactor is reinforced for his or her benevolence, encouraging more benevolent behaviors in the future. Evidence has also supported the idea that gratitude may inhibit people from engaging in destructive interpersonal behavior.

Gratitude is a key element of successful close relationships such as marriage. According to a study of long-term married couples, appreciation is one of the important factors in contributing to a satisfying marriage.[14] Another study of couples (who had been married for an average of twenty years) found felt or expressed gratitude significantly related to marital satisfaction.[15] Amongst newly-weds, couples expressing gratitude (and

10. Hill et al. *Examining the Pathways.*

11. Emmons and McCullough, "Counting Blessings versus Burdens."

12. McCullough et al., "Grateful Disposition," 112.

13. McCullough et al., "Is Gratitude a Moral Affect?," 249.

14. Kaslow and Hammerschmidt, "Long Term 'Good' Marriages," 15–38.

15. Gordon et al., "Have You Thanked Your Spouse Today?," 339–43.

other protective factors such as trust, respect, commitment, and affection) were more likely to have higher marital satisfaction, and even those who had been together for a relatively short time found gratitude predicted increased relationship satisfaction for both partners. In a series of studies, researchers found that individuals who were appreciative of their partners became more responsive and committed over time. Consideration of how much one's partner has invested into the relationship, both materially and emotionally, triggers feelings of gratitude, which, in turn, may lead to a deeper commitment.[16]

Expressing gratitude and being appreciative of one's partner is critical in maintaining a relationship, as it helps people to recognize the value of what they have, and promotes a desire to maintain the relationship. Gratitude helps to detect partners' selfless intentions, responsiveness and efforts at maintaining a close relationship. This reappraisal of a partner's positive qualities encourages relationship-enhancing motivations and actions. Perceived responsiveness to one's wishes and needs is crucial for the processes that are fundamental in close relationships, including intimacy, trust, and commitment.

At the heart of a Christian understanding of flourishing lies relationship with God. There has been some research about the impact this relationship has on gratitude, but there has been little research into the impact of gratitude on relationship with God. Drawing on the insights and resources that Positive Psychology provides, it seems feasible that activities that have been successful in improving interpersonal—or "horizontal"—relationships, may also be beneficial when applied to a "vertical" relationship with God. To this end, the author is currently researching whether gratitude, and specifically activities that have been shown to increase gratitude, enhances the perception of our awareness and relationship with God.

GIFTS

The purpose of this book is to explore the friendship between Positive Psychology and theology. Although there are clearly areas of disparity, and we need to maintain an awareness of these, there are also gifts that both fields can offer. Theology can offer Positive Psychology a deeper, more complete understanding of gratitude, as well as contributing to the wider notion of flourishing. Theology also offers a third type of gratitude for consideration,

16. For an overview, see Ford, *Gratitude Interventions*.

namely agent-triggered gratitude, where the benefactor *is* the benefit. Positive Psychology explores ways in which humans relate to one another, an important motif within Christian thought. Taking this concept of horizontal relationship and applying the findings to a vertical relationship—that is, a relationship with God—may open up new and exciting avenues of exploration that reignite and invigorate our faith. The following gifts are reflections on this theme and are written to stimulate discussion.

Gift 1: Gratitude in Adversity

Giving thanks to God when things are going well and then becoming angry or ungrateful in times of adversity does not appear consistent with the Christian life. St Paul spent a significant proportion of his ministry imprisoned for teaching the gospel (Acts 22:29; Col 4:3; Phil 1:7) and wrote to the persecuted church in Thessalonica, "Rejoice always, pray continuously, give thanks in all circumstances." Positive Psychology literature indicates that gratitude reduces the impact of negative emotions[17] and enables individuals to cope better with stress and trauma.

Even after a highly challenging life crisis, such as a cancer diagnosis, it may still be possible for individuals to experience positive change, known as posttraumatic growth (PTG). Although PTG is a relatively new term, the idea that great good can come from great suffering is timeless. Christians are encouraged to trust that "in all things, God works for the good of those who love him" (Rom 8:28) and the evidence indicates that positive outcomes can arise from an experience of adversity, leading to an increased appreciation for life in general. Not everyone experiences PTG, but the eschatological hope of a life beyond this one is promised to all who believe (John 3:16; Luke 23:43).

Gift 2: Indebtedness and Gratitude

McCullough, Kilpatrick, Emmons, and Larson[18] posit that people are most likely to feel grateful when (a) they have received a particularly valuable benefit; (b) high effort and cost have been expended on their behalf; (c) this expenditure was intentional rather than accidental; and (d) the expenditure

---

17. McCullough, et al., "Gratitude."
18. McCullough, et al., "Grateful Disposition."

was beyond what was expected. They also suggest a main characteristic of gratitude appears to be the desire of the recipient to return the favor to the benefactor. If we take these findings and apply this line of thinking to our relationship with God, we may find ourselves asking how we can repay such a valuable, costly, intentional, generous gift.

But is it about repayment and is that different to being grateful? Whilst some researchers have argued that gratitude and indebtedness are synonymous and that indebtedness is the essence of gratitude, most people experience indebtedness as an unpleasant psychological state. The focus of indebtedness is on (a) one's obligation to repay someone who has acted intentionally on their behalf, (b) fear of being unable to repay, and (c) concerns about how one might actually go about repaying. As Christians, we know that "it is by *grace* [we] have been saved, through faith—and this is not from [ourselves], it is the gift of God—not by works, so that no one can boast" (Eph 2:8–9). It seems we are unable to repay our benefactor.

Researchers have suggested that feeling indebted to someone leads to resentment, a sense of owing and an expectation to pay back. A person who feels indebted is less likely to be altruistic, compared with someone who feels grateful. Gratitude is more powerful than indebtedness as a motivation for future altruism and high pro-social behavior towards others. In addition, those who feel grateful, as opposed to indebted, have a better relationship with their benefactor.

Without wishing to make too big a presumption, these findings may prompt us to consider how we perceive and relate to God, and how we communicate him to others.

When Isaac Watts penned the final stanza to *When I Survey the Wondrous Cross*, he had in mind a grateful response to God's love and not an obligation to repay: "Love so amazing, so divine, demands my life, my soul, my all."

Gift 3: Increasing Gratitude

In seeking to understand a flourishing life at a personal and interpersonal level, Positive Psychology has developed practical interventions—intentional activities that lead to positive outcomes through the cultivation of positive feelings, behaviors or cognitions. These interventions facilitate wellbeing, positive emotions, creativity, growth, relationships, and other positive outcomes, underpinned by key theories within Positive

Psychology. Many of Positive Psychology's practical interventions align with biblical concepts of pro-social behavior such as kindness, forgiveness, and, of course, gratitude.

Positive Psychology interventions (PPIs) are empirically based, drawing on scientific research, and using both qualitative and quantitative methodology. PPIs do not all work the same way on everyone and in her book, *The How of Happiness*, Dr Sonja Lyubomirsky[19] describes the Person-Activity Fit Diagnostic. This twelve-question survey is designed to help you assess which interventions will be of most value to you.

Of the PPIs targeting increased wellbeing, gratitude interventions demonstrate the largest effects. Although wellbeing may not necessarily be an end that Christians seek in and of itself, these interventions, when viewed through a theological lens may serve as scientifically-based spiritual disciplines. The following encompass some of the most commonly recommended gratitude strategies.

The Gratitude Journal[20]

Keeping a gratitude journal is considered a popular and straightforward practice. In many studies people are simply instructed to record five things for which they are grateful. This should be done regularly (once or twice a week) and focus on recent experiences. The following strategies are recommended for greatest benefit:

- Being deliberate. Making a conscious decision to be grateful and being motivated to see positive changes.

- Quality not quantity. Spending time reflecting in detail on one or two experiences, rather than skimming through a list.

- Being people-focused. Focusing on people to whom you are grateful has a bigger impact than merely focusing on things.

- Life without good things. Imagining life without some of the blessings that we often take for granted is a good way to stimulate gratitude.

- Surprise! Surprise! Recalling events that were unexpected tends to generate stronger levels of gratitude.

---

19. Lyubomirsky, *How of Happiness*.
20. Emmons and McCullough, "Counting Blessings versus Burdens," 377.

- Enough is enough! Journaling once or twice a week, and keeping it fresh and enjoyable, is better than journaling every day.

The Gratitude Letter[21]

This involves thinking back into your past and remembering someone who did something for you for which you are extremely grateful. This could be a family member, friend, teacher, employer, coach, or a colleague, someone whom you have not expressed gratitude towards before. You may try selecting a person that you haven't thought about for a while or perhaps consider selecting God. Typical advice regarding gratitude letters is as follows:

- Write in the first person, as if you are directly addressing the individual.

- Grammar and spelling are not important.

- Be specific about why you are grateful to this person and how they have affected your life, giving concrete examples.

- Describe what you are doing now and how often you remember their efforts.

Some people may wish to visit the person and read the letter to them, or mail it. Others may wish to not deliver it at all. Either way, this intervention has been shown to raise gratitude and temporarily increase wellbeing.

Savoring[22]

Savoring is defined as "the capacity to attend to, appreciate, and enhance the positive experiences in one's life." It is a process, not an outcome, and it requires engagement on the person's behalf. It enables the individual to slow down and pay attention to their surroundings, feelings and experiences. Often we fail stop and notice the good things we have. Grateful people may possess the cognitive habit of savoring their life circumstances, and so savoring interventions help build the capacity to notice what, or whom, contributes to life's positive outcomes. A typical savoring intervention may involve suggesting that, o

---

21. Seligman et al., "Positive Psychology Progress," 410.
22. Seligman et al., "Positive Psychotherapy," 774.

Once a day, we take the time to enjoy something that we usually hurry through or take for granted (e.g., eating a meal, taking a shower, hugging a loved one). The effect can be enhanced if we then take notes on what we did, how we did it differently, and how it compared to our usual experience.

CONCLUSION

This chapter has begun to explore the multi-faceted nature of gratitude from both a psychological and theological perspective. A central theme within both fields, gratitude is a complex concept, with many nuanced understandings and elements. Evidence has shown that gratitude can be both measured and built through Positive Psychology interventions. These interventions, when viewed through a theological lens, can be referred to as scientifically-based spiritual disciplines. Theology contributes to a richer understanding of gratitude, whilst Positive Psychology equips believers with practical tools to live out the Christian faith.

More than four hundred years ago, St Ignatius of Loyola, the founder of the Jesuit Order, encouraged prayer-filled mindfulness by introducing what has been called the Daily Examen. This five-step practice encourages believers to review the day with gratitude, walking through the events in the presence of God, focusing on the gifts, large and small. It would appear that modern science has begun to study and uncover ancient wisdom. Now, with everyone talking about gratitude, it is an ideal opportunity for our faith to make a valid contribution to this discussion.

REFERENCES

Barth, Karl. *Church Dogmatics VI 1*. Translated by Geoffrey W. Bromiley et al. London: Continuum, 2004.

Edwards, Jonathan. *A Treatise concerning Religious Affections*. Northampton, Massachusetts, 1746.

Emmons, Robert A., and Michael E. McCullough. "Counting Blessings versus Burdens: An Experimental Investigation of Gratitude and Subjective Well-being in Daily Life." *Journal of Personality and Social Psychology* 84 (2003) 377–89.

Ford, Carla. "Can Gratitude Interventions Enhance Relationships with God?" Masters Thesis. University of Melbourne, 2015.

Gordon, Cameron L., et al. "Have You Thanked Your Spouse Today? Felt and Expressed Gratitude among Married Couples." *Personality and Individual Differences* 50 (2011) 339–43.

Hill, Patrick L., et al. "Examining the Pathways between Gratitude and Self-rated Physical Health across Adulthood." *Personality and Individual Differences* 54 (2013) 92–96.

Kaslow, Florence W., and Helga Hammerschmidt. "Long Term 'Good' Marriages: The Seemingly Essential Ingredients." *Journal of Couples Therapy* 3 (1993) 15–38.

Lambert, Nathaniel M., et al. "A Prototype Analysis of Gratitude: Varieties of Gratitude Experiences." *Personality and Social Psychology Bulletin* 35 (2009) 1193–207.

Lyubomirsky, Sonja. *The How of Happiness: A Practical Approach to Getting the Life you Want.* London: Sphere, 2007.

McCullough, Michael E., et al. "The Grateful Disposition: A Conceptual and Empirical Topography." *Journal of Personality and Social Psychology* 82 (2002) 112–27.

———. "Is Gratitude a Moral Affect?" *Psychological Bulletin* 127 (2001) 249–66.

Rusk, Reuben D., et al. *Gratitude or Gratefulness? A Conceptual Review and Proposal of the System of Appreciative Functioning. Journal of Happiness Studies* (2015) doi:10.1007/s10902-015-9675-z.

Seligman, Martin E. P., et al. "Positive Psychology Progress: Empirical Validation of Interventions." *American Psychologist* 60 (2005) 410–21.

———. "Positive Psychotherapy." *American Psychologist* 61 (2006) 774–88.

Spurgeon, Charles H. "Psalm 136." In *The Treasury of David.* London: 1885.

Wood, Alex M., et al. "Gratitude and Well-being: A Review and Theoretical Integration." *Clinical Psychology Review* 30 (2010) 890–905.

Chapter 9

Sailing Close to the Wind

J. HAROLD ELLENS

WHEN I WAS FIVE my beloved friend, Esther, burned to death. I was there. I could not save her. When she died, I died. Whoever I was before that, I never was again. I do not remember who I was before I lost her. I only remember that life was really pleasant. After that I remember nothing for two years. A shroud of blackness descended over me and shut me off. My brother said I was an automaton. Apparently I cried a lot, which annoyed him.

Then one bright and shining morning God saved me. I had a life-changing numinous experience. I came out of the horse barn and immediately was caught up in an intense light that enshrouded me. A pillar of ethereal brilliance lifted me off the ground, as it were. It shone around me, in me, and right through me. Instantaneously, I saw my whole life laid out before me. It was 1939 and life was dreadful—old folks were struggling with poverty, war was lowering, and little children were dying all around. In the numinous light I saw my life spelled out in terms of helping those in desperate need. I felt great elation, freedom, a towering joy. It was all revealed to me in an instant. I had this immense and intense sense of divine presence, heart-warming and healing; relief and clarity beyond words.[1]

My life has been a straight line of purpose from that moment to this. I have never felt distracted from that calling, never considered a different one. God lit up my life with such intense numinousness that the darkness was gone forever. I felt earnestly inclined to sail my boat close to the wind. I thank God for it. God has not averted suffering from my life, but God entered into all of it and turned it to my profit. I remained a neurotic kid, became an anxious adult, but I was steadied by the sense of clear calling and fervent focus.[2]

Numinous experiences are not uncommon. Illuminations of insight happen to most people at various times in their life journey. They range all the way from sudden "Aha!" moments to the radical, life changing events that direct one's destiny into a new and more creative direction.[3] Usually such surprises happen when we are wrestling with major quandaries and trying to solve specific problems. The preoccupation may be conscious to us or subconscious. It may even be totally unconscious, as it was in my case.

Such moments of revelation are not normally pursued, sought out, prayed for, struggled after, or consciously envisioned. They come to us un-asked, unanticipated, unbidden. Suddenly they appear, and we are never quite the same thereafter. Instead we are launched upon a constructive new course in our perceived destiny.

These extraordinary life experiences raise a number of important questions. Most important is the sizeable conundrum of whether the ex-periences are psychodynamic or spiritual. Are they natural to our inherent capabilities and faculties as human beings, or are they given us from some transcendent source? Do they come from inside us or from somewhere or someone, some force outside of us? Perhaps the answer is, somehow, that both dimensions share in the event or moment of revelation. Can these life-changing events be generated or motivated by an energy or agency inherent to the universe, that acts in cooperation with a vital capacity within us, to provide critically necessary insight at just the crucial moment?

Scientists are looking for answers on both sides.[4] The renowned sci-entist of Positive Psychology fame, Martin Seligman, is quite sure that the

1. Ellens, *Light from the Other Side.*
2. Ellens, *Understanding Religious Experience.*
3. Irvine, *Aha!*
4. Yaden et al., *Being Called.*

sources of our "callings" are inherent to humans or humanness. He plays with the idea that there might be some persons, agents, or forces out there in the future which are calling us forward into our destiny. However, he is sure that the matter can be explained in terms of a secular force that is natural and inherent to the material and psychological universes. I, myself, am more readily inclined to allow for some transcendent agency as the source of our illumination. This I made clear in the first line of my second paragraph above. It is true at this point that either of us may have the answer the right way around.

Is the correct perspective, then, that numinous experiences are basically human, or are they encounters with the divine? Whether they are simple or profound phenomena, are they psychic experiences or direct acts of God? Is the causative force or agency that drives this dramatic reshaping of our destinies transcendent or mundane? Positive Psychology, generally speaking, has pursued the secular and mundane possibility. This is more readily accessible scientifically than is a spiritual or transcendent hypothesis. It posits the notion that there are forces at work in our person or in the universe that envision a future for us, which is raised to the conscious level where it metamorphoses into a new personal imperative.

What is really going on in such a Positive Psychology approach? Seligman answers that question in an illuminating way.[5] He observes that Positive Psychology is devoted to developing "what makes life worth living." While clinical psychology is preoccupied with sickness and misery and its healing, Positive Psychology is busy drawing people out of that preoccupation and into a more joyful destiny. We have, after all, "evolved to escape misery." We have evolved to seek the future because we sense that what we want is in the future. Humans are drawn toward the future. The past and present often involve suffering and what we desire is a future that is more positive. "This asymmetry between approach and escape may be the deepest difference between psychology-as-usual and Positive Psychology, deeper even than the emphasis on misery versus wellbeing."[6] Positive Psychology calls this envisioning of a better future "prospection."

A Gallup poll in 2003 demonstrated that 41 percent of Americans say they have had "profound religious experiences or awakenings that changed the direction" in their unfolding life and destiny.[7] Seligman de-

5. Seligman, "How Are We Called."

6. Ibid., xvii–xviii.

7. Ibid., xxi citing Gallup, *Religious Awakenings*.

clares that science cannot avoid the question, "What is the Ground of these experiences?" Perhaps they are illusion. Perhaps they are real? "Can human beings really be visited by the future? The secular approach is that numinous experiences are merely efflorescent products of a Darwinian brain."[8] Such is the posture of Positive Psychology.

The spiritual perspective opens possibilities that have a rather different range and focus. It has a great deal in common with Positive Psychology. Both are sure that numinous experiences call us to our destiny, though psychodynamic experience may not explain their full range of process. Those callings are consistently constructive and have a compelling imperative about them. They are relatively common experiences, having similar characteristics cross-culturally and intra-personally. The spiritual perspective and Positive Psychology differ in trying to answer the question regarding the ground and agency by which these awakenings are provoked or driven.

Taking the perspective that numinous life-changing experiences are normal human events of a psycho-spiritual nature, opens us to the hypothesis that they come to us from and as a divine force. This suggests that the presence of the divine spirit is the dynamic force behind such illuminating and constructive events. If that is so, and they come to us unbidden as a gift from God, how can we keep our lives and spirits consciously open to that possibility? How can we live life open to the presence and power of God as Spirit, thus discerning how to sail our lives close to the wind (*ruach*: Hebrew for breath, wind, logos, spirit) of God, so to speak?[9]

PSYCHO-SOCIAL OR RELIGIOUS

Many of us have relatively frequent and significant experiences that we call spiritual, numinous, or mystical. By the term spiritual I mean to refer precisely to the universal irrepressible human hunger for meaning. Such numinous or mystical experiences provide us with an enhanced or new sense of meaning, leading to changes in destiny. For obvious reasons they are sometimes called para-psychological, paranormal, and psycho-spiritual events.

In the late eighteenth century, Thomas Clarkson had such a revolutionary and revelatory moment, in which he saw that the African slave-trade was an unmitigated evil and it needed to end. He was compelled by that

8. Ibid.

9. Genesis 1:1–3 and numerous other places in the Hebrew Bible.

psycho-spiritual conversion to mount the crusade that led to the abolition-ist movement and finally to the Act of Parliament that ended British slav-ing. As Irvine observes, it is hard to say whether Clarkson had the epiphany, or if the epiphany had him.[10] The potential of humans to experience such numinous moments and share them with other humans, is unique to our species and one of its most important talents.

In examining such events Levine notes that most folk do not con-sciously seek numinous experiences, but they form somewhere in their minds and emerge unbidden. He believes that our unconscious minds have unique lives and worlds, with embedded ideas and desires that emerge un-expectedly at crucial moments in our conscious lives.

Irvine addresses five domains in which sudden revelatory events come to human consciousness. They happen as religious, moral, scien-tific, mathematical, and artistic moments. He refers to these as domains in which breakthrough insights come to people at critical junctures, open-ing up entirely new vistas of reality and markedly changing their lives. A *scientific* breakthrough came to Einstein, where suddenly he saw clearly the insight that was the theory of relativity. The same was true for Archimedes, who solved the king's problem about the purity of the gold in his crown by discerning its weight compared with the water it displaced in the bathtub.[11] The crown was too light for the water it displaced. The jeweler had cheated.

Clarkson's revelatory moment about his calling to abolish slavery was a vision in the *moral* domain. Joseph Smith's vision to establish a new reli-gion lay in the spiritual or *religious* domain, as was the sudden conversion of C. S. Lewis on a motorcycle ride to London.[12] A French Mathematician, Poincaré, suddenly realized the solution to a geometry conundrum with which he had wrestled for decades and abandoned, and Mahler could not finish his Seventh Symphony until he went for a boat ride, and it came to him with the first stroke of the oar.[13] These illustrations can be multiplied infinitely in the domains of mathematics and art.

Irvine believes that the numinous moments in religion and morality are always unbidden, but that those in science, mathematics, and art are bidden. Joseph Smith described his miraculous calling in a manner similar to my experience at age seven. "I saw a pillar of light exactly over my head,

---

10. Irvine, *Aha!* 6.

11. Ibid., 4.

12. Myers, *Conversations,* 94. Compare Irvine, *Aha!* 23.

13. Irvine, *Aha!* 3.

above the brightness of the sun, which descended gradually until it fell upon me . . .."[14] Saul of Tarsus, Mohammed, David Brainerd who was a missionary to the Native Americans, Jesus, and Mary the mother of Jesus, all testified to such supernatural experiences that led to a life-changing sense of calling.

Valerie L. Myers investigated calling experiences from a somewhat different perspective. Her book is a comprehensive assessment of calling from the point of view of managers and work enterprises. She declares at the outset that "Modern management scholars generally agree that a calling entails engaging in work that is intrinsically rewarding because it is aligned with one's passion, core interests, abilities, and perceived destiny. Consequently, work in a calling is energizing, elicits commitment, and sometimes benefits society."[15] It is her claim that this perspective derives from Max Weber's notion of the Protestant work ethic.[16]

Weber contended that the Protestant Reformers' sense of the religious dimension of calling, a divinely-revealing life-changing experience, had been weakened and displaced in Enlightenment culture by psychological and developmental notions. Bellah et al. make essentially the same claim in their very influential work, *Habits of the Heart*.[17] They highlighted the significance of institutions in creating community and society, in turn damping down individualism and interior focus. This represents a material and externalized sense of call, as adaptation to one's social and commercial set in life. While the Reformers thought of calling as a numinous experience moving one to religious belief, behaviors, service, and embracing ordinary work as a sacred call, modern and postmodern perspectives envision calling more as our "fit" for our work and our society.[18]

Weber viewed this fatal shift in the meaning of calling as producing a culture of "Specialists without spirit" which he abhorred.[19] It represents a drift in the worker culture from conceiving of work as a "sacred ethical calling toward a secularized, individualistic, utilitarian calling."[20] Psychological analyses discovered that the strongest sense of the nature of personal calling

14. Ibid., 5.
15. Myers, *Conversations*, 1.
16. Weber, *Protestant Ethic*.
17. Bellah et al., *Habits of the Heart*.
18. Myers, *Conversations*, 1–12.
19. Weber, *Protestant Ethic*, 182.
20. Myers, *Conversations*, 26.

was as a transcendent guiding force and not as their person-environmental fit in society or identification with their work.[21] This led Hagmaier and Abele to conclude that most people who describe being called to a life-changing degree, feel that God has called them through an inner voice to a new course of action, and given them the determination to do it.

Dik and Duffy noted that this call usually includes pro-social and altruistic behavior and affords one a sense of purposeful destiny, in keeping with the Reformers' perceptions.[22] It is a sense of the sacred in life, which often reflects a theological cosmology—that is, a worldview in which the presence of God is a palpable reality in daily life. However, it can also be the case that the numinous experience, perceived as a divine visitation, changes a person's world-view from atheism or agnosticism to a fervent faith perspective. Myers concludes with the following:

> First, secularization denudes calling of practical relevance in life.
>
> Second, transcendent or religious dimensions are essential but may be internal.
>
> Third, callings span one's life and roles. One may have multiple callings.
>
> Fourth, calling gives one a sense of destiny, duty, and ethical design to life.
>
> Fifth, calling is sustained by communal or collective cosmologies.

These five truths inform one's moral commitment to excellence; provide a coherent framework that clarifies one's values, sense-making, and coping; fosters spiritual wellbeing, renewal, and wisdom; and complements and corrects work cosmologies.[23]

NUMINOUS EXPERIENCES AND THE LIFE SPAN

Humans are innately driven to find life meaningful or to create meaning in it. We long for life to form a coherent picture. This need is irrepressible and universal. We intuitively and unconsciously weave all the individual stories of our lives into a meaningful master story, editing out minor or peripheral narratives and elaborating those that are central. We interpret its meaning

---

21. Hagmaier and Abele, "Multidimensionality."
22. Dik and Duffy, *Make Your Job.*
23. Myers, *Conversations,* 87.

as we go along. When a numinous, life-changing event overtakes us, it is paranormal in that it does not fit smoothly into our master story—its special illumination radically changes the flow and direction of the master story. In the ancient world people perceived all paranormal experiences as important divine interventions in their lives. They saw them as gifts of guidance from God. They took them seriously and spent considerable energy on trying to discern and ritualize their methods and meanings.

Conversely, in the modern world the quest for understanding is not preoccupied with issues of meaning and purpose, as much as it is focused on the practical problems of cause and effect, testable by empirical science. The spiritual world has largely been relegated to the world of myth and speculation; left to priests and theologians. As a consequence, the human spirit has been starved, making rather urgent the occasion of the breakthrough of the transcendent.

I am a Panentheist. It seems to me that our prevalent human moments of visionary illumination are the initiatives of the Divine Spirit, pervasive in all aspects of the material world. The Divine Spirit's purpose, apparently, is to awaken us to, and keep us in touch with, the sources of transcendent meaning that lie within and beyond all of us all the time. These illuminations of God's Spirit make us aware of dimensions of reality otherwise unknown to us. The Spirit is a dynamic force or energy in us and beyond us. It is my experience that it pervades not only the material world but equally the moral and spiritual universes in which we exist. As I have said elsewhere, "I believe it is related to or identified with the life force in all organisms, perhaps even the energy that keeps the electrons in orbit in a rock. That dynamism is, in my view, the phenomenon that may rightly be named God as Holy Spirit."[24] In my view, our numinous life-changing experiences are instances of the energetic divine presence, persistently relating to us as Spirit. When they occur they infuse our psyches, minds, affects, and bodies. They give us our sense of destiny, direction, and duty.

When such numinous moments of the Spirit have tracked me down and illumined my life with God's presence and power, they have simply infused me, without any act or response or obedience on my part. His presence and power were just there, radically changing me. I was set on courses that I have never felt like second-guessing or altering. It was not as though I responded in any way to the events and felt led to the life laid out before me. Spontaneously, and in the same moment that the light embraced me in

24. Ellens, "Normalcy," 145.

each event, my life was full of meaning, and the meaning was always made clear to me. My life has been a straight line from those numinous moments to this.

We should be far less surprised than we are by those moments of the Spirit. If we remember them, share them with others, and keep track of them, we can become so aware of their frequency and impact that we will create the awareness that we live in a world in which the Divine Spirit is constantly alive to us and our personal lives. We will then have consciously cultivated a Culture of the Divine Spirit.

A CULTURE OF THE SPIRIT

I think there are eight facts or characteristics of the Culture of the Divine Spirit. First, we can experience that presence in *tangible* ways. Second, we can profitably *hold ourselves open* to its intimations; sailing our lives close to the wind. Third, we can *notice the presence* in ordinary and extraordinary experiences. Fourth, we may *identify* those experiences as the presence of that spiritual dynamo. Fifth, it is natural and normal to name those events as *moments of the spirit*. Sixth, *explaining* such events to each other will raise our consciousness of their presence in our lives. Seventh, we will *recall* that those events continue to happen frequently. Eighth, we will find it natural to *maintain the awareness that we live* all the time within the force field of that dynamo of Spirit. We will *develop a consciousness* of living in the matrix of the active presence of God's Spirit in us and around us, and we will come naturally to think of ourselves as constantly vivified by that life force.[25]

It is surprising that we do not have a greater awareness of the frequency and impact of paranormal experience upon human lives. Certainly that is because in the action-religions of the Western World—Judaism, Christianity, and Islam—the doctrinal and behavioral experiences of religions and spirituality are totally prescribed and predictable; what should be believed as religious truth, what should be carried out as religious ritual, and what should be expected as spiritual experience. "One would think that religious communities would be particularly interested in the frequency and meaning of paranormal experiences that constructively change people's lives and enhance their understanding of their spirituality. It is the case, however, that the prescribed nature of most religious life squelches openness to the

25. Ibid., 147–48.

spirit and to the reality and importance of the numinous experiences."[26] There may be another reason why we are not more aware of the moments of the Spirit. Paranormal experiences are very difficult to describe, define, or fully comprehend. They are mysterious and personal. People are hesitant to report paranormal experiences for fear that others will think them strange. Some might even consider them psycho-pathological. However, such experiences are most likely explainable as personalized moments of spiritual illuminations, caused by the Spirit that pervades all facets of our world. Enriching moments of the Spirit happen in many people's lives as we have noted repeatedly. However, it takes the eyes to see them, the ears to hear them, and openness of the spirit to share them. That is necessary if one is to recognize them for what they are, take them for real, and celebrate them. Otherwise we tend to dismiss them as abnormal moments to be quickly repressed and forgotten.[27]

A CULTURE OF SCIENTIFIC UNDERSTANDING

It is important to create a culture of openness to the investigation of moments of spiritual illuminations and life-change. This requires, as I mentioned, sailing our lives close to the wind of the Spirit, *ruach*, the breath of God, so to speak. We may find that what we have called the paranormal is really much more normal than we think. If we cultivate a Culture of the Spirit in which we keep track of our numinous experiences we may discover that we have a world of data that falls into typical paradigms, categories, patterns, and organizable phenomena. This would give us an ample basis for an empirical or phenomenological science of the paranormal. We might very well have the kind of data from which we could develop hypotheses, theories, and laws about numinous events.

We need to develop collection and management systems relevant and sensitive to this kind of data. We can assume that reality in the world of the paranormal is orderly and lawful as in all other aspect of creation. The reason we think it is so mysterious is because we have not enlarged our paradigms to include it, nor created the systems to study it. "Life's constant change and our widening experience demand an expansion of our paradigms. Failing to expand them obstructs our scientific inquiry into the unknown. Investigation of the paranormal is the threshold waiting for us

26. Ibid.

27. Ibid., 148–49.

to cross over, equipped with a new and broader [outlook]. Truth is open-ended and requires a courageous open-ended quest."[28]

REFERENCES

Bellah, Robert N., et al. *Habits of the Heart: Individualism and Commitment in American Life*. Updated Edition with a New Introduction. Berkeley: University of California Press, 1996.

Dik, Brian J., and Ryan D. Duffy. *Make Your Job a Calling: How the Psychology of Vocation Can Change Your Life at Work*. West Conshohocken: Templeton, 2012.

Ellens, J. Harold. *Light from the Other Side: The Paranormal as Friend and Familiar (Real Life Experiences of a Spiritual Pilgrim)*. Eugene, OR: Resource, 2011.

———. "The Normalcy of the Paranormal: Numinous Experiences Throughout the Life Span." In *Being Called: Scientific, Secular, and Sacred Perspectives*, edited by David B. Yaden et al., 143–62. Santa Barbara: Praeger, 2015.

———. *Understanding Religious Experience: What the Bible Says About Spirituality*. Westport: Praeger, 2007.

Gallup Organization. *Religious Awakenings Bolster Americans' Faith*. January 14, 2003. Online: http://www.gallup.com

Hagmaier, Tamara, and Andrea E. Abele. "The Multidimensionality of Calling: Conceptualization, Measurement and Bicultural Perspective." *Journal of Vocational Behavior* 81 (2012) 39–51.

Irvine, William B. *Aha! The Moments of Insight that Shape Our World*. New York: Oxford University Press, 2015.

Myers, Valerie L. *Conversations about Calling, Advancing Management Perspectives*. New York and London: Routledge, 2014.

Seligman, Martin E. P. "How Are We Called Into the Future?" In *Being Called: Scientific, Secular, and Sacred Perspectives,* edited by David B. Yaden et al., xvii–xxvi. Santa Barbara: Praeger, 2015.

Weber, Max. *The Protestant Ethic and the Spirit of Capitalism*. London: Routledge, 1992.

Yaden, David B., et al., eds. *Being Called: Scientific, Secular, and Sacred Perspectives*. Santa Barbara: Praeger, 2015.

28. Ibid., 160.

Practical Perspectives

Chapter 10

Grief Experiences

Potential Catalyst for Post-traumatic Growth and Wellbeing

GILLIES AMBLER

Figure 1: Gillies and Sandra celebrating the birth of their only child Nigel

GRIEF COMING, READY OR NOT!

This is a photograph of my wife Sandra and me at the birth of our only child, Nigel, in 1974, in Leamington Spa, England. How proud we were embarking on parenthood and a future filled with delightful surprises. Who could have foreseen that Sandra would contract bowel cancer, dying seventeen months later, leaving a husband and son with broken hearts? Not only was I grappling with the loss of my wife, but I was also struggling to come to terms with raising our son away from our families and friends back in Australia. It would have been impossible to conceive then that twenty-seven years later Nigel would die in a car accident.

In the 1970s, academic research into grief was in its infancy. Nobody introduced me to Kubler-Ross's emerging research into the stages of grief. I was not even aware of the concept of grief. As a topic of research, Seligman's theory of wellbeing and its focus on positive emotion, engagement, relationships, meaning, and accomplishments (PERMA)[1] was some decades away, as was Positive Psychology, the scientific study of what goes right in life.[2] What I did understand after Sandra died in 1976, was that a fog had descended on my life. I could no longer see clearly the way ahead. Life had been stripped of meaning. I experienced alienation from the world I once called home. I was repeatedly told, "You are young, forget Sandra, move on, and find someone else to marry," advice that compounded my loss and slowed my path back to everyday life.

I was an advocate of the Enlightenment. I loved philosophy, majoring at university in physics, mathematical physics, and pure and applied mathematics, which I taught with passion at a large high school. This knowledge was meaningless in the face of such a major loss. My left-brain strengths of logic, ability to synthesize facts and order knowledge with analytic skill, proved powerless in the face of this tragedy.

Intuitively I began to write poetry, surprising me with the intensity that flowed line by line. With no mentors to guide me, I returned to prayer, my adolescent faith relationship with Jesus and the Psalms, especially those that grappled with the subject of loss. Charry eloquently highlights the power of the Psalms to enable people who are languishing to flourish once again.[3] They yielded insightful concepts and images that enabled me to

1. Seligman, "Flourish."
2. Peterson, *Primer*.
3. Charry, "Flourishing and Languishing."

identify some of my confusing responses, while offering hope that, through God's grace, I could flourish once again. I struggled to articulate consciously what was happening to me. My right-brain processes were being awakened, stirring creativity and imagination, birthing a grounded spirituality and allowing a dialogue with many complex dimensions of being human, less accessible to the strict framework of scientific research. I did not abandon analysis, logic or a passion for order. This was an unsophisticated attempt to integrate right and left-brain processes, while struggling to make sense of this traumatic loss.

With a profound sense of call, I returned to Australia in 1979 to train as a Uniting Church minister, now traversing the dangerous and complex terrain of loss, well on the way back to everyday life. Falling in love with and marrying Wendy in 1982 completed my journey back to wellbeing. Love possesses great healing power. I found little help from experts or books on grief when it would have been most beneficial. Not surprisingly, one of my passions on entering the ministry in 1988 was pastoral care, especially for people lost in grief.

In 2001, police informed us that Nigel, our son, had died in a car accident in Brisbane. My friend grief emerged again. This was heartbreaking, as I had now lost my "first" family. This tragic event, however, did not shake my foundations as severely as that first time. I had discovered ways to travel this confusing and complex path towards wellbeing and a loving life, honed from reflecting on my grief and many years of counseling. This journey, however, was still arduous and demanding and would test many of my core beliefs and spiritual principles. Wendy persuaded me to enroll for a doctorate exploring the ways I had discovered to heal my broken heart following Sandra's death, and how to embrace these and new ways to wholeness a second time.

OPENING DIALOGUE WITH POSITIVE PSYCHOLOGY

The *Flourishing in Faith: Positive Psychology and Theology Conference*[4] provided me with the opportunity to share my approach to grief and wellbeing with Positive Psychology. I shared research findings from my thesis[5] and

4. The conference was held jointly by St Barnabas College, Adelaide, and St Peter's College, Adelaide, South Australia from September 29–30, 2014.

5. Ambler, "Transcending Grief."

later self-published book.[6] I discovered that research into grief parallels trends in psychology. In the twentieth century both have largely focused on the negative and most demanding of life experiences and responses. My thesis explores positive ways to grow through brokenness towards wellbeing. My autoethnographic case study demonstrates Charry's assertion that languishing challenges and encourages self-reflection, through the poetic narrative as in the case of the Psalms, encouraging a development of life skills and acquiring the wisdom to flourish.[7] As I share briefly from my doctorate on my two grief experiences and journeys towards healing and wellbeing, I invite you to reflect on this question:

Do personal, evocative narratives of grief journeys towards wellbeing, accompanied by analysis yielding key insights, have a complementary role alongside the scientific approach of Positive Psychology?

REFLECTING ON PERSONAL GRIEF IN ACADEMIA?

Employing the recently approved qualitative methodology of autoethnography enabled me to narrate, reflect, and analyze my two grief experiences in an academic setting. In their groundbreaking article Ellis and Bochner describe autoethnography as "an autobiographical genre of writing and research that displays multiple levels of consciousness connecting the personal to the cultural."[8]

Autoethnography enabled me to widen my understanding of "narrative" to include photography and artwork, alongside poetry and prose, to further convey and analyze the complexities involved in overcoming grief storms. Ellis and Bochner assert that evocative narratives occupy a significant place in qualitative research. They enable the individual to describe:

> Stories that create the effect of reality, showing characters embedded in the complexities of life's moments of struggle, resisting the intrusion of chaos, disconnection, fragmentation, marginalization and incoherence, trying to preserve and restore the continuity and cohesiveness of life's unity in the face of unexpected blows of fate that call one's meaning and values into question.[9]

6. Ambler, *Grief Wounds.*
7. Charry, "Flourishing and Languishing."
8. Ellis and Bochner, "Autoethnography," 740.
9. Ibid., 744.

Although autoethnography applies rigorous criteria, including verification principles[10] at the academic level, it is a method employed by everyone throughout their life. It is this dialogue between the self and our many communities, as well as the consequent forms of knowledge, which enables us to develop our understanding of the world, our self and others, both individually and corporately. This continual interaction is illustrated by the following diagram.

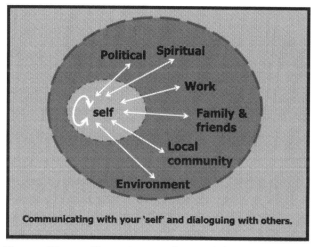

Figure 2: Diagram illustrating autoethnography's complex dialogue

In employing autoethnography, I focused on some of the complex dimensions of my "self" (auto), in dialogue within multiple social settings (ethos) by adopting a rigorous research process (graphy). Key characteristics[11] include:

- the ability to write evocatively in the first person to evoke compassion, understanding, and action in the reader

- adopting a participant-researcher stance embracing subjective and objective approaches to the narrative and its analysis, as well as inter-subjectivity in dialogue with others

10. One principle, peer review, employed in my thesis and this paper establishes a group of people with expertise who offer a critique of the method, presentation, my authenticity, and transferability of my insights.

11. For a more detailed understanding see Ambler, "Transcending Grief," Chapter 4. For a comprehensive discussion of autoethnography see Chang, *Autoethnography*.

- conveying experiences which hopefully assist others, leading to further communal dialogue
- sharing life experiences in an academic context which encourages self-analysis
- reflection and discovery
- employing any genre which contributes to this search for meaning.

Adopting this approach, I created an evocative narrative followed by an analysis of my personal grief experiences. This led, through resilience and a search for meaning, to post-traumatic growth and wellbeing or, as I prefer, spiritual growth leading to healing and wholeness.

INSIGHTS FROM MY NARRATIVE CAMEOS

In sharing briefly from my doctorate, I will explore how befriending grief, listening to, and valuing the multiple ways I responded to its wounding, can become a catalyst for wellbeing. I adopted, and now advocate, embracing a multi-genre approach to narrating any story, including historical data, poetry, photography, artwork, spirituality, theology, insights from significant others, and findings from academic research. Woven together they open up pathways through grief terrain to wellbeing. I will illustrate this through two cameos.[12]

I wrote many poems following Sandra and Nigel's deaths. Each was formed before it arrived in my consciousness. Each revealed dimensions of the grief experience, and hinted at and highlighted ways towards healing. I was not, however, as aware of these insights following Sandra's death, as I was when Nigel died in a car accident some twenty-five years later. Counseling and caring for others in grief in those years, while reflecting intuitively on my own experience, however, had yielded a wealth of insight, and key principles, which coalesced during my doctorate.

In the first cameo, I will contrast two poems, the first related to Sandra and the second following Nigel's death.

---

12. Many more are detailed in Ambler, "Transcending Grief," chapters 4–6.

Loneliness and Despair My Constant Companions

Loneliness, despair
Why are these two my companions?
Love, laughter,
Where have they gone?
Happy New Year, the people say.
I can't see what for
I struggle for happy new day.
I find life hard
Don't you?
So little in it comforting
So few to comfort me.
Why do I need so much love?
Is it strange?
Why do I find so little?
Have people changed?
A New Year
Oh, not 365 days long.
What lies ahead in so much time?
How many barriers are in mine?
How much of a battle will this year be?
How much strength will it take from me?
What will I feel like one year from now?
Will I be stronger?
Will I be sad?
Will it be happy?
Or will it be as bad
As the one I've just had?

This poem, written in January 1987, highlights my comprehensive loss of love, meaning, and happiness. There is the loss in my relationships. Who could have replaced the love that flowed so significantly from my wife Sandra who loved me as I was? There is a loss of meaning as I struggled to find fulfillment in each day, let alone the year. The future seemed filled with uncertainty. I wondered if I had the strength to carry on; in some ways, I didn't want to. Loneliness and despair, my two constant companions, epitomized my loss.

Reflecting on this poem, thirty years later, I discovered that there were sixteen questions (highlighted in italics) in only twenty-seven lines of poetry. Questions dominate the poem! All sixteen questions are negatives expressing my loneliness, sadness, pain, and loss of love; yet also highlighting a search for meaning. By way of contrast, there are only nine questions in the poetry following Nigel's death, and they are all positive. This poem does not contain answers, yet help comes with the questioning process itself. Another discovery! Reflecting on this poem, I discovered that help comes from:

- asking negative questions,

- expressing grief responses, especially negative ones,

- searching for meaning,

- sharing our experience sensitively with others and reflecting together. This for me came from reading my poems to friends,

- themes such as seeking love, happiness, and healing which are latent within the poem; even though I was living in grief's shadow, and

- truthfully acknowledging the present experience.

It never occurred to me at the time to reflect on what they were conveying. I didn't know that writing poems was healing in itself. I didn't realize how crucial it is to share honestly who we are. I now believe that "telling it as it is" contributes to the possibility of breakthroughs.

So, embedded within this poem is a latent seed: grief as the loss to personhood. Amazingly, I wrote over thirty-five poems in that first year as a bereaved husband, all flowing from deep within my being. Without realizing it, writing about my "loss to personhood" was cathartic in itself. In my doctorate, *I described grief as loss to personhood, where personhood includes who we are and all the ways we relate to the world.* It provides a comprehensive understanding of grief. My thinking was influenced by Cassell's concept of personhood.[13] Whenever we reflect on our losses in prose, however, we can only list them linearly. Grief is multidimensional, so the challenge is to present these losses in a multifaceted way. The schema below provides a guide to many of the losses that can occur following a grief event. It is not intended to be an exhaustive list, rather, illustrative in general of the many possible losses. It would be even more realistic in 3-D!

13. Cassell, *Nature of Suffering*.

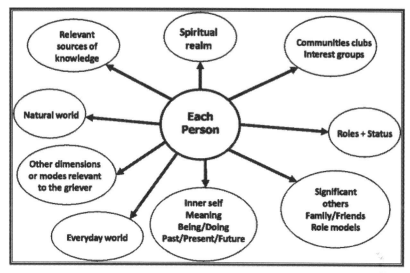

Figure 3: Schema illustrating grief as loss to personhood

Since we can experience many or possibly all of these losses simultaneously, or in complex ways, within brief periods of time, the schema underscores grief's complexity and diversity. This multidimensional and constantly changing experience of grief requires a multifaceted approach to healing.

In 2003, after a morning of wading through articles on grief and feeling almost overwhelmed by concepts, interpretations, and academic debates, this sentence: "Love wills love, as love must do" entered my consciousness. Within a few minutes the following poem emerged, encapsulating much of my understanding of grief, love, and life.

Love Wills Love

Dedicated to my families in this world and the next,
from whom I have learnt to love and treasure life.

Love wills love, as love must do.
Love lives truth, does it live in you?
Love lives on in sunshine and rain.
Love lives long by embracing pain.
Love sings songs, as love must do.

Love sings songs, does it sing for you?
Love sings low in the depth of your heart.
Love sings me: come sing your part.
Love is myst'ry, as love must be.
Love wills life in you and me.
Watch love grow within, without.
Breathe love in and share it about.
Love seeks peace, as love must do.
Love needs peace each journey through.
Love lives peace in a world of doubt.
Love wills peace: though some hate it out.
Love seeks love, as love must do.
What's life's purpose for me and you?
Love must nourish the whole, the part.
Love's revealed through words of the heart.
Love must die, as love must do.
Love on a cross, the world in view.
Love embraces pain and sin.
Love transforms, lets eternal in.
Love's transcendent, as love must be.
Love beams out through eternity.
Love came down to die on a tree.
Love so suffers to set us free.
Love arose, as love must do.
Love rose Christ: love raises you too.
Love so silent, so deep, so strong.
Love will rise to right each wrong.

The poem marked a significant turning point for me, with its focus on
love rather than grief, life rather than death, healing rather than wounding. What a contrast! The first poem narrates my loss of love, whereas the
second asserts the power of love to bring healing, meaning, and wellbeing. It was surprising to discover that the most dominant descriptive word
was "love" which occurred 238 times in the two personal narratives, twice
as frequently as words related to the concept of "grief." Even in the first
narrative "love" provided a major key to reconnecting with everyday life.

Surprisingly the concept of love as a powerful way of assisting growth towards wellbeing is rarely mentioned in academic grief research.

I reflected on this understanding of love's power to bring healing, seeking a succinct description. My core understanding came from a synthesis of three sources; Jesus' second commandment to love your neighbor as you love yourself,[14] Peck's understanding of the significant role willpower exercises in spiritual growth[15], my understanding of grief as loss to personhood, as well as my experience in providing counseling assistance to women traumatized by domestic violence. Eventually, *I described love as the will to nurture your personhood as you seek to nurture another's.* When wrestling with grief the focus needs to be on nurturing your "self" and deciding who can be trusted to assist you. At other times, this order can be reversed. My narrative, along with dialogue with others, and insights as a spiritual director and pastoral counselor, led to my description of spirituality. *I described spirituality as the personal integrated search for meaning, nurtured by love, open to the transcendent, which transforms (or positively changes) one's personhood.*

Seligman's theory of wellbeing, highlighting as key concepts positive emotion, engagement, relationships, meaning, and accomplishment (PERMA)[16], shares much commonality with my descriptions of spirituality and love. I believe there could be fruitful dialogue between qualitative case studies, in particular autoethnographic studies, and Positive Psychology. One benefit of my research is that it offers ways to journey through grief towards wellbeing, making a personal contribution to the psychology of being positive and, hopefully, to Positive Psychology. Further case studies would enhance such insights. Another advantage to my descriptions of grief, love, and spirituality is that they could be adopted by anyone, whether secularist, atheist, agnostic, Christian, or a member of another religion.

Autoethnography allowed me to choose any genre that yields meaning. Photography has always been a passionate hobby. While Sandra was in hospital over many months, I decided to photograph our home, Nigel, and places of interest to her. The photograph below was taken in Febuary 1976. Although I did not know it at the time, I had captured Sandra saying her last goodbye to Nigel with a last tender kiss.

14. Matthew 22:39.
15. Peck, *Road Less Travelled*, 126.
16. Seligman, "Flourish."

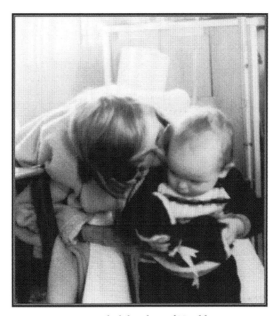

Figure 4: Sandra's last kiss of Nigel her son

I remember that, as Nigel and I walked towards the door of Sandra's room, we turned and waved goodbye. Sandra's eyes were focused on Nigel with an intensity that seemed to belong to another world. There was a deep longing in her eyes that frightened me. It was as though she was drawing in every detail and memory of Nigel to take on her journey beyond life. Two grief counselors responded to this powerfully evocative image, with its almost ethereal haze. One reflected that this inability to care for your child would probably be one of motherhood's most painful experiences. The other shared how deeply troubled she became, the mother within her crying with the pain of goodbye and the nurse in her remembering the poignancy of dying children drawing in every detail of their parents. Both reinforced my contention that grief cannot be contained by cognitive analysis alone. My experience cannot be completely expressed by rational thought, let alone Sandra's experience of saying a final goodbye to her son.

Although reason assisted me in describing, analyzing, and reflecting on these lived grief experiences, I am now aware that some forms of knowledge, though they include rational dimensions, go beyond rational thought processes. These forms of knowledge I have termed "supra-rational." *I asserted that grief is supra-rational, including forms of knowledge accessible by reason as well as knowledge beyond the reach of reason alone.* Some aspects of major lived experiences are "known" by the senses, the body, the heart, and the soul/psyche, yet cannot be put into words, and hence cannot be comprehended by reason alone. Consequently, there are dimensions to lived experience that are inaccessible to the mind alone. Stake describes a tacit knowledge of that which is remembered by our being when we subtract all we have conceptualized in words, symbols or rhetorical forms.[17] The grief event captured in Figure 4 is one significant example.

Although it is important to describe, order, systematize, and analyze grief (or other significant dimensions of lived experiences) I am now aware that there is much that is non-logical, unpredictable, boundary-breaking, and chaotic. Knowledge of these aspects can be conveyed in a multitude of art forms, including sculpture, mime, painting, photography, pottery, and music. Consequently, a comprehensive understanding of grief experiences needs to include some of these nonverbal modalities. That is why my personal narratives and subsequent analysis contained images and photography.

Quantitative studies of groups of bereaved or grieving people have yielded many important empirical insights, which often assist in policy-making. For me, they did not help to find a way to wellbeing. Qualitative research with a focus on case studies and testimonies yielded much more helpful insight.

In my doctorate and subsequent lecturing at university I struggled with two questions:

Firstly, how could I utilize the strengths from my scientific training with newly discovered right-brain skills, including creativity and spirituality? And secondly, can quantitative and qualitative research into grief complement each other?

Grief is supra-rational. It includes dimensions that can be analyzed and understood through the power of reason and empirical methods, yet to more fully understand its complex dimensions we need to access other forms of knowledge. Another genre that conveys meaning beyond the powerful yet limiting scientific empirical framework, is art. One of the verification principles I employed was to form a group denoted by the term "member checks." This is a group of people who have grown through significant grief experiences and can articulate an understanding from their journey towards wellbeing. I invited an artist to create pencil sketches that were evoked in her as she resonated with my narratives.

17. Stake, "Case Study Method."

Figure 5: Journeying through grief to wellbeing

One significant aspect of art is that it draws multiple meanings from observers. For me, the artist portrays grief work as a journey that we begin by expressing our responses of pain, loss, sadness, brokenness, loneliness, fear, and meaninglessness. This loss is expressed pictorially in the tears that become pools of water, representing the intensity of the grief experience. The artwork underscores the principle that, as we express our grief, and in whatever form, it can become a pathway to wellbeing. As we journey, we discover that our expressions of grief become glimmers of light, represented here by tears being transformed into candles. In the candlelight, which is vulnerable and can flicker or be extinguished by winds of grief, it becomes possible to look towards the horizon that brings hope. Slowly, as we focus not only on our grief but also on the possibility of healing, we are able to trek towards meaning and loving life again.

Can my narrative, insights, inferences, and principles, gained from my doctorate and years of counseling, assist others? And can they inspire and help people on their journey through brokenness to loving life again?

These are legitimate questions. The Enlightenment paradigm is skeptical of any knowledge claims outside the boundaries of reason, observable facts and empirical analysis. The narrative of Jesus' life, ministry, teachings, and role model, as portrayed in the Gospels, have been embraced by countless people across all continents and cultures for nearly 2000 years. Such questions, however, as they relate to my project, remain. Many concerns are raised in the research community concerning the ability to transfer principles, concepts, and insights, particularly from single or small case studies. Silverman, however, asserts that qualitative research is capable of producing principles which can be generalized in some way and possess resonance with others.[18]

WHEN THE RUBBER HITS THE ROAD: WOMEN TRAUMATIZED BY DOMESTIC VIOLENCE ROAD TESTING MY INSIGHTS

I will now turn our attention from theory to praxis and two further cameos. For over twelve years I have been privileged to provide counseling support for many women severely wounded by domestic violence. My experience of loss sharply contrasts with women who have experienced rape, death threats, and other forms of physical, psychological, spiritual, and economic violence. Can my story, insights, and principles be embraced by such women? My experience has been "yes." I have been overawed seeing women I have counseled finding ways towards healing by adopting some of my insights. I will share the stories of two women, who though crushed and severely traumatized by their heart-wrenching experiences, have discovered pathways towards wellbeing.

Sometimes I show an image or photograph to the women I support at the local domestic violence service (DVS) and invite them to respond. Images can play a significant role, especially for someone who has been so controlled and traumatized by words. Words direct us, whereas images invite us to respond. For over ten years Josie (pseudonym) had been controlled in almost every aspect of her life by her cruel, violent, and narcissistic partner. After listening to her incredibly tragic story, I invited her to respond to the following image, in which the artist in my doctorate had conveyed my heartbreak.

18. Silverman, Doing Qualitative Research.

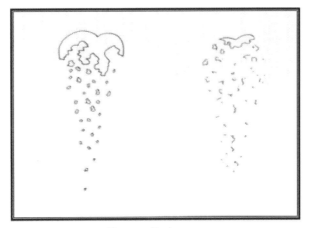

Figure 6: Brokenness

Instantly it resonated with her. She talked about her broken heart and longing to be loved. In tears, she explained that the right-hand image conveyed her present brokenness and fragility. Then she surprised me by saying, "What happens when you turn the image upside down?" As I turned the image around, she exclaimed, "That's my way forward. The image is telling me to open my heart to the ways that love can bring healing."

Figure 7: Vulnerably open to healing

I was astounded. I had reflected on this image for years, never thinking of turning it upside down or wondering is it the right way up? Sometimes those we care for not only resonate with some of our insights, but they also enrich them. Images are supra-rational, providing us with pathways to healing that include words, yet go beyond words.

In 2013, I was invited by a DV case manager to counsel a young woman gripped by fear from a short-term relationship with a particularly violent and brutal man. Many months later she wrote a brief account of her story, which was included in a display organized by the Zonta Club of Adelaide.[19] Angie's (pseudonym) story begins:

> He told me he would hurt me so badly I would never dance again. After he had said this, I started planning my escape. Unfortunately, at this stage, I was completely isolated. It felt like I was trapped in a prison of fear.

Months earlier, Angie had been very reluctant to stay at the DVS. She would demand to leave after two weeks if she was not satisfied. The only person she could trust was her partner, "trusting" through sheer terror of being murdered if he knew she had deserted him. Despite all my grief experiences, there is always a significant degree of vulnerability in counseling such women. How can I help? What key is required for each woman to unlock her door to new life? How can trust be established?

Angie spoke softly into her tears through the first session. Was she frightened to voice her experience? I understood little of what she said. I listened intently and shed tears of compassion. The few words I did speak had taken me a lifetime to articulate. I had no idea if she would want to see me again or if I had helped her. Could she, would she, find support in any of my spiritual principles? Months later she wrote about this first meeting and her subsequent journey towards wellbeing. With Angie's permission, I share from her reflection:

> Once upon a time, there was a girl who was lost in a deep sea of grief and all she could see was darkness. Traumatized by fear and terrorized by demons of the past. This girl was filled with emptiness and surrounded by loneliness . . .
>
> It was suggested I speak with Rev. Dr. Gillies Ambler; I had never really spoken to a minister before . . .
>
> Instantly he gained my trust and respect. I knew somewhere deep down; this man could help me . . .
>
> "Grief wounds. Love heals." "Love heals grief wounds" these words Gillies wrote down on a piece of paper. These words—the

19. This story can be viewed with many others on http://www.zontaclubofadelaide.org.au.

title of his book is what I live by today; these words are the words I use to comfort others who have experienced grief. This book has given me an understanding of how important it is for love to embrace grief. I underestimated the power of love.

I have been overawed and deeply moved by correspondence from people who have been assisted, changed, and even transformed from reading my doctorate[20] and my book,[21] *Grief Wounds. Love Heals. Insights of a Bereaved Husband and Bereaved Father.* To be trusted by grievers to assist them traverse dark grief storms and so enable them to experience wellbeing has been deeply meaningful and truly awe-inspiring.

CONTINUING DIALOGUE

The death of my wife and only son had a devastating impact on my person and many of the ways I related to the world. My spiritual (or post-traumatic) growth from brokenness to wellbeing has been transformational. Without these two traumatic grief events, I would never have been challenged to dig so deeply and profoundly, out of sheer necessity, to embrace wellbeing. Travelling from disconnection to reconnection, loss to gain, despair to hope, and loneliness to love, has enabled me to step over wellbeing's threshold, embracing life with a renewed passion. A peer review member highlighted my courage to transcend grief, contending that my role modeling of a journey from wounding to wellbeing offers hope to others.

Positive Psychology is the scientific "systematic study of the structure and behavior of human interaction through observation and experiment."[22] Through scientific analysis it has enriched our understanding of key characteristics at the macro level of wellbeing and associated concepts such as happiness, hope, love, joy, meaning, and purpose. Positive Psychology has established many programs of wellbeing in communities, with school-based programs being common examples. I would also assert that we need people to role-model ways to embrace wellbeing, especially for those who have been stopped in their tracks and sent tumbling into valleys of grief or dark personal hells. Throughout life each person has to rise to challenges, including:

20. Ambler, "Transcending Grief."
21. Ambler, *Grief Wounds.*
22. White, "Introduction to Positive Psychology."

156

- How am I to journey towards wellbeing, in spite of life's challenges?

- How can I embrace fuller dimensions of wellbeing?

Richardson argues for the importance of narrative in academic research.[23] She asserts, and I agree, that narrative and the scientific-logical method form two complementary, irreducible ways to interpret reality. Each has its distinctive frameworks, methods, and verification principles.

Qualitative research methodologies, including autoethnography, complement quantitative methods and the empirical approaches of Positive Psychology, by exploring grief and wellbeing from personal perspectives. Personal narratives and case studies provide a "human face" to wellbeing. On such personal journeys many, if not most, look for mentors and role models who have fleshed this out, by integrating negative and positive experiences with theoretical principles. Many seek life-inspiring stories as they reflect upon negative life experiences, seeking a sense of wellbeing. These are some of the most significant ways we personally seek meaning and explore ways to uncover, discover, and embrace wellbeing.

It is my hope that this single personal case study, alongside other people's profound personal journeys from brokenness to wellbeing, will not only generate and enrich a dialogue with proponents of Positive Psychology, but also inspire others to strive for and experience wellbeing, despite all that life's negativities have thrown at them. I rest my case and leave you, the reader, with these questions:

Do personal, evocative narratives of grief journeys towards wellbeing, accompanied by analysis yielding key insights, have a complementary role alongside the scientific approach of Positive Psychology?

Could you create and reflect on your own evocative narrative and so yield personal insights that will enable you to more fully embrace wellbeing and as a consequence assist others?

REFERENCES

Ambler, Gillies. *Grief Wounds. Love Heals. Insights of a Bereaved Husband and Bereaved Parent.* Adelaide: Self-published, 2010.
———. "Transcending Grief—Journeying to Loving Life Again. An Autoethnographic Case Study of One Bereaved Spouse and Parent." Doctor of Ministry Studies Thesis, Melbourne College of Divinity, 2007.

23. Richardson, "Narrative and Sociology."

Cassell, Eric J. *The Nature of Suffering and the Goals of Medicine.* New York: Oxford University Press, 1991.

Chang, Heewon. *Autoethnography as Method.* Walnut Creek: Left Coast, 2008.

Ellis, Carolyn, and Arthur P. Bochner. "Autoethnography, Personal Narrative, Reflexivity: Researcher as Subject." In *Handbook of Qualitative Research,* edited by N. K. Denzin et al. Thousand Oaks: Sage, 2000.

Peck, M. Scott. *The Road Less Travelled: A New Psychology of Love, Traditional Values and Spiritual Growth.* London: Arrow, 1990.

Peterson, Christopher. *A Primer in Positive Psychology.* New York: Oxford University Press, 2006.

Richardson, Laurel, "Narrative and Sociology," *Journal of Contemporary Ethnography* 19 (1990) 116–35.

Seligman, Martin E. P. "Flourish: Positive Psychology and Positive Interventions." The Tanner Lectures on Human Values. University of Michigan, 2010. Online: http://www.isbm.at/pics/Flourish_Seligman.pdf

Silverman, David. *Doing Qualitative Research: A Practical Handbook.* Thousand Oaks: Sage, 2000.

Stake, Robert E., "The Case Study Method in Social Inquiry." In *Case Study Method: Key Issues, Key Texts,* edited by R. Gomm et al., 18–26, Thousand Oaks: Sage, 2000.

Chapter 11

Flourishing in a Broken Body

An Interview with Professor Shane Clifton

SHANE CLIFTON AND MATTHEW P. ANSTEY

MATTHEW: SHANE, WHEN WE asked you to write a chapter you said that unfortunately you were too busy (writing a book, I understand, on disability, flourishing, and faith). So the editors thought it would be great to interview you. Since you are a Christian theologian with a severe disability, it makes for a fascinating conversation. You have published your lived experience over several years in your memoir: *Husbands Should Not Break*. There is an added interest since you are in a Pentecostal church and lecture at Pentecostal theological college, so you have had to wrestle with the whole issue of "prosperity doctrine," which asserts that if we obey God, we will be blessed, typically with health and wealth. So I thought a good way to begin this open-ended conversation with you, would be to go through PERMA because that's the headline of Positive Psychology: positive emotion, engagement, relationships, meaning, and accomplishments.

Shane: That's great, Matthew.

Matthew: But before we get to that, could you give us some understanding of your accident, where you are today and what life is like for you now?

Shane: I'm married to Elly, I've got three teenage boys and on October, 7, 2010, I was holidaying with my family on the south coast of New South Wales, at a little town called Nowra. We were at a church facility that had a skateboard/push-bike jump set up for the youth group. My kids were using it so I decided I'd have a go and I jumped on a push-bike. I landed badly and broke my fourth and fifth vertebrae, which left me as an incomplete quadriplegic. Quadriplegic means a spinal cord injury that affects four limbs, incomplete means I've had some recovery. I have movement in my biceps, but no triceps and nothing really below the chest. But on the right side, I've had some recovery so I can use my hand.

So I'm a quadriplegic, full-time wheelchair, carers in the morning. I spent about seven months in the hospital. After the hospital, you have to get used to being at home. I went back to work about a year later. I teach theology at Alphacrucis College. It's the national training college of the Australian Christian Churches, a Pentecostal denomination. I work at half-time. I'm Dean of Theology there so in one way I'm really fortunate, I had a job that I could go back to. Not only that, in some strange way, theology is about the problem of pain, isn't it? It's a fundamental Christian topic so I've spent five years thinking about the problem of pain, I've written a memoir which partly explores it, and I recently had a journal article published in *Theological Studies* on the problem of pain.[1] So weirdly my injury and my teaching and my research have been able to go together.

You spend seven months in a hospital; you are desperate to get home, and you think to yourself that when you do, life will return to normal. When I did get home, I realized what I'd lost. I was desperately unhappy, for obvious reasons. I don't think I had clinical depression, and while I saw the psychologist a couple of times, I didn't find it helped me all that much. So instead I investigated the virtue tradition. I devoured the work of Thomas Aquinas and spent time reading Aristotle. Recently, I have studied the work of Alisdair McIntyre, books like *After Virtue*. More recently I have read his book *Dependent Rational Animals*, which attempts to translate the virtue tradition for disability.

I filled my head with this virtue tradition, which has similarities with Positive Psychology. It's sort of a wrestle. It's really about happiness. We

1. Clifton, "Theodicy."

think the virtue tradition is about ethics, but it's about happiness. Virtues are habits of character that enable you to succeed, to live a life of purpose and meaning, to live a happy life. So virtues are connected with happiness. Then in the midst of reading this virtue tradition, I came across a video by Martin Seligman, I'm sure you've seen the TED video that he did there.[2] I suddenly realized this amazing connection between Positive Psychology and the virtue tradition. Then I began to think through the way in which both of those traditions could help me, not only wrestle with my loss but maybe find happiness or meaning or purpose. So both of those traditions became very important in my recovery over the next few years. They still are. I'm often reading, thinking, and writing about them.

Matthew: How similar are those two traditions—virtue and Positive Psychology?

Shane: Martin Seligman likes to imagine that he's developed a new psychology and he hasn't. In my opinion, Positive Psychology puts some empirical proof around the virtue tradition that existed for thousands of years before him and, to be honest with you, is much richer than Positive Psychology. The problem with Positive Psychology is it tries to reduce everything to empiricism, and I don't think that you can really reduce notions like happiness and concepts like virtue to empirical measurement techniques. I think you lose too much when you do that. But Positive Psychology adds empirical support to the virtue and some new ways of thinking. So I do like the idea of bringing together a really philosophical, ethical tradition with a science. They go well together.

Matthew: Seligman's popularized Positive Psychology and not many people read Aristotle, or Aquinas.

Shane: He does make it much more accessible, that's very true, which is a great thing.

Matthew: Have you thought about the times we're in? Does it seem to you that the emergence of Positive Psychology comes at a time with a decline of organized religion? Although it's not all doom in spirituality, is it one of these ideas that is right for the time? There is a hunger for it, isn't there?

Shane: Oh, obviously. It succeeded I think because the contemporary world has lost a reason for living, so we wonder what are we doing with our wealth, with our wellbeing? Historically, much of our meaning was derived from religion, from faith in God which gave you a purpose. Now we live in

2. Seligman, "New Era."

an increasingly secular society. People don't know what they're spending their time doing and the great thing about Positive Psychology is talking about happiness. Everyone's interested in happiness.

Matthew: I was interested in hearing you say you "devoured" Aquinas. Do you think before the accident you devoured anything in that sense? Did the accident give you a drive in some way to search and almost hunt for something?

Shane: Yes. I've always been a reader; I'm a theologian and theological curiosity has always been a part of my background. This, however, was the first time I think that I'd read a tradition for very personal existential reasons.

Matthew: I know in your own writing too, you've turned to the method of autoethnography, reflecting on your life. Have you stopped to think that for many great theologians biographies were a critical part of development?

I suppose the bigger question—what I'm trying to get at is—if theology's just doctrine, just ideas, why is it that personal experience has such a profound influence on what I believe is some of the great theology of the world? Have you thought about that?

Shane: Oh, look, I call myself a theologian, but I don't pretend to be the sort of theologian that is spending time debating the nuances of Trinitarian theology. I don't want to be too harsh on abstract theology, it has its place, but the best theology is thinking about the existential crisis of life. So theology by its very nature is asking, "Where are you God in this difficult, troublesome, problematic life?" Theology in that sense is one of the great disciplines and it's a shame that it's in decline because where else are we thinking about the meaning and the purpose of life in the face of all of the crises that we face in the world? So, I'm pleased to be a theologian for that reason.

Matthew: Having trained as a professional theologian, do you think that shaped the way you responded to the cataclysmic accident?

Shane: Oh, absolutely. I mean I'm rare the way in which I dealt with the accident, which was to read Aristotle and Aquinas. That's not because I'm special, it's just I've had a particular background, and that's the way I processed my loss. In writing my memoir *Husbands Should Not Break*,[3] I processed my loss. So reading and then writing my story was the way in

---

3. Clifton, *Husbands Should Not Break.*

which I've been able to deal with the injury so far and to rehabilitate. You know, I'm doing much better now than I was two or three years ago.

Matthew: In what sense?

Shane: Well, psychologically. In the first couple of years, there were so many difficulties. The injury has so much effect on life. People imagine it must feel horrible to be in a wheelchair. No, the wheelchair's fantastic. It's liberating. You're not trapped in a wheelchair. The wheelchair is what gets you out and about.

The problem of the spinal cord injury is the effects on marriage for example. How do you relate to the mutuality of marriage when it feels like you can no longer contribute to looking after a house, doing the cooking, driving your kids around? We've been married now twenty-five years, so, it's been like I've had to start again in working out what it is to be a husband. As you can imagine, the injury also has a dramatic impact on sexuality and physical intimacy, and that is very hard to adjust to.

Similarly, I've had to rethink how to be a parent. I did this injury while riding pushbikes and skateboards with my children. I was a surfer so I'd take the kids surfing. How will I be a father? I had to work out how do I be a Dad when I can't do those physical things. Simple things, like what do I do with my kids on the weekend?

One of the reasons I spent so much time reading these ancient sources is because I'm stuck in front of the computer not knowing what to do with my time. So your life changes in really fundamental ways. Reading these resources is a way of processing that, especially since Positive Psychology and virtue are about wellbeing, happiness, succeeding, and notions like gratification. Reading Seligman on pleasure, especially where he talks about notions like savoring, became life-giving to me. These books gave me very practical insights for me to wrestle with in my life.

Matthew: What about the empirical stuff? Lots of gems there?

Shane: Look I shouldn't dismiss that. My problem is when I compare Alasdair MacIntyre to Martin Seligman. It feels like chalk and cheese, but you're right. I also had some very practical things that I needed to respond to and Seligman was really helpful, so I don't want to dismiss what he's done, even if I prefer the depth of the virtue tradition.

Matthew: You said before you love this combination of science and philosophy. Maybe part of the problem is that sometimes in Positive Psychology, it's just science. They're not aware of the riches of those other traditions.

Shane: I've read works on rehabilitation. I have read scientific journals, also considerably on Positive Psychology, and spinal cord injury and their journals are so boring. I mean, there'll be around 7000 words in a journal article, and there's probably only three paragraphs you need to read, the introduction and the conclusion, because the whole middle section is statistics. They do all of this work to come to one or two conclusions related to a couple of statistical comments.

I do love science, and I do love empiricism, but I get a bit cynical with empirical research. You can't reduce life to the numbers in the way that sometimes psychological researchers try to do.

Matthew: Shane, this strikes me as slightly ironic: empirical science saved your life in many ways. If you had this accident in many countries, in many locations, even our country in other locations, it could have been a different story. Also, you're in an amazing fancy wheelchair. Do you think about that as well?

Shane: Yes. I'm evidence driven, but you also need people dealing with questions of faith and prayer as well as seeking solutions backed by empirical proof. So, we need both.

Matthew: You have talked about still having to face potentially life-threatening complications. Does this link into an ancient idea, which positive psychologists these days tend to call "mindfulness," this idea of living in the present? Do you find you're living more in the present now because of this? Has your experience changed your views of the horizon so you don't look forward?

Shane: Maybe, but in some ways, I'm still and always have been goal driven. I am still, weirdly enough, not thinking about death. I want to travel, I'm writing books, I'm thinking about my next publication. So, in some ways, because I had this injury at forty personality-wise I'm not disabled. I'd formed my theology. I had an established marriage. So, many things in a sense were in place at the time of my injury and as a result, I'm the same but different. On the one hand my life is very different, but on the other hand I haven't changed all that much. I have the same personality and approach to life. Now I just have to deal with a different set of circumstances.

Matthew: Have you, out of curiosity, spent time with other people suffering various types of disability? Have you tried to mentor them, because you do seem quite psychologically robust and mature?

Shane: Look, I'm not a counselor. I was never going to be the person who was going to walk fifty people through their injuries. Apply your gifts and your skills; my gifts are in scholarship and I've got this unique opportunity now to apply my scholarly interest and gift to disability. For example, I've been appointed an honorary associate of the Faculty of Health Sciences at Sydney University, working with their center for disability, policy, and research. I've done some work on spinal cord injury and happiness with them and in the process interviewed five or six people. This means I have met some amazing people with disabilities. I've done some work with CBM, which is a brilliant Christian ministry encouraging the church to think seriously about the way it deals with disability. But I've spent more time with my head in books than with disabled people. Even as I say this, I'm challenged to do better from here on in!

Matthew: In your struggle has there been tremendous loneliness and the fact that others just don't get it? How much has that been an issue?

Shane: I don't think it's been a big issue. One of the interesting things, of course, that Positive Psychology tells you is that personality has a lot to do with a person's resilience. There's a set point for resilience and happiness, you could almost guess beforehand how well a person will or won't cope because a lot of those things are based on personality.

I was at the Prince of Wales Spinal Unit a couple of weeks ago doing a presentation on Positive Psychology. We were interested in resilience and happiness, and I said to them up front, the truth is that a lot of the skills that you need to flourish after the injury are ingrained. You either have the right personality or not—but that's not completely true. I do think individuals can change. I do believe virtue can be developed and I think you do get that from Christianity, don't you?

You know, as Christians, we have to believe people can change otherwise what the hell are we doing? So I do believe that we can make decisions, we can pray, we can invite the Holy Spirit to help the transition, to help us find a new meaning and a new purpose. What are some of the ways in which Christianity can bring change that maybe sometimes Positive Psychology's pessimistic about? Well, I think Christianity can provide a new basis for meaning, purpose, and hope. I'd like to believe that Christianity can transform vice into virtue strength. So that, when we are talking to people everything isn't just pre-set as to whether they will or won't succeed. We can take responsibility for our future.

Matthew: That's very wise. Shall we now talk about PERMA? P is for positive emotion. Of course, it's a mistake to think this is about being happy. The list of the core things includes love and peace, and very clearly your experience of love in the family is a key part of the whole way you cope. How do you feel about that?

Shane: Positive pleasure, positive emotion I think this is the biggest challenge with spinal cord injury. Because of all the things that I received positive emotion from they're all the things you lose. On the day of the injury, I was surfing. Where were the places where I got that hit of positive pleasure? Surfing and golf were my two sports. Sex, another example. Playing with your kids. I was sporty, so I'd run in the morning. All of these were avenues for positive emotion and I really felt like I'd lost them.

You work hard all week but then you come to the weekend. The weekend's where you're looking to get relief, where you get to go and do those things that give positive emotion. I'd wake up on a Saturday morning and think, "What the hell am I going to do with myself today?" So, it was a big challenge. When you read Aristotle and Aquinas, Aristotle particularly, his ethics, for example, was really down on positive emotion. They're so focused, Aquinas, on the love of God, and Aristotle, philosophical reflection, that they forget that you have to have a little fun in life. Sometimes I think these guys put positive emotion so far down that they thought it was almost irrelevant. One of the things I like about Seligman is he doesn't dismiss it. I really like Barbara Frederickson's idea that positive emotion gives you a set of resources that will enable you to succeed in other things.

So, for me, I had to wrestle to find avenues for positive emotion. This transition in thinking just takes time. You've got to accept that these losses have occurred and that you can't get those back. Just like anyone who's had a loss, you first of all have to grieve, and it's hard to experience joy while grieving. But with enough time things get better. And Seligman really helped me, by talking about the skills of savoring and mindfulness. It's taken me a few years, but I've gradually started to learn to savor the simple things in life.

I developed some new pleasures, expensive Scotch for example! So I have a lovely Scotch collection! Seligman talks about mindfulness and some of those techniques. I've never been very good at practicing mindfulness. My son is trying to get me into meditation, for example, and maybe I'll keep trying. I think prayer can be a form of meditation for some people, but often I feel like I'm not spiritual enough to do that justice. But over time, I've learnt to find pleasure in enjoying my kids having fun, or I go disabled surfing, as I did today. For many years, the idea of lying on a surfboard and being pushed in tiny waves sounded horrible to me because you know, that was what I did for sport. I surfed with big waves. But five years down the track I'm able to set that aside now and just enjoy being in the water. So, you do learn to savor a humbler sense of enjoyment.

Matthew: Shane it sounds as though if you were reviewing PERMA that you'd give a tick to P (positive emotion)?

Shane: Absolutely. Definitely. I think they get that right, unlike Aquinas and Aristotle.

Matthew: Richard Rohr says that you spend your first forty years of your life looking for acceptance, but your next forty looking for authenticity.

Shane: Yes, I like that idea. That's exactly right. Because you do, you find a way to live again; you find a way to experience pleasure and meaning and happiness. So, that's P.

Matthew: So, E—engagement is interesting, being in the flow, that sense of time distortion which you can get from reading a novel or daydreaming. As I was preparing this, I imagined that in a way engagement is something that wouldn't be so affected. What's your experience?

Shane: Yes, that has been the easiest for me. Spinal cord injury affects different people differently. Because a lot of engagement or gratification comes from a person's work, one of the challenges of a spinal cord injury is that employment rates drop. They say that of 80 percent of people with a spinal cord injury who were working before the injury, the employment drops to around 30 percent after. You think about the drastic impact it has upon them. It doesn't just affect money, although there's a lot of poverty with a disability. It also affects a person's happiness because it affects their gratification and flow. What are they doing if they're no longer working?

Now a lot of young men engage in sport. That's why disabled sport is really important. When you've lost the physical, often putting the effort into sporting activities becomes a way of earning engagement, gratification, and flow. In my case, again it was writing and reading. So I wrote and published my memoir for example, of around eighty-six thousand words. I also published another bunch of essays, so most of my engagement has come from writing. I was also able to keep teaching and working at Alphacrucis College, and I love my work. So through my work I have been able to remain engaged with others—so engagement has been relatively easy for me.

I also blog a bit. Recently we had mental health day and I'd been reading a book by Joseph Prince, who thinks mental illness can be defeated by right-thinking. He's a very well-known Pentecostal preacher from Singapore, who has spoken in Australia and written a book on mental health.

Basically, his attitude is that if you have faith, you think right and if you think right, you don't need to see a psychiatrist. So I wrote a blog going to town on this way of thinking because I think it shows no understanding of the challenge of mental health and gives a completely false view of faith. We tend to have faith as the belief that God will heal you. A belief that you'll be able to experience some sort of perfect psychological and physical health. Whereas faith is trust in God whatever the circumstances. The object of faith isn't healing or psychological health. The object of faith should be God.

Matthew: Pentecostalism, in its popularized form, does it affirm that wellbeing means the absence of any ill health? Does it mean total wellbeing?

Shane: Yes, that's right. I think in some ways this dilemma is Christian, not just Pentecostal. I think many Christians who read the Gospel stories seem to believe that Jesus heals everyone. So I think this tension is part of Christian faith. Maybe it's more obvious in Pentecostals because they tend to emphasize healing more, although I have found that the spiritual practices of churches have more in common nowadays.

Matthew: Engagement, so another tick for PERMA. Now, to R—relationships. You've mentioned already that's been a huge thing, you've mentioned your three sons and your wife.

Shane: Yes, look, the R's interesting because when Seligman first wrote *Authentic Happiness*, he didn't have R in it. It was just pleasure, gratification, meaning. That's all it was. He didn't include relationships so there was a big gap. Look, an emphasis on relationships is one of the great things about Christian communities, and you see this in non-Christian communities as well. You couldn't get through a spinal cord injury well on your own. You do see in hospitals, some lonely people and they have it the hardest. In the seven months I was in the hospital, my wife and family lived up at the hospital. My parents came and stayed in our house. The church and work people visited. I believe prayer, for example, is an expression of relationships. I was prayed for by people around the world and I think that's something really beautiful.

Matthew: What about now? You obviously have formed many new relationships. For example, you have carers in the home every day whom you have the opportunity to relate to. What's that been like?

Shane: Look, I'm not sure whether I'd quite relate that to PERMA's relationship. It's very functional in terms of carers. There is a certain fencing a lot of the time. I love my carers, don't get me wrong, but it's a job. I try to live in my own world while that's going on. But look, here is what's true:

disability often requires you to deal with dependency. We're often dealing with these different forms of gratification or engagement. Seligman and the virtue tradition say that to succeed in gratification and engagement, you need to exercise virtues or strengths.

If your character is dominated by vice, then you won't succeed either in engagement or relationships. So, if you're an angry bastard, for example, you'll drive people away, and you'll be lonely, and even your carers will find it more difficult to care for you. You do see this in the hospital, people who are just yelling at their nurses. The nurses put up with it but then when you get back to your home, if you treat carers that way, well, why would they come the next day? So, you'll have this constant turnover of staff. As a consequence, I've had to learn new virtues. I've had to learn to become a lot more patient. I was a forty-year-old, driven male. Patience is not something some career people really have in abundance. Whereas when you do live in the medical establishment and it takes you a couple of hours to get ready in the morning, you have to try and pick up these skills. These skills help you both in terms of flow and engagement but also in relationships as well.

Matthew: It certainly sounds like you would definitely say this is a critical part of human flourishing. Of course, Christian faith has been saying that forever. Seligman didn't think of that. You're a systematic theologian who undergoes this catastrophic accident. Has it exercised you? Do you see meaning differently now?

Shane: That's been one of the things that I've really wrestled with. When I was in the hospital, I spent time with my PhD supervisor, Neil Ormerod. He is a close friend. We wrote a book together before the injury. During my hospital stay, he visited me almost every week, and we often discussed the problem of pain and also that other critical question: "Where's God?" Both are questions I've thought and written about. The journal article I mentioned earlier was very important to me personally.[4] I spent a lot of time on it. I rewrote it about twenty times and eventually decided it's what I wanted it to be. So I really wrestled with meaning . . .

Matthew: Why the wrestle? Why did it need to be rewritten?

Shane: Well, because I kept reading something new, then I'd realize I'm not quite happy with part of the answer because it's just such a big question. The truth that I struggled with believing in was not only "Is God just?" I also spent a lot of time saying, "Well, I'm not sure I believe in God at all." An interesting challenge, for a theologian, isn't it? You go into the

---

4. Clifton, "Theodicy."

classroom and you teach the doctrine of the Trinity, and you think, "Well I can tell you about the doctrine of the Trinity but I'm not sure whether the Trinity exists." It's just a doctrine I can explain to you. So I wrestled and still do.

Matthew: Have you ever been *that* honest with your students?

Shane: Yes.

Matthew: I gather these questions became increasingly significant after the accident?

Shane: Much more acute. It's not just a theological game, is it? It's very real. The truth is, this far down the track, I'm mostly fairly comfortable with faith. I still experience a lot of doubt, I'm far less sure about the existence of God than I was before the injury, which is a weird thing for a theologian to say. But it worries me less than maybe it did a couple of years ago because I think faith actually isn't about certainty, that's science. Faith isn't the opposite of doubt, maybe faith is learning to be comfortable with your doubt, even trusting God when you're not always sure you believe in him. That's a sort of a weird irony.

Matthew: So finally A for accomplishment, achievement, that's a big one.

Shane: It's interesting. Seligman didn't have that in his original but to a certain degree, I don't really differentiate achievement from gratification and flow. I think achievement comes as an end product from gratification and flow. I'm not big on the achievement thing. Look it's nice to succeed in life. I don't want to be a failure, but I don't think it's as significant as the other factors.

Matthew: So for you we could probably leave it at PERM!

Shane: Yes, we probably could!

Matthew: I've also thought about PERVA. Changing M to a V for a vocation because it strikes me your sense of vocation seems to have strengthened dramatically through all these experiences. You've mentioned quite a few times that working with the disabled, developing policy, lecturing, and writing, that you're really clear about what you want to devote yourself to.

Shane: Yes. Now regarding vocation, Seligman includes that in gratification but it's a bridge, isn't it, between engagement and meaning because hopefully the thing you get gratification in, is driven by meaning, isn't it? Vocation's a great word for that, because it's about living, it's about working whether as a volunteer or paid for a call. I like that Christian word "call."

Matthew: That's right. Shane, a couple more questions on Positive Psychology. Do you ever wake up some days and just think "Negative Psychology," especially when your mornings are a struggle?

Shane: Look, I am not always upbeat of course. So I'm as up and down as anyone. More often than not, night times are harder than the mornings. I'm exhausted, I get a lot of pain so pain doesn't help. I know, however, there are people who have got a lot worse pain than me. I think there are some things that get me down so exhaustion and pain are probably when I'm no good. Sometimes, the hard times can be on holiday, so it can come at weird times but the down days are a lot less than they were a few years ago.

Matthew: Shane, in this book we're talking about theology encountering Positive Psychology and you've talked about how you don't think there's much original in that. It's made popular ideas Christianity has had in our tradition for over a thousand years, but we've got really slack at articulating it or perhaps we've taken it for granted. So two questions then. First, what's theology's biggest gift to Positive Psychology, and second, what do we bring to the table that they've missed, if anything?

Shane: Well, firstly I think we bring a rich tradition of thinking about both meaning and virtue and a belief or an understanding of vice. It's interesting Seligman spends all of his time on virtue and strength and doesn't talk about vice. I think that's weird. Back with Aristotle's, though Aquinas deals with it as well, understanding of virtue as the mean between vice of deficiency and vice of excess. For Aristotle and Aquinas, the virtue is the mean, the midpoint between. So, for example, the virtue of generosity is like the midpoint between the deficiency of generosity, which is stinginess, and the excess of generosity, which is profligacy, just giving it all away. Or patience, for example, the deficiency is impatience, but the excess would be apathy, never pushing for any change. So, I think Christianity gives a much richer understanding of virtue and vice and secondly also makes the claim that God can help change us.

Matthew: You said before that transformation is a reality, it's a renewal of body, soul, and mind.

Shane: It's interesting because we don't use the word "virtue" much in the Christian tradition. But it's all through it. The word we often use is "fruit of the spirit." So, the fruits of the spirit are virtues. So spirituality is about character and so, I think, Christianity brings this idea that God changes us and then the spirit can help develop the virtues in us and transform our character. I think that's pretty important because, in a sense, Positive

Psychology describes what occurs whereas Christianity, I think, is better able to provide ways of thinking, ways of transforming a person so they can develop and become happy.

Matthew: I'll give you my answer and then I'll give you a right of reply. I think one of the gifts of Positive Psychology to Christianity, particularly for Protestants, is challenging us to focus on wellbeing. Unfortunately, we've become too obsessed at times with sin and vice.

Shane: Yes. So, look I think, these notions of flourishing and wellbeing are a good reminder to us of what actually salvation is. If I was to define salvation now, I would talk in terms of flourishing. Salvation isn't going to heaven. What is it to be saved? It's to flourish. So all of these things we've actually been talking about; living a life of meaning, vocation, relationship. All these things are salvation, aren't they?

REFERENCES

Clifton, Shane. *Husbands Should Not Break: A Memoir about the Pursuit of Happiness Following Spinal Cord Injury.* Eugene: Resource, 2015.

————. "Theodicy, Disability, and Fragility: An Attempt to Find Meaning in the Aftermath of Quadriplegia." *Theological Studies* 76 (2015) 765–84.

Seligman, Martin E. P. "The New Era of Positive Psychology." *TED*. February 2004. Online: https://www.ted.com/talks/martin_seligman_on_the_state_of_psychology.

Chapter 12

"I Came that You may Have Life, and Have it Abundantly"

Drawing on the Resources of Faith to Help School Communities Flourish

LISA SPARGO

SCHOOLS MAKE SIGNIFICANT INVESTMENTS each year in designing and facilitating their pastoral care and personal development programs, with the quest for new and better resources central to this process. However, are we continually searching for something new while overlooking the resources already available to us? The introduction of Positive Psychology into many schools has provided us with a fresh vocabulary from which to speak about wellbeing, but contained within these new terms there is a reflection on humanity facing many of the same fundamental struggles of every generation. With this in mind, it is clear that religious tradition is able to speak into and complement Positive Psychology in faith-based schools. Chaplains continue to occupy a key role in nurturing personal development through their preaching of the faith both within and beyond the context of worship,

173

through their administration of sacred rites, and through their engagement with wider society as they seek to help their communities to flourish. Here, the emphasis is placed on the Christian school context, by way of example, but it is my hope that the discussion in each section will bring to mind for chaplains of all faiths the comparable theological concepts, scriptures, and rituals available to them from their own tradition.

SPIRITUALITY, WELLBEING, AND THE ROLE OF CHAPLAINS

Chaplains indeed have a key role to play in any wellbeing program a school may offer, not least because Seligman himself highlights the value of spirituality in his own writings on Positive Psychology.[1] A faith-based school will benefit greatly if they continue to see chaplains as key players in the area of student wellbeing, even if they also adopt Positive Psychology as a model for pastoral care. This is because spirituality, however it may be understood, is indeed an aspect of human life, and in order to flourish, our "whole" self needs to feel nurtured. I imagine Seligman would agree wholeheartedly with these sentiments expressed by John Cox:

> If human beings are spiritual as well as physical, emotional, moral, social and intellectual then it is part of what makes up a "whole" person and should be included in their education. At its simplest the spiritual includes a sense of otherness beyond the immediate and physical: an other that not only exists but can in some way be related to. It includes the wonder and creativity, or awe and excitement, working more often through the imagination and intuition than through the rational. It enhances experience through what is perceived as the transcendent. Spirituality is an appreciation and cherishing of what is good, joyful, truthful and beautiful, and, in relationship with others, of what is generous, creative, loving. The spirit of a person is seen in acts of courage and perseverance, in dealing with both setbacks and praise, in endeavor and enquiry. The human spirit, no less than the physical body, has needs that must be met if it is to be healthy and develop. At root there is the need to be loved and to love, to feel warmth and appreciation, to have opportunities for giving as well as receiving, to have a sense of belonging. The spirit will not flourish if it does not have the

---

1. In a number of his publications, Seligman lists Spirituality (or Transcendence) as one of the six virtues that underpin the twenty-four character strengths.

opportunity to be stimulated and express itself—be it through art, through writing, through music, through dance, or through physical activity.[2]

To my mind, there is a striking parallel here between the goals of Positive Psychology and the ministry of chaplains, and for this reason both may find their work enriched and enhanced when they are afforded the opportunity to work collaboratively rather than distinctively. The language Seligman gives to aspects of wellbeing carries a clear resonance with Christian theology, and indeed, the theology of many different faith traditions. When we allow them to speak together, in similar but different words, we hear very clearly that, while much has changed in our society, many of the underlying human struggles remain the same. Faith-based schools that adopt the Positive Education program for their pastoral care will find it greatly enriched if they continue to look to the chaplain for guidance and input.

In exploring how chaplains may interact with Positive Education I have focused here on the five aspects of Seligman's PERMA model of wellbeing, namely: positive emotions, engagement, relationships, meaning, and achievement. In all five aspects of the PERMA model chaplains have much to offer a school from the theological vocabulary, the Scriptures, and the sacred rituals and traditions of the Christian Church. I will also highlight some of the key character strengths,[3] which I believe fit within each aspect and which have a significant crossover with theology.

1–POSITIVE EMOTIONS

The first area Seligman names as significant for wellbeing is *positive emotions*, referring to "hedonic feelings of happiness."[4] Many of the character strengths named by Seligman connect with multiple areas of PERMA, but perhaps those with closest association to positive emotions are forgiveness, gratitude, hope, humor, prudence, and self-regulation.

The resonances here with Christian Theology are quite striking and indeed our scriptures provide us with a wealth of resources for speaking about human emotion along the full spectrum. These resources include

---

2. Cox, *More than Caring*, 110–11.

3. Park et al., "Strengths of Character."

4. Kern et al., "Multidimensional Approach," 2.

concepts such as faith, hope, and love; fruits of the spirit/gifts of the spirit; thanksgiving; confession; forgiveness; peace; hope and fear; and grace.

This list is by no means exhaustive, but it highlights the fact that much has been written, both in the Bible and in the broader realm of Christian theological thought, on this subject of human emotion. At the very heart of the Christian faith is the story of the Incarnation; the story of God dwelling among us, living human life, and experiencing the range of human emotions we all face in response to the joys and sorrows we experience. Christian theology, and therefore our preaching and teaching of the faith, will often find its focus here, for in seeking to know and understand God we return again and again to the mysterious truth that God knows us and what it is that we experience in human life. When a traumatic event occurs within the school community, chaplains may draw on the scriptures to teach about the sanctity of human life; of the pain of loss; of God's unending love, care, and protection; of the importance of healthy grieving; and, most importantly, of the hope we hold. Chaplains are called upon to address moments of sadness, grief, and distress, but their role in nurturing wellbeing in a school community stretches far wider than this. When they speak of the Prodigal Son making the journey home, for instance, they teach vital lessons on the importance of confession and forgiveness in our life, and of the freedom which comes to us in showing grace to others.

Not all teaching comes through words; very often, ritual and symbolism are the most powerful tools available for nurturing positive emotional health and wellbeing. The very nature and shape of the funeral rite allows for the remembrance and honoring of the deceased, feeling the pain of loss, supporting one another and, finally, commending the deceased into God's safe-keeping. Funerals are not by nature joyful or cheerful events, but where faith, hope, and love can be experienced they may be deeply healing experiences that enable those who mourn to continue living their lives fully.

In a similar vein, the sacrament of penance or confession holds something of a negative connotation, despite the wonderfully positive impact it may have on someone's life from that time forward. For this reason, I rather prefer the contemporary terminology of reconciliation for this sacrament, for it focuses our attention more keenly on the desired outcome and not simply on our sins. It has not been my experience to date that many have felt the need to confess to me their sins and seek forgiveness, however I have found this is one theme I return to, time and again, in my preaching. In part, I mention the importance of confession and forgiveness because it leads us into reconciliation with God and with one's neighbor, and in part it is because the impact of guilt and shame on mental health cannot be over stated. In order to flourish we must not be held back by our past sins. The rite of reconciliation may be one way that chaplains help individuals to be free of their past and live into their future. Ash Wednesday and Lenten rituals also offer similar opportunities for refocusing our lives.

As a key sacrament of the Christian church, chaplains can offer the Eucharist as an opportunity to encourage a culture of Thanksgiving in their community. Thanksgiving and gratitude are the antithesis of despair and discontent, and necessarily add to the building of positive emotional health. Of course, the Eucharist is not the only way to build such a culture. I have seen a group of Year Three classroom teachers successfully do this through the implementation of gratitude journals for their students. Each day, these students would spend time recording at least three things they were thankful for, and while some days may have proved more of a struggle, nevertheless these students learnt to look for things to be thankful for each day. Such simple, yet profound, rituals can have a tremendous impact upon the emotional health of a school community.

2–ENGAGEMENT

Seligman's second area of focus in the PERMA model is *engagement*, which may be understood as "psychological connection to activities or organizations."[5] In close association with engagement are the character strengths of awe, curiosity, and judgment.

Chaplains are well able to contribute to this area of student wellbeing for they bring a wealth of knowledge of both the importance of engagement and also of disciplines that can foster such a way of living. Through their liturgy chaplains endeavor always to allow the "still small voice of God" to be heard amongst the noise of the world, so that the divine may seem close at hand rather than distant and aloof. Key themes to be found in the Bible and Christian theology that encourage us to live with purpose and depth of engagement include: liturgy, prayer, and worship; contemplation; transcendence; sacredness; divinity; retreat; and Sabbath.

Traditional and contemporary Christian rituals have a role to play in nurturing Engagement. Prayer and worship may take on an infinite variety of shapes, but always at the heart is the full engagement of those present,

5. Ibid.

for liturgy is indeed the work of the people and necessarily requires active and full participation. Sometimes it will be making a change that allows for greater engagement, but at other times the familiarity of words and actions may better allow worshippers to become fully absorbed in the experience. Music, drama, and dance can also add richness to any liturgy and draw worshippers towards a recognition of divine presence and transcendence that dramatically increases their perspective in all areas of life.

Sybil MacBeth in her book, *Praying in Color*, explores ways of prayer that primarily involve drawing and coloring, but does not exclude the use of words, be they spoken or written. As she notes:

> Praying in Color is a way to pray with your eyes, your ears and your hands. It invites your mind, your heart, and your body into the prayer. You can use words or you can be quiet. What matters is that you want to be closer to God.[6]

Praying in Color creates a space wherein participants may be fully engaged in the art of prayer and meditation, and are enabled to more deeply reflect on their lives and those things that are important to them. In a similar way, Sr. Anthony MacDonald, in her book, *To God on a Magic Carpet*, identifies that children are able to more fully engage when their contemplative nature is given freedom to emerge:

> For many years I have been praying with children using the traditional prayers we all know and love, such as the "Our Father" and "Hail Mary." But . . . in today's world children are bombarded with noise from all sides. They have little opportunity to find a place of quiet to sit and think. Yet children are natural contemplatives. One need only to think of a child's openness to awe and wonder: their delight in creation as they observe a starlit night, wildflowers, and birds singing.[7]

Anyone who has spent time with young children will attest to the truth in this. Meditation and contemplative exercises exist in all faith traditions, with many similarities to be found among them as well as unique characteristics in each. Christian meditation may involve the use of icons or other items as a visual focus, or a passage of scripture that may be read over slowly and repetitively. Lectio Divina, or divine reading, is another a way of prayerfully approaching the scriptures so that we might hear what

---

6. MacBeth, *Praying in Colour*, 38.

7. Macdonald, *To God on a Magic Carpet*, 1.

God is saying to us in our life at that time. Chaplains may incorporate such practices into their pattern of worship, or through the offering of a meditation space in the school. The offering of retreats also opens up a space for people to take time away from the busyness of life. Schools that teach Religious Education using Peter Vardy's "Five Strands Approach" also have an opportunity to introduce contemplative practices through the affective strand, which encourages stillness.

> The affective approach seeks to redress the imbalance when education solely stresses the cognitive. In the 1970s, some Philosophers of Education stressed the idea of 'Rational Autonomy' as an educational aim, but emphasis on this alone can develop the rational side of human nature at the expense of the emotional and affective, closing people off to religious possibilities . . . . This can give an alternative perspective to materialism and help students to gain inner confidence and to recognize the value of silence, gentleness, compassion, concern for others, and personal responsibility, as well as achievement, success, recognition, and reputation. Many young Australians' lives are filled with noise (CD player, video, television, computer game, and so forth) making the ability to be still more important than ever. Through this, they may come to know themselves and to find peace an increasingly valuable part of their lives . . . . Life for both adults and children is increasingly frenetic. There is a tendency to want to "keep children busy" as this avoids them getting into mischief. "The devil makes work for idle hands to do" may be implicit in many teachers' thinking. However, a central dimension of religion is that it affects an individual's subjectivity and that time is needed for silence and reflection.[8]

From other faith traditions we can learn many techniques for fostering stillness beyond those commonly seen in the Christian tradition. The growing popularity of coloring books for adults reveals a need for greater stillness in society generally, and not least within our schools. The simple act of coloring in focuses and quietens our mind and is a slow, meditative task not dissimilar to the practice of making of sand mandalas in Buddhism. This is one practice I have introduced with some of my students over the past year and they have enjoyed the opportunity to relax and unwind at the end of some religious studies lessons. It hasn't been a silent activity, for that is too much to ask many twelve and thirteen-year-old boys, but it has been a quiet activity. There have even been times when this space has

---

8. Dialogue AustralasiaNetwork, "Five Strands."

opened up deeply philosophical, theological, and ethical conversations that may otherwise not have found their voice among the busyness of our curriculum. Most importantly, though, it has afforded them an opportunity to stop, to unwind, to be still and to refocus—and all of this, I hope, recharges their batteries and enables them to engage more fully in whatever the rest of their day holds.

3-RELATIONSHIPS

The third area focuses our attention on the positive *relationships* that lead us to feel "socially integrated, cared about and supported by others, and satisfied with one's social connections."[9] Seligman's character strengths of citizenship, love, humility, and social intelligence connect closely with this area, and indeed with numerous aspects of Christian theology that speak of relationships and their importance in human life. Important aspects include: people of God; the Body of Christ; ecclesiology; humility; respect; love; community; Eucharist; and Trinity.

As I reflect on the relational side of Christian faith, I am reminded of the stories of John the Baptist—especially that of Jesus' own baptism—but also of other recorded baptismal events, such as that of the Ethiopian Eunuch. I can also picture Jesus welcoming the little children and sternly warning anyone who would turn them away. As indeed St. Paul writes, the Church is one body made up of many parts, each unique and gifted in a different way. With these and other scriptures guiding them, chaplains are called upon to set an example of open, gracious, and unconditional hospitality to all whom they encounter, and thereby instill such values in others. They are pivotal in establishing such a culture within a school community, and where such a culture exists it is more likely that each individual will have a healthy sense of their own value.

With relationship a central aspect of Christian theology, it is perhaps not surprising that an array of rituals have developed which enhance this sense of community among members. Andrei Rublev's icon "The Hospitality of Abraham" has long been viewed as a symbolic representation of the triune God and therefore is known commonly as "The Trinity." Clear to many are the Eucharistic elements in this icon, which serves to remind us of the "unifying" nature of the Holy Communion, which draws us together with God but also with each other. Baptism and Confirmation, likewise,

9. Kern et al., "Multidimensional Approach," 2.

provide for sacramental experiences of community where individuals may come to know themselves welcomed into relationship with God and with the whole Body of Christ. Within the life of a school community there are regular cycles of welcome and departure, and each of these are opportunities re-invigorate the sense of community among all members, whether they be students, parents, staff or ex-students.

Chaplains are often called upon to speak meaningful words into a time of transition or change, or to perform some kind of ritual action. Some occasions call for use of traditional words and actions, but other times they call for tremendous creativity as we encounter scenarios for which no prescribed liturgy has yet been crafted. Traci Smith,[10] in her book, *Seamless Faith*, offers a wide range of rituals and new traditions, many of which focus on the relationships which sustain us and bring life to us—welcoming a new baby, beginning school, graduation, and moving out of home. Ceremonies are also included for the occasion of a pet's death. What is common in all of these is the care and nurture of those involved and affected most deeply. Perhaps the most profound role the chaplain has in these times, however, is creating the space for gathering, for often the words and actions themselves are second to the greatest ritual of all—the coming together of the community. Even if nothing else were said or done, this gathering together in a moment of joy or sadness has a kind of sacramental nature.

4–MEANING

Seligman's fourth area in the PERMA model is *meaning*, referring to "believing that one's life is valuable and feeling connected to something greater than oneself."[11] Tied into this sense of meaning are the character strengths of creativity, perspective, integrity, spirituality, vitality, and fairness. This is perhaps the greatest area where chaplains can have significant input, not simply because of the reference to the spiritual life, but because of the core values seen within Christianity and the fundamental value placed on each individual's life and being.

Each and every day, chaplains seek to help their school community, and the individual member therein, to recognize, value, and celebrate their life and existence. When a sense of purpose or meaning is lost, chaplains draw on the richness of Christian theology to help them remember and

10. Smith, *Seamless Faith*.

11. Kern et al., "Multidimensional Approach," 2.

see again what was always there. This is perhaps the most crucial area for enabling one to flourish, for without a clear sense of meaning in their life they cannot experience positive emotional health, feel engaged in what they are doing, build relationships that enhance their life, or feel any sense of achievement. Some key ideas from the vocabulary of Christian theology that concern meaning include: vocation; discernment; sanctity of life; service; justice; compassion; mercy; and faith.

The scriptures abound with wisdom and sentiment on the meaning, value and purpose of life, generally and specifically. From the psalmist we are reminded that we are all knit in the womb by God and created perfectly and unique. Jesus expands on this by reminding his followers that their lives hold even greater value than that of the plants or the birds, and if God provides all that they need to be sustained, how much less should we worry ourselves about our own most basic needs. Many of the Commandments also remind us of the sanctity of human life.

Chaplains can encourage students to see the meaning of their own lives and to begin to discern their own unique vocations. Scripture passages including Samuel's call and Jesus calling the disciples can provide a space for students to reflect upon and discuss their sense of giftedness, their dreams, and their identity. With this may come anxieties, uncertainties or feelings of inadequacy. Inspiration may be drawn from Jonah, who didn't particularly like the idea of following God's call to go to Nineveh, or from David, who was an unlikely choice of king by the world's standard. These characters offer a refreshing "humanness" to what can too easily be presumed a spiritual exercise devoid of these human responses. We think of Mary, who, at first glance, seems to accept the strangest of messages from an angel with hardly a quiver of doubt or confusion. In truth, vocational discernment is rarely a simple and smooth path, and chaplains play a crucial role in guiding and supporting students along the way. From the viewpoint of vocation as growing into the person one is called and created to be, chaplains can also remind students that careers are but one part of their life, albeit an important one. While the focus of schooling is so often placed on future study or employment goals, chaplains may help to broaden student's perspectives so that they may look to the future with a clear sense of who they are and the values which will shape their whole life, not just their choice of career.

Values such as service, justice, compassion, and mercy can be encouraged in students through chapel and religious education classes, but they cannot begin to shape their lives in isolation from real-world experience and application. Chaplains are often the instigators and encouragers of social justice initiatives within the school community, though of course not without the help and assistance of many others. Chaplains remind the community of the needs of others and provide a myriad of ways to allow students an experience of life outside of their familiar world. Whether this be locally or internationally, any opportunity for students to become aware of the struggles faced by others broadens their perspective, and can have a profound impact upon them. They may feel an increasing sense of gratitude for all that they enjoy in life, and from this place of gratitude a desire to make a difference in the lives of others.

Finally, this spirit of service can also be fostered within the school community. Traditional Lavabo services can be used in many ways in a school context, beyond that of Maundy Thursday. At Guildford Grammar School, the Headmaster has incorporated the washing of the prefects' feet into their Induction Service at the start of each year. The powerful symbolism in this act reminds the students that all are called to serve one another, not least those who hold positions of power and authority.

5-ACCOMPLISHMENT

Seligman's final area in the PERMA model is *accomplishment*, meaning "making progress toward goals, feeling capable to do daily activities, and having a sense of achievement."[12] Connected with achievement are the character strengths of bravery, leadership, love of learning, and persistence.

To experience a sense of accomplishment, I believe we must first have a clear sense of meaning and purpose in our life. Without this, we won't be able to set goals or live our life with any sense of direction, and without goals or direction there will be no markers along our way to suggest progress, growth or change. Christian theology has much to say about the meaning in our lives and one idea with crossover to accomplishment is vocation. Where discernment of our vocation feeds into our sense of meaning and purpose, perhaps our greatest sense of accomplishment in life will come with living into that vocation. Other key ideas from Christian theology that connect with the area of accomplishment are as follows: vocation—lived into; courage; pilgrimage; journey; discipleship; Sabbath; ordination; and marriage.

12. Ibid.

The Bible provides us with many examples of people who have persevered and achieved their goals, despite all kinds of adversity. The story of the Exodus and the journey towards the promised land is a formative narrative in the Jewish and Christian community's sense of identity, and, being filled with raw human emotion, it is a story that can resonate with students today. Like the Israelites, our students can find themselves exhausted by the seemingly unending journey towards their goals. Challenges can also make students want to return to their comfort zone rather than striving for something new. Taking the voice of Ecclesiastes, chaplains can help students to learn that there is indeed a time for everything, including a time for failure and disappointment, just as there is for success. Embracing and accepting this reality will also foster healthy positive emotions and will thereby ensure that their sense of meaning is not shaken by any apparent failure. Chaplains can help their students to see that the journey itself is equally as important as the goal they are seeking. Were it not for their wanderings in the desert, the Israelite community would not have fully appreciated the promised land when they arrived.

Moses also sets a striking example for students to be team players and contributors to the greater good, even if they can't be the ones to completely solve an issue on their own. While he led the Israelites out of Egypt, and persevered for many years in the desert, Moses never reached the promised land. He never enjoyed what God promised to the people, but if it were not for his leadership and perseverance, perhaps the Israelites would still be enslaved in Egypt. Through their encouragement to join in service activities, chaplains can help students to be outwardly focused and courageous enough to make even small differences, in the knowledge that every individual effort contributes to the overall solution.

Using rituals and traditions, chaplains can help schools to mark the accomplishments made by individual members and groups. Beginnings and endings are milestones along life's journey and these can be marked in various ways. Commissioning services for new staff can affirm their vocation as teachers and ancillary staff, as well as their call to serve in a particular place. The American tradition of the "blessing of the backpacks" can be an equally meaningful ritual for students and their families as they begin school. These beginnings are accomplishments just as much as any ending. Graduations, resignations, and retirements also call for sincere acknowledgement, as they are profound markers of the accomplishment that has come with change and growth.

Beginnings and ending are extremes on the accomplishment spectrum though, and it is the middle part that is something akin to the Israelites forty years of desert wanderings. In this space, the labyrinth can be a powerful symbol of journey, perseverance, patience, and striving. The labyrinth can also help schools to slow down, become focused, and act intentionally. Alongside this, the importance of retreat and Sabbath cannot be emphasized strongly enough. Schools are busy places, with calendars filled to capacity and students and staff alike under tremendous pressure. While everyone is setting goals and working furiously towards them, chaplains who keep at the forefront of their minds the need for rest, can breathe life and peace into their school community. Retreat programs can also provide much needed time away from the worries of school life and help all members of the community to refocus their priorities on the most important concerns. Interestingly, many schools do adopt the name "retreat" for many and various gatherings, when in fact these are often anything but a time for rest. Schools are indeed busy places but amongst this busyness we all "need a time and place to just rest and be."[13] Chaplains can open up such spaces, but perhaps one of the most significant things chaplains can do is value "Sabbath" times in their own life and be a model to others.

FINAL THOUGHTS

Positive Psychology offers a new way for schools to consider how their pastoral care of students may be delivered, with the aim of guiding all students to flourish. No one could argue against the significance and value of this. For faith-based schools adopting this program, however, it is important to acknowledge and celebrate the work already done in the school, not least by chaplains, who from the framework of faith are working towards achieving the same goal. Positive Psychology and chaplaincy need not been seen as unrelated, and certainly not as opponents, but rather as allies in the work of student pastoral care. As Jesus said, he came into the world that we may know and experience life abundantly and fully (John 10:10)—in other words, that we might flourish. I imagine Seligman and other proponents of Positive Psychology would find a resonance between these words of Jesus and their own mission.

13. Nye, "Spirituality," 69.

REFERENCES

Cox, John. *More than Caring and Sharing: Making a Church School Distinctive*. Buxhall: Kevin Mayhew, 2011.

Dialogue Australasia Network. "Five Strands: Becoming Fully Human—The Five Strands Approach to Religious and Values Education."

Kern, Margaret L., et al. "A Multidimensional Approach to Measuring Well-being in Students: Application of the PERMA Framework." *The Journal of Positive Psychology* 10 (2014) 262–71.

MacBeth, Sybil. *Praying in Color*. Kids' ed. Brewster: Paraclete, 2010.

Macdonald, Sr. Anthony. *To God on a Magic Carpet: Meditating with Children*. Richmond: Spectrum, 2008.

Park, Nansook et al. "Strengths of Character and Well-being." *Journal of Social and Clinical Psychology* 23 (2004) 603–19.

Nye, Rebecca. "Spirituality." In *Through the Eyes of a Child: New Insights in Theology from a Child's Perspective*, edited by Anne Richards et al., 68–84. London: Church House, 2009.

Smith, Traci. *Seamless Faith: Simple Practices for Daily Family Life*. St. Louis: Chalice, 2014.

Chapter 13

Character Strengths and Christian Wisdom

JAMES NELSON

INTRODUCTION

CHARACTER STRENGTHS OFFER GREAT insight into human values, authenticity, wellbeing, and engagement. These strengths (*Values in Action*) and their overarching *virtues* may also offer a hermeneutic for studying the Bible. This essay will explore a practical model for applying this principle in schools, showing those parts that enable Christians and non-Christians a common language for humanity, love, engagement, and wellbeing, and a common text within which to build pedagogy, culture, and community. This positions the Bible as an excellent reference point for paragons of these human values and a relevant teaching point for human flourishing.

WHY TEACH CHARACTER STRENGTHS AND VALUES IN SCHOOL?

Central to our missions and ministry in Lutheran schools we seek to nurture individuals who are aware of their humanity, and are open to the influence of the Holy Spirit and the possibility of growing in and living according to a cohesive worldview. This can be nurtured in our communities, which reflect characteristics of God through core values, especially *love, justice, compassion, forgiveness, service, humanity, courage, hope, quality, and appreciation*. We believe in the Bible as authority for Christian faith and the Holy Spirit as the vital life energy of each person as source of *wisdom* and *courage* for their lives.

Christian Wisdom and Character Strengths

To read Torah is to read *wisdom* and the limits of wisdom found in early people of God. Old Testament narratives are of *courage* before overwhelming odds, because they served the Lord of Hosts. Their doctrines of *humanity* and *justice* shaped ancient history because their God was just. Later in the prophets, there are warnings for *humility* and *temperance*, as they were obedient to the God, who brought them out of Egypt and will be faithful to lead from Babylon. These same prophets spoke of *transcendence* and redemption by the power and grace of Jehovah. With this brief overview it is possible to imagine the development of a rich curriculum for teaching Positive Psychology (beginning with character strengths) and teaching Christian theology.

HOW TO TEACH CHARACTER STRENGTHS AND VALUES

Virtues are those universal, core characteristics valued by moral philosophers and religious thinkers. Strengths are the psychological ingredients of specific routes through which virtues are displayed as persons take action towards these virtues. Peterson and Seligman (2004) emphasize that the learning of character strengths fits well with a study of role models, or paragons, such that we have a vision of how people have put these strengths into action, and reference points for people to learn from, apply, and then reflect on. As a Christian teacher, it seems that there is a responsibility to revere the Bible and understand the role-modeling of values that occurs in sacred scripture. As a Christian teacher, there is ample opportunity to use the faithful, God-fearing and persevering Biblical characters, as well as more recent Christian characters. This provides insight into humanity in relationship to God, sustained in the struggle and journey through life. As a Christian teacher, there is always the exciting prospect of speaking of sacred scripture, its broad narratives and its specific features relating God to humanity, in a way that engages and challenges a wide range of thinkers. Creating a range of experiences, reflections and connections to these characters which are exposed in chapel each week, positions students amidst a developing and engaging curriculum of pastoral care, values in action, and Christian wisdom.

Our School's Experience

The job of interpreting Bible characters and stories for an audience comes with great responsibility to preach Christ alone (1 Cor 1:12, 17) and so there is serious caution about simply attempting to find scriptures to fit only certain positive psychological presentations, or to "sanctify a humanistic doctrine." But the personal challenge is that character strengths simply offered an opportunity to delve deeper into biblical characters with a new sense of adventure and ultimate reverence for God. Character strengths offered a common language that people of different ages, worldviews, and demographics could engage with, and that teachers with different epistemological views on scripture or ontological views on our students and our adult population might still have in common. Values in Action became a mantra that our college was already applying to service programs, leadership development, visible culture enhancement and community engagement, so that when it was introduced into Christian Studies, outdoor education, and chapels, there was a synergizing effect. Values in Action and character strengths offered a small set of terms and focus areas that could act as headings that provided synergy for our educative practices. This coalescing of ideas has helped teachers wrestling with "change fatigue" and the range of extracurricular programs, to find some sense of solidarity in our approach to pedagogy, care, reporting, and cultural development. It has been a powerful tool for many in the college and has helped to promote staff and student wellbeing.

A PRACTICAL GUIDE

The following sections outline a practical model for presenting a reasonable Christian curriculum through chapels over the course of a year. The term-based schedule uses the six *virtues* and twenty-four *character strengths* as themes and is repeated and developed annually. The rest of this essay is essentially an overview of how this is accomplished, with a few practical examples of links to curriculum and sample discussions with pastoral care teachers. Hopefully it will show how it can be developed in dialogue with teachers and how it engages students in reflections and conversations about their learnings. Those parts that are in first person represent dialogue between teachers.

Term 1

Focus: Wisdom: creativity, curiosity, open-mindedness, love of learning, perspective. Courage: bravery, persistence, integrity, vitality

The virtue of wisdom relates more to cognitive strengths (creativity, curiosity, open-mindedness, love of learning, and perspective), while courage relates to emotional strengths (bravery, persistence, integrity, and vitality).[1] Many philosophers consider wisdom to be the core virtue and Christian theology aligns with this. Socrates alludes to humility and open-mindedness as the beginning of wisdom, and, according to the author of Proverbs, wisdom begins with a fear of God. "Fear" as expressed in this context means "awe and wonderment," an experience we may experience with great music, incredible sunrises, and accepting the sense of unconditional love and acceptance of Christ. "The beginning of wisdom as knowing that you know nothing" fits with an openness to "fear and wonderment as the beginning of wisdom" in the Judeo-Christian tradition. As we build a learning culture, and as we encourage and celebrate actions that move teachers and students towards wisdom, love of learning, curiosity, and integrity, we are doing something vital and life-giving.

Early Term 1 presentations will orient the community towards the characters and narratives of Joseph and Moses in the Old Testament, who offer us insight into *wisdom* and *courage*. As we move into Lent, Jesus' *wisdom* and *courage* will be exemplified for us as we consider the importance of Christ in history and Christ in relationship. Most obvious to me is the

---

1 Niemiec and Wedding, *Positive Psychology at the Movies.*

courage (*bravery, integrity, vitality,* and *persistence*) of some Old Testament characters, but different presenters may find *wisdom* to be more evident in their prayer, study and preparation for chapels, and be inspired by Heb 12:1 to draw upon these characters and their witness. *Persistence* is a *Habit of Mind* in focus this term, also a strength we can all develop. The Bible speaks to how we can experience and have perspective on this in Rom 5:3–5, ". . . we can rejoice in our sufferings, knowing that suffering produces endurance, endurance produces character and character produces hope." The experiences of Joseph, Moses, and Jesus are identified in chapels this term and will add some narrative and meaning to this essential experience and faith in action.

An Example—Home Group Exercise

Courage: "The exercise of will to accomplish goals in the face of opposition, either external or internal." Describe a time you acted courageously. Why was it courageous? What were you thinking and feeling? Describe what led up to the action, the action itself, and the outcome of your action.

Directions: To introduce the concept of courage and explore its various forms and definitions, allow students five minutes to write on scrap paper, then answers may be traded with other students who may read them out loud. *Do not* put your name on the paper. When finished, trade papers twice to preserve anonymity. Most commonly this triggers thoughts around stepping outside of comfort zones, trying something new, standing up for others, taking responsibility in a negative situation.

Discussion: Describe "physical, moral, and psychological" and mark on whiteboard. Have students classify the statements into these headings. Ask students to find common features in each story; "willing/intentional, noble/worthy goal, risk/difficulty."

Term 2

Focus: Humanity: love, kindness, social intelligence. Justice: teamwork, fairness, leadership

The virtue of humanity consists of the interpersonal strengths of *love, kindness,* and *social intelligence.* Peterson and Seligman[2] distinguish these

---

2. Peterson and Seligman, *Character Strengths.*

from the *justice* strengths in that the humanity strengths are one-to-one and interpersonal, while the justice strengths are one-to-many and broadly social. The humanity strengths involve relationship building, particularly the tending and befriending of others. *Justice* is a broad virtue that involves three character strengths: *citizenship, fairness,* and *leadership.* This virtue encapsulates the concept of interaction between an individual and society. Care includes the domain of justice, but goes beyond this to include compassion, empathy, and understanding. Researchers find that women are more likely to use *care* reasoning and men are much more likely to use *justice* reasoning.

Chapels pick up on aspects of these themes. As Term 2 chapels will cover a sort of "church history" curriculum, you may notice that all the examples of people who are making a difference to *humanity* and fighting for *justice*, are inspired by the work of Christ and enabled by the Holy Spirit. What will hopefully come through is the passion of the Holy Spirit behind the loving actions for humanity. Martin Luther King may have made a famous speech about a dream where all were created equal, but the social change was inspired by his reading of John 1. John Bunyan writes in this context, yet his story inspires Christians and others feeling persecuted to persevere and fight the good fight across cultures and for the love of what is right and good. These messages may well be powerful in the minds of our students as they respond to the human needs or justice issues they will confront in life. There are numerous connections to our curriculums that should also be explored.

Head, Heart, and Hands is a metaphor within our strategic documentation; it is the focus of our school's mission and Lutheran Education Australia's (LEA) vision statement. What does it mean for you? As a Health and Physical Education teacher, as a Head of Department, as a math teacher, as a mentor or coach? Consider how reflecting upon the service of missionaries, evangelists, and reformers in church history (which will come through in chapels this term) might help link the ideas of faith, values, and passions guiding people to live out lives of service and vocation—the link between heart (faith, emotions, intuition) and head (conviction, pragmatism, reason) and hands (service, leadership, teamwork). Reinforce that the ideals, scriptures, and messages of chapel should not just remain in our memory, but lead us to feel strongly about issues, which might then lead to actions of love in our world. Consider that we should begin with small actions of love and justice, and develop habits, strengths, and characteristics that enable us to continue to love others, serve, lead, work in teams, and seek justice in our different areas of life. Also, note how great things have been achieved, how often great sacrifice is required, that justice is worth pursuing despite the peer pressure against such a cause, and that truth and love for humanity is more worthwhile than selfish gain.

Example of How Movies Can be Used to Teach Humanity and Justice

Love, kindness, and social intelligence are all key themes in movies and you may find a range of inspirations from film this term as stimulus for pastoral care, broadening and deepening your understanding of human nature. You may describe or show clips from *Amelie* (2001) to discuss *kindness*; or Helen Hunt's character in *As Good As It Gets* (1997) showing *compassion*; *Charlie and the Chocolate Factory* (1971/2003) for Charlie's *compassion, kindness,* and *altruism. Pay it Forward* (2000) is used in the Christian Studies curriculum, so many students are able to reflect on the *altruism* displayed in this film. From twentieth-century thinkers, you may draw upon C. S. Lewis and his discussion of four loves; E. Fromm's postulation that *care, responsibility, respect,* and *knowledge* are basic elements essential in all types of love; and of course scripture, such as "Greater love has no man, that he would lay down his life for his friends" (John 15:13).[3]

    Citizenship is exemplified in *Hotel Rwanda* (2004), where the lead character explains his actions as "obligation to help one's neighbor." *Coach Carter* (2006), *Remember the Titans* (2000), *We are Marshall* (2006), *Rudy* (1993), and *Cool Runnings* (1993) offer a sporting perspective to illustrate individual and team challenges, and show growth and liberty through persevering with *team work* towards valued community goals.[4]

Example of Chapel Reflections in Class

C. S. Lewis's novels speak of the tremendous value of knowing what is valuable to ensure you persevere in life's journey and adventure. In his *Narnia* series we might be encouraged as children (or as adults) to fight against what is wrong in our world and hope for newness and renewed ideals amongst humanity. In his science fiction we might see how humans are

---

3. Niemiec and Wedding, *Positive Psychology at the Movies.*
4. Ibid.

designed with a spark of the divine. In his theology he challenges us to discover love, not in romantic or self-serving ways, but in God's unconditional "agape" acceptance of us. This love experience brings a peace that passes all understanding, is a power source that will light our ways in the darkest of experiences, will warm us when we are cold and brittle. Bunyan's "pilgrim" may also remain in your memory as a powerful analogy to keep you persevering on the journey when there are distractions, side tracks, and people who want to drag you away from the path you are called upon, to make a positive and healing difference in others' lives.

Examples of "Easy Chats" Discussion Starters

- *Describe* to the class the most loving person you know. *Explain* how they express their love for humanity.

- *Describe* the most upright and just person you know. *Explain* how they show unwavering support for the virtue of justice.

- Make a *judgment* regarding which of these two virtues has had the most significant bearing on the shaping of your life until now. *Reflect* on how you will cherish this experience and how will you take committed action to pursue it further.

- *Service*: Are you inspired to serve in your community when you are adult?

- *Action*: What skills or what values will you take with you that might help people in need?

Example of Link to Curriculum

In English, the Year Tens are studying a Voices of War unit this term. The unit doesn't focus as much on the factual military, political, and historical approach to war as it does on the often-overlooked voices of war, the stories and poetry of people who have been connected to war, whether they be frontline soldiers, parents of soldiers, leaders, or innocent victims caught up in the conflict. In amongst the texts, we will discuss how, despite the violence confronting people in war, virtues of *forgiveness* and *compassion* have often rung through, and how many people's actions during war were driven by what they believed was *right* (e.g., fighting Hitler's regime because they believed that what he was doing to *humanity* was wrong—the pursuit of *justice*). We will also examine anti-war texts and discuss how writers have expressed their attitudes regarding the injustices often associated with war, the reasons they carried such opinions, and references to the ulterior motives many people believe have shadowed the actions of nations. The goal of the unit is to expose students to many perspectives of war, not just the popular ones, the western ones, the "allied" perspective, and students will contrast the "voices" heard throughout the unit.

As far as characters showing *love* and *courage* go, there will be strong correlations drawn to the various stories we examine (e.g., amongst the texts, we will watch the film *Life is Beautiful* and we will read some of Anne Frank's diary entries). Encourage students to reflect on their emotional reactions to the stories and characters, have them notice and discuss how these emotional reactions affect motivation to learn more and engage with historical characters in English.

Term 3

Focus: Temperance: forgiveness/mercy, prudence, self-regulation, modesty/humility

The virtue of *temperance* is developed with action relating to *forgiveness, humility, prudence,* and *self-regulation.* These pro-social changes in our motivation shape our character towards strength and love. Empathy for others facilitates forgiveness and this requires great strength and *bravery*; for some of us this comes through experience of being forgiven by Christ. When we forgive we are no longer held captive by the affect associated with imagery of the offensive act or fantasies of retaliation.

Example of the Theme of Temperance in a Chapel Service Outline

Chapels pick up on aspects of these themes. Term 3 chapels will savor some of the lasting values from Paul's letters in the New Testament. After Christ's resurrection and ascension, a rapid movement between people of faith transpired. As faith communities grew, there was a need to help make sense of faith in light of Christ's revelation. Then, and as is the case today, Paul's letters helped shape our understanding of the deep mystery of living as spiritual and physical beings. The messages of *temperance* help shape our living and our faith so as not to remain like impulsive children in our faith, but to grow in the experience of God's grace and goodness, filling our lives and pouring into the community. As we meditate on Paul's words (inspired by God and illuminated by the Holy Spirit) it may be that our lives are transformed for God's glory and the benefit of others.

Example of Reflection during Pastoral Care Sharing with Staff

While temperance is the virtue that keeps us from excesses, forgiveness is the value in action or character strength to experience and act upon. We experience forgiveness as a "means of grace" from others, we gift it to others, we are freed by it existentially, and we are liberated spiritually by Christ's work for us. This ties in with examples of Ubuntu theology and the Peace and Reconciliation Commission in South Africa, which further embed shared understanding of restorative practices and justice from the crime and punishment realm, but are applicable in our cultural practices in Lutheran Education. How can we practice behaviors that free our spirit from anger, resentment, and psychological inflexibility and offer hope of restored relationships?

Example of a Home Group Activity that Explores these Themes

Spirituality Application: Life can be characterized as a journey involving all aspects of ourselves as human beings, including the spiritual. We should expect times of difficulty and challenge, as well as times of peace and connectivity. Questions, doubts, isolation, and lack of faith are normal parts of this journey and spiritual development. Our response to these struggles can lead to stagnation or growth, disconnection or purpose, and as such we should anticipate facing these and following a path of spiritual progress and transformation.[5] Students might interview someone who has experienced a difficulty in their life, in terms of "spiritual struggle." According to Johnson and Hayes (2003), 26 percent of the adolescents in their study experienced "considerable distress resulting from religious or spiritual problems." An interview may help emerging adults normalize the experience of pain as part of development, help them articulate and explore their own struggles,

---

5. Pargament, Spiritually Integrated Psychotherapy.

create psychological flexibility and add to their belief about ways they may deal with adversity in their life.[6]

Easy Chats

- *Describe* to the class the most humble/forgiving/faithful person you know. *Explain* how they express their values in community.

- *Describe* the most modest and gentle person you know. *Explain* how they show unwavering support for the virtue of temperance.

- Make a *judgment* regarding which of these two virtues has had the greatest bearing on the shaping of your life until now. *Reflect* on how will you cherish this experience and how will you take committed action to pursue it further.

Term 4

Focus: Transcendence: appreciation of beauty, gratitude, hope, spirituality

The virtue of *transcendence* is experienced by those who move beyond the ordinary range of human experience and understanding. The strengths that accompany this virtue help the individual make connections with the universe and provide a deeper sense of meaning and purpose. Peterson and Seligman[7] emphasize the connection that goes beyond interpersonal; appreciation of beauty connects to excellence, gratitude connects to goodness, hope to the future, humor connects to pleasure, spirituality connects to the sacred or divine. But appreciation can be awe and wonder, which is like fear and amazement, at God's glory and magnitude, and yet also consciousness of God's grace, gift, and gospel, helping Christians from languishing to flourishing as a realization of dependence. Although we are taught through life to be independent, we learn to hold these in tension and know a certain interdependence.

6. Froh and Parks, *Activities*.
7. Peterson and Seligman, *Character Strengths*.

Example of How these Themes Might Be Communicated through Chapel

Chapels pick up on aspects of these themes. This term focuses on the virtue of transcendence and the character strengths of *hope, humor, gratitude, spirituality*/sense of meaning, and *appreciation of beauty*. I think of the transcendent understandings we have as Christians, informed by a Bible that reveres a God who is infinite and yet reveals a baby in a manger. Also of the "Theology of the Cross" perspective of what witnesses thought was a heretic being crucified, yet it was God's glory revealing itself. I think also of the transcendent reality we live in by faith, in the "Kingdom of God" and yet also with other world views and systems of meaning around us and "in" us. I think about the nature of prophecy in the Old Testament of Messiah coming, as well as prophecy in New Testament about the end of the age (putting our current reality into a "new" perspective), both of which are such essential aspects of our faith. I think about the lead up to Christmas and how this is corrupted by commercialism, requiring us to transcend "other" promotions of what is meaningful, and seek God in faith and prayer for how we should be celebrating Christ's birth. I also think of the ways in which we will wrap up a year with students and community, making sense of, making meaning of the year that was (full, ups and downs, conflicts and resolutions, learning and celebrating), to help give it some possible framing perspectives. I wonder about how and when we might express things to the students as the graduating class wraps up this chapter of life and prepares for the next.

Example of How Teachers Might Personally Reflect on These Themes

Gratitude will transform relationships. Gratitude will transform experiences. Gratitude will transform our character. Christians living in grace and gratitude are empowered to love their communities with an intense spiritual reality. What gets in the way of you living with a perspective of gratitude? What might be great about living and acting upon the value of gratitude? How does gratitude convey an appropriate response to faith and grace?

CONCLUSION

Good education is the most moral thing we can offer our students. Values are essentially a conception of what is desirable. The values espoused by a school are helpful for students and teachers as we continue to grow and experience life. Those values expressed within a *Lutheran* school lead us to reflect on ways we experience some of the characteristics of God, further enhancing the emphasis. Education for *eudemonia* must include a curriculum of values, to help shape notions of what is meaningful and positive for relationships. Making our values explicit is indeed now a requirement for all Australian schools. As we embed and exemplify core school values into our shared practice, we are also shaping student norms to those which are amenable to learning and behaving well, that students might grow in integrity and persistence, hopefully in preparation for lives of service, love, and vitality. This is important in our character development, our growth of social capital, and the development of our virtuous organizations. And, as teachers and leaders living out these values, we might experience a greater sense of authenticity and influence (i.e., living out what we see as valuable). Paul offers clear direction in Phil 4:8:

> Whatever is true, whatever is good, whatever is right, pure and lovely, whatever is admirable; if anything is excellent or praiseworthy, focus on these things.

REFERENCES

Ciarochi, Joseph, and Louise Hayes. *Get Out of Your Mind and Into Your Life for Teens: A Guide to Living an Extraordinary Life*. Oakland: New Harbinger, 2012.

Froh, Jeffrey J., and Acacia C. Parks, eds. *Activities for Teaching Positive Psychology: A Guide for Instructors*. Washington: American Psychological Association, 2012.

Lutheran Education Australia. *Lutheran Lifelong Learning Qualities: A Vision for Lutheran Schooling in Australia*. 2005.

Pargament, Kenneth I. *Spiritually Integrated Psychotherapy: Understanding and Addressing the Sacred*. New York: Guilford, 2007.

Peterson, Christopher, and Martin E. P. Seligman. *Character Strengths and Virtues: A Handbook and Classification*. New York: Oxford University Press, 2004.

Niemiec, Ryan M., and Danny Wedding. *Positive Psychology at the Movies: Using Films to Build Virtues and Character Strengths*. Ontario: Hogrefe, 2008.

Seligman, Martin E. P., and Mihaly Csikszentmihalyi. "Positive Psychology: An Introduction." *American Psychologist* 55 (2000) 5–14.

Wilson, Kelly G., and Troy DuFrene. *Mindfulness for Two: An Acceptance and Commitment Therapy Approach to Mindfulness in Psychotherapy*. Oakland: New Harbinger, 2009.

Chapter 14

Understanding the Role of Hope and Faith in Flourishing

Piloting a Measure of Christian Hope

James Patrick Burns, Jameela Conway-Turner,
Christopher Staysniak, Melaine Malcolm,
Matthew T. McGonagle

HOPE IS CONSIDERED AN essential protective factor against depression. It is also a key variable associated with positive physical and mental health-related outcomes and overall life satisfaction. As well as its reported association with decreased levels of depression, it is considered central to the recovery from and prevention of further depressive episodes.[1] Yet, definitions of hope vary from an ability to monitor feelings about a positive future (optimism), to more profound transcendent appreciations of self, others, and the world, as well as the belief that all things will work out for

---

1. Michael et al., "Hope Theory"; Cheavens, "Hope and Depression"; Valle et al., "Analysis of Hope."

the good or some future eternal good.[2] Varying definitions of hope have left researchers continuing to question what the construct of hope consists of, and what role it plays. Efforts to understand and appreciate the role of hope for individuals have evolved over time and have included both secular and religious notions of hope.[3] Scholars in the fields of medicine and mental health in particular have questioned how these definitions might relate to one another. This study seeks to determine whether there is a difference between secular and religious concepts of hope and if so how this difference might impact future studies in this area.

While the taxonomy of hope differs along secular and religious lines, it is important to determine whether these differences can be identified through assessment. Such assessments could aid in understanding how a different perspective on hope can allow it to be accessed and utilized for better emotional and psychological functioning. In part, the benefits of hope have already been suggested by studies linking secular notions of hope to positive adolescent and college student development. For example, Varahrami and colleagues demonstrated the importance of hope in these populations as part of healthy psychosocial functioning.[4] In this study college students who exhibited hope-filled thoughts had a more positive relationship psychosocial development. Multivariate analyses revealed that these students were also better able to maintain a sense that their life was meaningful and worth living. That is, "the greater someone's positive resolution of the stages of development, the more strongly they perceived their own life to have meaning and purpose."[5] Not surprisingly both of these variables, meaningfulness and worthfulness, are correlated to hopefulness.

Additionally, Curry et al. explored the role of hope in academic and sporting achievement, illustrating a positive relationship between hope and Grade Point Average (GPA).[6] According to this study being more hopeful was a significant predictor of higher GPA semester to semester for the athletes. Hope was also significantly predictive of overall GPA for all college students (athletes and non-athletes). Similar to Curry's findings, studies involving non-student athletes have also reported a correlation between

2. Carver and Scheier, "Hopeful Optimist"; Sethi and Seligman, "Optimism."
3. Sympson, "Rediscovering."
4. Varahrami et al., "Relationship."
5. Ibid., 1.
6. Curry et al., "Role."

being hopeful and a variety of achievement markers.[7] Taken as a whole, these studies suggest that for adolescents, hopefulness (at least as understood within the secular context) is overall positively correlated to indicators of both cognitive flourishing, as well as satisfaction and wellness, and regardless of extracurricular activity.

These and other such studies over the last twenty years point to a resurgence of interest in the effect hope has relative to an individual's ability to draw upon hopefulness as an internal resource and an intensifier of cognitive ability. For example, Snyder and colleagues, in defining hope as a set of cognitive beliefs, highlighted the important role it plays as a mental resource.[8] In particular, they highlighted two important components: "agency" related to goals (in particular the developmental lessons of the self as an author of causal chains of events) and "pathways" to these goals (thought of as developmental lessons through which we can learn and correct future action aimed at goal attainment). Together, pathways and agency allow an individual to construct a realistic and flexible conduit to the desired goal. Still other scholars consider hope as correlated to or "subsumed under" optimism—the belief that one has or will have the means to do what is required to actualize expectations.[9] Other researchers have developed an integrative theory of hope, consisting of four elements: attachment, mastery, survival and spirituality.[10] In this conceptualization, a greater sense of hope is associated with greater trust and openness. Mastery relates to the ability to pursue higher goals, incorporating a sense of self-empowerment and collaboration. Survival involves the ability to enlist coping strategies and to self-regulate. Spirituality integrates a faith perspective and/or a sense of cosmic or divine meaning.

Still others suggest that in real life situations, decisions depend on comparisons of a person's danger perception with their indicators of hope. Bruhn suggests that such indicators can be assessed as a value proportional to the probability of an event and its expected outcome/payoff/benefits.[11] This proportionality can be an essential resource in the healing process though it appears limited by the intensity with which one approaches the

7. Snyder et al., "Will"; Snyder et al., "Hope."
8. Snyder et al., "Will."
9. Peterson, "Future"; Ai et al., "Faith-based and Secular Pathways."
10. Scioli et al., "Prospective Study"; Scioli and Biller, "Hope."
11. Bruhn, "Therapeutic Value."

expected outcome. Nevertheless, Bruhn encourages the development of practical strategies that stimulate hope.

In contrast to this, Nietzsche characterized hope as, "the most evil of all evils because it prolongs man's torment" by leading him to believe in the possibility of things changing or even improving, despite evidence that this is not likely to happen.[12] In fact, he believed a hope-filled person would be far worse off than someone had not been hopeful at all. Thus, Nietzsche would say that hoping puts an individual in a worse position because it promises something that does not exist, that is, an eternity where there is no more pain or sorrow. In contrast, Seligman suggests that hope may guide us through difficult personal changes, albeit tempered with an understanding that there are certain things beyond our control.

For the most part, these theories have concentrated on what could be termed "secular" hope. Described in this way hope is associated with the belief that one has a way and the means to do what is required to realize one's desired expectations and to that end one can sustain movement along those selected pathways. However, more ancient understandings of hope illustrated in the Greco-Roman worldview hold out hope as a virtue. In this context it was thought of as a remedy of sorts for enduring prolonged suffering. According to such a framework, the individual extolled about the potency of hope as a means to endure pain. For example, in the story of Pandora hope allowed Pandora to believe that something greater might be possible, even if it was accompanied by continued suffering.

By way of comparison, Christians understand hope as an essential component of appreciating the transcendent. In many ways, this conceptualization of hope is closer to more traditional and ancient understandings of hope as a virtue. According to the Christian rubric hope is understood as one's desire for the afterlife, conceived variously as the kingdom of heaven or eternal bliss. Christian hope is therefore that virtue whereby one places trust in Christ's promise to save them.[13] In this sense, hope is an enduring attitude related to the belief in God's goodness and power to bring good out of desperate circumstances, even if these circumstances fail to demonstrably change in the here and now.[14] This notion relies not so much on one's strength, but on the help of the grace offered by God. Accordingly, hope is

12. Nietzsche, *Human, All Too Human*.

13. Verback, "Signification"; Marcel, *Philosophy*, *Mystery*, and "Structure"; Pieper, *Faith*.

14. Pieper, *On Hope*; Tilliette, "Notes"; Strukelj, "Hope."

the confident expectation of divine blessing and a blessed vision of God; counter-intuitively it also incorporates the fear of disappointing or offending God's love and goodness out of personal selfishness or lack of generosity. Whereas the secular concept of hope expects things to change and relies on the agency of the individual to promote such changes, Christian hope relies more heavily upon maintaining a set of hopeful beliefs that good will eventually come and suffering will eventually end, if not now then later, even if later is after this life. And even when one is unlikely to achieve the desired outcome presently or in the future. In this sense, hope incorporates an appreciation for the ability to delay the fulfillment of expectations.

This study seeks to differentiate between secular concepts of hope and religious concepts. This contrasts those scholars who consider that hope is related to or "subsumed under" optimism and heavily reliant on personal agency, with those who understand hope as an enduring attitude related to the belief in God and God's goodness and the power to bring good out of desperate circumstances. This pilot study seeks to demonstrate the reliability and validity of a self-report measure that conceptualizes hope related to self, hopefulness in others and hopefulness in God or the transcendent, which roughly correlate to three constructs of hopefulness regarding temporal, humanistic and Christian themes.

METHOD

Data Collection and Sample Participants

Participants from a variety of undergraduate classes at a large private university in New England were recruited for this study, which was approved by the University Institutional Review Board (IRB—the mission of which is to protect the rights and welfare of people who take part in research). All one hundred and two participants were administered a four-part survey including (1) a demographic questionnaire, (2) the Trait Hope Scale, (3) the Satisfaction with Life Scale and (4) the Christian Hope Scale. The survey was designed to take approximately fifteen minutes to complete and participants were asked to complete all items. Only completed surveys were analyzed in the study. Informed consent was obtained from each participant and instructions were printed at the beginning of each section. Participants were allowed to choose between an electronic or paper version of the survey in order to maximize the sample size. The researchers used Qualtrics for the electronic administration of the survey. Data from completed paper forms was entered into Qualtrics by research staff and subjected to dual data checking for accuracy.

The demographics section of the survey included questions regarding gender, marital status, age, race, religion, current student status, and employment status. Also, the importance of religion and the degree of activity in faith community were assessed, information necessary in exploring a Christian construct of hope. Other studies have demonstrated the usefulness of such questions in scales measuring the extent to which religious individuals employ potential religious resources.[15] Study participants were offered the opportunity to enter a draw for one of ten twenty-five dollar gift cards upon completion of the survey. Participants were made aware that all of their responses would be confidential.

Of the initial 102 participants taking the survey, eighty-three participants provided valid and usable responses and remained throughout the process. Participants ranged from eighteen to thirty years of age. In the event a participant failed to respond to an item, mean response rates were used. This was only allowed for those surveys that had three or fewer unanswered questions. The sample was comprised of slightly more males (54 percent) than females (46 percent). The largest group of respondents was between eighteen and twenty years of age (48 percent). The vast majority of the respondents indicated that they were single (88 percent), with just over three-quarters reporting they were full-time students (76 percent). Slightly more than half of the respondents were Christian (54.2 percent). Thirty-seven percent of respondents reported not being involved in a faith group at this time.[16]

Measures

Trait Hope Scale. Developed by Snyder, the Trait Hope Scale is also known as the adult hope scale (AHS). It comprises twelve items and includes two subscales. One subscale (four items) is designed to measure Agency, while the other subscale (four items) measures Pathways. Four additional filler items are included. The scale is designed to measure Snyder's cognitive model of hope, involving goal-directed energy or belief in one's capacity

15. Ai et al., "Faith-based and Secular Pathways."
16. See Table 1.

to initiate and sustain actions (agency) and the planning of ways to achieve goals (pathways).[17] Participants respond using an eight-point scale ranging from definitely false to definitely true. The agency and pathway subscales are derived separately and then added together for the total Trait Hope Scale score. Cronbach's alpha coefficients were acceptable (total scale range 0.74 to 0.84, individual subscales above 0.63.)[18] Several studies have verified the very good reliability and validity of the scale.[19]

Satisfaction With Life Scale. Developed by Diener and colleagues,[20] this scale assesses individual satisfaction with life as a whole. Life satisfaction refers to a process of judgment in which individuals assess the quality of their lives by their unique set of criteria.[21] A comparison of one's perceived life circumstances with a self-imposed standard or set of standards is presumably made, with the level of life satisfaction reflecting the degree to which conditions match these standards. Therefore, life satisfaction is a conscious cognitive judgment where the criteria are determined by the individual. The scale does not assess satisfaction within specific life domains, such as health or finances. The scale contains five items to which participants respond using a seven-point scale ranging from strongly disagree to agree strongly. The total score from the items are then added together for the final Satisfaction with Life score—the higher the score, the more satisfied the individual. Test-retest correlations were very good (0.82 to 0.87).[22]

Christian Hope Scale (CHS). This scale was developed by Burns, Conway-Turner, Staysniak, Malcolm, and McGonagle in 2012, seeking to measure conceptualizations of hopefulness according to a Christian rubric that includes an appreciation of the transcendent (Christian themes), ability to delay satisfaction (humanistic themes), and focus on eternity and meaning of suffering (temporal themes).[23] It was hypothesized that all three constructs would be related to hope as a Christian virtue. The theoretical basis was derived from Christian scholars such as Marcel, Tilliette, Verhack, Servais, and Von Balthasar.[24] All themes involved hope for oneself,

17. Snyder et al., "Will."

18. Carifo and Rhodes, "Construct Validities."

19. Snyder et al., "Will"; Snyder, *Handbook*; Carifo and Rhodes, "Construct Validities."

20. Diener et al., "Satisfaction."

21. Shin and Johnson, "Avowed Happiness."

22. Saunders and Roy, "Relationship."

23. Burns et al., "Christian Hope Scale (CHS)."

24. Marcel, *Philosophy and Mystery;* Tilliette, "Notes"; Verhack, "Signification";

hopefulness in others and hopefulness in God or the transcendent. The scale originally included forty-nine items. However, through an earlier pilot process, it was determined that two questions would be dropped for lack of clarity, a further nine were reworded for precision, and three were split into two separate questions, leaving a revised scale of fifty items. This scale was determined to have internal consistency with reliability ranging from 0.89 to 0.91. The scale reported a Flesch Reading Ease of 77.4 with a Flesch-Kincaid Grade Level of 5.0 and Passive Sentences rating of 13 percent. Since the survey is distributed to individuals who vary not only in age but also education level, the readability was considered acceptable.

ANALYSIS

Exploratory Factor Analysis

Latent factor structure of the fifty-item CHS was analyzed utilizing exploratory factor analysis (EFA). This procedure assesses the inter-correlations between variables to create factors.[25] EFA often reduces the test items to produce a measure that better fits the construct. Tabachnick and Fidell[26] outline the steps for this procedure. The first step involves choosing an extraction process. Principal components factor analysis (PCA) was chosen in order to reduce the number of items in the test.

Next, the number of factors extracted was assessed. Fabrigar et al.[27] discussed the use of eigenvalues greater than 1.00 and Catell's Scree test was applied.[28] Both procedures were applied to avoid over-extracting factors. The authors utilized both procedures to determine the correct number of factors to extract. This process resulted in thirty-three items related to three factors.

Following this step, to better understand the factor loadings, a Varimax rotation with Kaiser Normalization was employed to constrain the structure to a zero-order correlation between the factors. From this the

Servais, *Theologie* and "Restlessness"; and Von Balthasar, "Christ" and "Communio-Ein."
25. Tabachnick and Fidell, *Using Multivariate Statistics*; Kahn, "Factor Analysis."
26. Tabachnick and Fidell, *Using Multivariate Statistics*.
27. Fabrigar et al., "Evaluating."
28. Catell, "Scree Test."

items that constituted factor structures were determined. Items that loaded highly on one factor and minimally on another were retained. For this pilot only items that load above 0.50 were retained to ensure practical significance.[29] The dataset was assessed for normality and missing data before extraction.

Reliability

Inter-item reliability was employed to determine the utility of the factors. Tabachnick and Fidell[30] suggest that factors that produce alpha coefficients above 0.7 are considered to be meaningful. This was the cut-off used to estimate internal consistency.

Construct Validity

Evidence for construct validity was determined by assessing the practical relationship between the CHS subscales and theoretically related measures.[31] Convergent validity evidence was gathered in this pilot by utilizing a theoretically similar measure that correlates with the CHS. It was hypothesized that the CHS subscales would correlate to some degree with Snyder's Trait Hope Scale and to a lesser degree with the Satisfaction with Life Scale.[32] Divergent validity was assessed by examining the correlations between CHS and age, race, and student status, all of which were hypothesized to have weaker correlations than the Trait Hope Scale or the Satisfaction with Life Scale.

RESULTS

Preliminary results revealed that three factors were generated with appropriate eigenvalues. Constraining the scale items to these methods revealed that the three factors accounted for 48 percent of the total variance. The results can be fitted into three constructs with minimum loadings of 0.50;

---

29. Hair et al., *Multivariate Data Analysis.*

30. Tabachnick and Fidell, *Using Multivariate Statistics.*

31. Campbell and Fiske, "Convergent"; Messick, "Test Validity"; Rubin and Babbie, *Research Methods.*

32. Snyder, *Handbook;* Diener et al., "Satisfaction."

twenty-three items for Christian Themes (eigenvalue = 17.48), seven items for Humanistic Themes (eigenvalue = 3.39), and three items for Temporal Themes (eigenvalue = 2.86).[33]

Reliability

Cronbach's alpha was used to estimate the reliability of this sample's scores across the three factors. Christian hope themes revealed high internal consistency (α = .97) across the twenty-three items. The Humanistic and Temporal factors also revealed high to moderate internal consistency (α = .81, .61, respectively). These results further confirmed the latent factor structure and utility of these subscales.

Construct Validity

Convergent validity was established by measuring the correlation between two theoretically related measures and the CHS, while discriminant validity was established by correlating three theoretically unrelated measures.[34] Bonferroni's correction was utilized to correct for experiment-wise error rate. Cohen's cutoff scores were utilized to determine the strength of relationships (i.e., -.10 to .10 weak correlation, -.3 to .3 moderate correlation, -.5 to .5 strong correlation).

The results revealed convergent validity evidence for the subscales. First, Christian Themes were correlated with the Trait Hope Scale and Satisfaction with Life Scale. The Trait Hope Agency subscale revealed a moderate positive correlation (r = .35, $p<.01$) with Christian Themes and a smaller yet positive relationship with the Trait Hope total score (r= .25, $p<.05$). Likewise, the Satisfaction with Life Scale revealed a moderate correlation with Christian Themes (r=.34, $p<.01$).

Next, similar to the correlations with Christian Themes, Humanistic Themes and Temporal Emphasis were correlated with the Trait Hope Scale and Satisfaction with Life Scale. Humanistic Themes demonstrated moderate correlations with Trait Hope Total Score (r = .25, $p<.01$), the Trait Hope Agency subscale (r=.23, $p<.01$) and the Satisfaction with Life Scale (r = .32, $p<.05$). Temporal Emphasis had an inverse correlation with the Trait Hope

---

33. See Table 2.

34. Rubin and Babbie, *Research Methods*.

Scale and Satisfaction with Life Scale. The Trait Hope Agency subscale (r = -.23, $p<.01$), Trait Hope Pathways subscale (r = -.32, $p<.05$), Trait Hope Total Score (r = -.32, $p<.05$) and Satisfaction with Life Scale score (r = -.30, $p.05$) all had moderate negative correlations with Temporal Emphasis, while Trait Hope Negative subscale had a strong negative correlation (r = -.47, $p<.05$).[35]

Discriminant validity was established by correlating the CHS subscales with theoretically unrelated measures. It was hypothesized that age, race, and student status would be unrelated to the measures. This was found to be the case for all three factors when correlated to these three items.[36]

DISCUSSION AND CONCLUSION

Hope, both from secular and Christian perspectives, has been understood to be a significant part of being able to deal with and recover from various kinds of adversity. In addition, individuals who are considered more hopeful tend to address the effects of mood disorders better. Yet, for some religiously affiliated individuals, hope appears to have an even greater effect in terms of both resilience and recovery, suggesting that there is a difference in how certain individuals (in this case Christians) understand and process hope. This study validated the CHS as a reliable measure of the less well-understood construction of hope from a Christian perspective. This construct was conceptualized by the authors as reflecting a distinct understating of hope compared to previous measures of hope and optimism. It suggests that for religiously affiliated individuals (particularly for Christians), a more sensitive measure of hope can be useful.

The original CHS measure consisted of fifty items that were categorized into three components. The latent factor structure of the CHS was examined using EFA, more specifically the PCF analysis. The PCF analysis revealed a three-factor structure that comprised thirty-five items. As expected, Christian and Humanistic Themes, along with Temporal Emphasis, were found to be the three main factors. The thirty-five item CHS was found to have high reliability and construct validity.

The validation of the CHS can be understood as a helpful addition to the assessment literature as it fills a previously unexplored gap. While assessing hope utilizing a Christian rubric explores a less conventional

35. See Table 3.
36. See Table 4.

research approach than that exploring the relationship between hope and psychological wellbeing and flourishing, it is nonetheless important because of the significant number of individuals espousing a Christian worldview. Further, the capacity to assess Christian hope in religiously involved individuals, offers Christian and non-Christian therapists and counselors an additional resource as they seek to help clients access avenues of hope. It is likely that Christian hope, given hope's association with individual wellbeing and life satisfaction, may play an important role in mental health and resiliency.[37]

The sample size of the current study is an obvious limitation as is a pilot study's inability to more broadly randomize the participant pool. Further, confirmatory factor analysis (CFA) would likely strengthen the use of CHS by verifying the hypothesized latent factor structure. Future research plans include procedures to validate and confirm the latent factor structure and this will allow researchers to utilize the measure in conjunction with studies on mental health and wellness. It will also add a resource for therapists to use when working with a diverse range of individuals who increasingly present with spiritual concerns (not solely Christian), in helping to address their mental health issues. It is likely that understanding hope, and particularly Christian hope, as a resource for clients to utilize who are disposed to such will offer an additional low-cost intervention strategy that is likely to reduce or mitigate the impact of certain serious mental illness symptoms.

REFERENCES

Ai, Amy L., et al. "Faith-based and Secular Pathways to Hope and Optimism Subconstructs in Middle-aged and Older Cardiac Patients." *Journal of Health Psychology* 9 (2004) 435–50.

Bruhn, John G. "Therapeutic Value of Hope." *Southern Medical Journal* 77 (1984) 215–19.

Burns, James, et al. "Christian Hope Scale (CHS)." Unpublished manuscript, School of Education, Boston College, Chestnut Hill, MA (2012).

Campbell, Donald T., and Donald W. Fiske. "Convergent and Discriminant Validation by the Multitrait-multimethod Matrix." *Psychological Bulletin* 56 (1959) 1–25.

Carifio, James, and Lauren Rhodes. "Construct Validities and the Empirical Relationships between Optimism, Hope, Self-efficacy, and Locus of Control." *Journal of Prevention, Assessment and Rehabilitation* 19 (2002) 125–36.

Carver, Charles S., and Michael F. Scheier. "The Hopeful Optimist." *Psychological Inquiry* 13 (2002) 288–90.

37. Pattyn and Van Liedekerke, "Anxiety."

Catell, Raymond B. "The Scree Test for the Number of Factors." *Multivariate Behavioral Research* 1 (1966) 245–76.

Cheavens, Jen. "Hope and Depression: Light through the Shadows." In *Handbook of Hope: Theory, Measures, and Applications*, edited by C. R. Snyder, 321–40. San Diego: Academic, 2000.

Curry, Lewis A., et al. "Role of Hope in Academic and Sport Achievement." *Journal of Personality and Social Psychology* 73 (1997) 1257–67.

Diener, Ed, et al. "The Satisfaction with Life Scale." *Journal of Personality Assessment* 49 (1985) 71–75.

Fabrigar, Leandre R., et al. "Evaluating the Use of Exploratory Factor Analysis in Psychological Research." *Psychological Methods* 4 (1999) 272.

Hair, Joseph F., et al. *Multivariate Data Analysis.* 5th ed. Upper Saddle River: Prentice Hall, 1998.

Kahn, Jeffrey H. "Factor Analysis in Counseling Psychology Research, Training, and Practice: Principles, Advances, and Applications." *The Counseling Psychologist* 34 (2006) 684–718.

Marcel, Gabriel. *The Mystery of Being, Vol.1, Reflection and Mystery.* Translated by G. S. Fraser. London: Harvill, 1951.

———. *The Philosophy of Existence.* Translated by Manya Harari. New York: Carol, 1948.

———. "The Structure of Hope." *Communio* 23 (1996) 607–8.

Messick, Samuel. "Test Validity and the Ethics of Assessment." *American Psychologist* 35 (1980) 1012–27.

Michael, Scott T., et al. "Hope Theory as applied to Brief Treatments: Problem-solving and Solution-focused Therapies." In *Handbook of Hope: Theory, Measures, and Applications*, edited by C. R. Snyder, 151–66. San Diego: Academic, 2000.

Nietzsche, Friedrich. *Nietzsche: Human, All Too Human: A Book for Free Spirits*, translated by R. J. Hollingdale. Cambridge: Cambridge University Press, 1996.

Pattyn, Bart, and Luc Van Liedekerke. "Anxiety and Uncertainty in Modern Society. *Ethical Perspectives* 8 (2005) 88–104.

Peterson, Christopher. "The Future of Optimism." *American Psychologist* 55 (2000) 44–55.

Pieper, Josef. *Faith Hope Love.* San Francisco: Ignatius, 1997.

———. *On Hope.* Translated by Sister Mary Frances McCarthy. San Francisco: Ignatius, 1986.

Rubin, Allen, and Earl Babbie. *Research Methods for Social Work.* 6th ed. Belmont: Thomson Higher Education, 2008.

Saunders, Shaun A., and Cherie Roy, C. "The Relationship between Depression, Satisfaction with Life, and Social Interest." *South Pacific Journal of Psychology* 11 (2000) 9–15.

Scioli, Anthony, et al. "A Prospective Study of Hope, Optimism, and Health." *Psychological Reports* 81 (1997) 723–33.

Scioli, Anthony, and Henry Biller. "Hope, Attachment, and Love." Paper presented at *Works of Love: Scientific and Religious Perspectives on Altruism.* Philadelphia, 2003.

Sethi, Sheena, and Martin E. P. Seligman. "Optimism and Fundamentalism." *Psychological Science* 4 (1993) 256–59.

Servais, Jacques. *Théologie des Exercices Spirituels: H. U. von Balthasar interprète Saint Ignace.* Paris: Culture et vérité, 1996.

———. "Restlessness and Anxiety: Towards a Christian Discernment." *Communio* 34 (2007) 224–42.

Shin, Doh Chull, and D. M. Johnson. "Avowed Happiness as an Overall Assessment of the Quality of Life." *Social Indicators Research* 5 (1978) 475–92.

Snyder, C. R. *Handbook of Hope: Theory, Measures, and Applications.* San Diego: Academic, 2000.

Snyder, C. R., et al. "Hope and Academic Success in College." *Journal of Educational Psychology,* 94 (2002) 820–26.

———. "The Will and the Ways: Development and Validation of an Individual Differences Measure of Hope." *Journal of Personality and Social Psychology* 60 (1991) 570–85.

Strukelj, Anton. "Hope does not disappoint." *Communio* 23 (1996) 2.

Sympson, Susie C. (2000). "Rediscovering Hope: Understanding and Working with Survivors of Trauma." In *Handbook of Hope: Theory, Measures, and Applications,* edited by C. R. Snyder, 285–300. San Diego: Academic, 2000.

Tabachnick, Barbara G., and Linda S. Fidell. *Using Multivariate Statistics.* 5th ed. Boston: Pearson, 2007.

Tilliette, Xavier. "Notes and Reflections on the Virtue of Hope." *Communio,* 23 (1996) 441–47.

Valle, Michael F., et al. "An Analysis of Hope as a Psychological Strength." *Journal of School of Psychology* 44 (2006) 393–406.

Varahrami A., et al. "The Relationship between Meaning, Hope, and Psychosocial Development." *International Journal of Existential Psychology and Psychotherapy* 3 (2010) 1–13.

Verhack, Ignace. "The Signification of Hope for the Present Time." *Communio,* 23 (1996) 431–40.

Von Balthasar, Hans Urs. "Christ: Alpha and Omega." *Communio* 23 (1996) 465–71.

———. "Communio-Ein Programm." *Communio,* 1 (1972) 4–17.

Table 1: *Demographic Descriptive of the Sample*

	Frequency	Percentage		Frequency	Percentage
Gender			**Employment**		
Male	45	54.2	Full-time	15	18.1
Female	38	45.8	Part-time	49	59.0
			Unemployed	19	22.9
Age			**Religion**		
18–20	40	48.2	Christian Orth.	4	4.8
21–23	29	34.9	Christian Prot.	45	54.2
24–26	9	10.8	Christian Cath.	10	12.0
27–30	5	6.0	Muslim	1	1.2
			Hindu	1	1.2
Marital Status			Agnostic	8	9.6
Single	73	88.0	Atheist	8	9.6
Married	3	3.6	Other	6	7.2
Divorced	1	1.2			
Committed Rel.	6	7.2	**Importance of Religious Belief**		
			Not at all imp.	4	4.8
Race/Ethnicity			Very unimp.	7	8.4
African-American	2	2.4	Somewhat unimp.	5	6.0
White, Non-Hisp.	55	66.3	Neither	10	12.0
Hispanic	6	7.2	Somewhat imp.	23	27.7
Asian	13	15.7	Very Imp.	22	26.5
Other	2	2.4	Extremely imp.	12	14.5
Multicultural	5	6.0			
			Involvement in Faith Community		
Student Status			Not at all	31	37.3
Full-time	63	75.9	A few times a year	20	24.1
Part-time	16	19.3	Monthly	10	12.0
Non-student	4	4.8	Weekly	22	26.5

Table 2: *Factor loads* for the component items in Christian Hope Scale*

Question number	Items (central idea)	Component 1	2	3
h45	Faith in the power of God's love assures me there is perfect heaven	.914		
h37	Death not the end because Jesus destroyed death's power	.905		
h47	Trust in God's mercy to all, including self	.888		
h38	Liberation from this life's tragedy in next life	.869		
h50	Consoled by God, allows me to reach out to others	.864		
h18	Able to accept current difficulties because of better world to come	.857		
h16	Next life inspires me to think and act better towards others	.855		
h15	Things will get better because of Jesus' Resurrection	.853		
h24	Limits of this life in life to come because of Jesus' act of salvation	.852		
h43	Jesus came to save humans (body and soul) for life of glory	.852		
h33	Desire relationship with God	.851		
h19	Can give up comfort now because of Jesus' example and promises	.840		
h46	Christ's death and rising allows all creation to be saved	.828		
h23	There is nothing after this life	-.823		
h39	Grounded in relationship with God	.808		
h49	Believe in everlasting mercy beyond death	.789		
h34	God desires all of creation to be redeemed through Jesus	.781		
h2	Believe we will be free of human limitations one day	.758		
h1	Something beyond self is capable of fulfilling me	.653		
h11	Anchored in something beyond myself	.594		
h8	Get through problems because suffering's purpose to be revealed	.527		
h3	I seek fulfillment regularly	.519		
h36	Purgatory shows God's mercy	.518		
h44	Trials in life are way to prepare me for something better	.397		
h6	Temporary fulfilment is the only fulfillment to be found	-.334		
h27	Try to accept others, imperfections and all		.738	
h29	I appreciate my life		.645	

h26	Try to accept myself, imperfections and all	.638	
h28	Am forgiving towards others	.635	
h40	Can be cheerful in desperate situations	.624	
h48	Believe in new beginnings, even in failure	.606	
h32	Want what is good for others	.511	
h41	Believe all things work for good, even without knowing future	.492	
h9	Can accept world is imperfect	.423	
h17	Believe service to others important for fulfilled person	.382	
h14	"Absence makes the heart grow fonder" true for me	.339	
h21	Very afraid of death		.682
h22	Death is the end of everything; this is frightening		.650
h20	Attached to material things, happiest when have all I want		.582
h35	Believe in Purgatory (to make up for sins before heaven)		.485
h12	Can delay current fulfillment because of better future		-.426
h10	Way to get through life is to escape suffering		.410

Note: factor extraction method = principal component analysis;
rotation method = varimax with Kaiser normalization
*Factor loads with module less than 0.33 were omitted from the Table

Table 3: *Construct Validity Spearman's rho Correlations*

	Christian Themes	Humanistic Themes	Temporal Themes
Satisfaction with Life Scale	.340**	.320**	-.295**
Trait Hope Scale (Total)	.248*	.247*	-.324**
Trait Hope Agency Subscale	.349**	.226*	-.231*
Trait Hope Pathways Subscale	.073	.158	-.315**
Trait Hope Negative Subscale	-.011	.011	-.471**

Note. $* = p \leq .05$, $** = p \leq .01$

Table 4: *Discriminant Validity Spearman's rho Correlations*

	Christian Themes	Humanistic Themes	Temporal Themes
Age	-.208	-.086	-.209
Race	-.087	.036	.063

Student Status	.032	-.161	-.045

Note. *= p ≤ .05

Printed in Great
Britain
by Amazon